To Jerry and Gerrie White

*who have been an inspiration to
my entire family of an enduring
faith in the Lord Jesus Christ.*

With Special Thanks to Brian and Linda Rowberg

*There are not words enough to thank Brian and Linda for their
incredible perseverance and encouragement in editing. They
have labored with me for over seven years, helping me soften,
clarify, and articulate my thoughts. Without their experience
and dedication, this book would have been vastly inferior to
what it has become. Thank you, dear friends, for entering into
the yoke with me.*

Contents

Part 3
Applying Doctrine to Life

Foreword

Understanding Biblical doctrine is required for a God-honoring life. Only right thinking leads to holy and righteous living.

The Bible is our only source and final authority for God's truth (doctrine) as we see from 2 Timothy 3:16. It alone is the written record of God's self-disclosure, and this finds its perfect, beautiful, and complete expression in the Person of Jesus Christ (Colossians 2:9). He is all the fullness of God disclosed in human form, and in that disclosure as a genuine human being Jesus reveals what every human being is supposed to be (John 1:14). Jesus Christ is both revelations: God revealed perfectly, and a human being living as God purposed. If we are to know God intimately and to live like Jesus humbly, then we must know the truth, richly found in Christ the living Word (2 Peter 3:18). This knowledge comes through accurate understanding of the truth, revealed in the written Word by the Holy Spirit. Such understanding requires carefully and diligently applying our minds and hearts to study, meditation, and application of the essential theological truths so indispensable to true Christianity (2 Timothy 2:15). Neglecting this pursuit leads to spiritual anemia in Christians, their families, and their churches.

Bishop J. C. Ryle of England (1816-1900), whose sound and respected Biblical teaching still speaks through his excellent books, wrote, "It was doctrine in the apostolic ages which emptied the heathen temples, and shook Greece and Rome. It was doctrine which awoke

Christendom from its slumbers at the time of the Reformation and spoiled the Pope of one-third of his subjects. It is doctrine which gives power to every successful mission, whether at home or abroad. It is doctrine—doctrine, clear ringing doctrine—which like the rams' horns at Jericho, casts down the opposition of the devil and sin."

False doctrine was a constant threat to the New Testament church. Paul wrote Timothy a solemn charge to preach the word at all times by reproving, rebuking, exhorting, and instructing. He then cautioned Timothy, "For the time will come when they will not endure sound doctrine; but wanting to have their ears tickled, they will accumulate for themselves teachers in accordance to their own desires" (2 Timothy 4:3).

We live in that day Paul foretold. False teaching has always been a threat to the stability and health of the church, but today in much of Christendom it is epidemic. There exists obvious and blatant heresy in some places; but in more subtle ways for evangelical Christians, much teaching today is man-centered instead of God-centered. The present trend focuses on what we need for a happy life rather than on what truly pleases God and exalts Jesus Christ. This trendy teaching emphasizes how to be blessed, feel good about yourself, and prosper in life, as if God exists solely for the sake of the believer.

With this off-center emphasis, many Christians ignore and keep silent about numerous core and vital truths because they make us uncomfortable. These neglected but very essential truths are the ones that convict us and humble us and make us ashamed. But this shame is necessary before we can wholeheartedly turn to the Savior for His ministry of grace and mercy that will free us, heal us, and transform us.

We must be anchored in this clear Biblical doctrine: God alone is the center of the universe and all things are from Him and through Him and to Him, for His glory forever (Romans 11:36). The plain path to a life of profound love, fullness of joy, and an ocean of peace is marked by sound Biblical doctrine. We need the whole gospel! We must have a thorough mental grasp and a deep heart revelation by the Holy Spirit of who God is, what He is like, what He has done, and what He will yet do. We must know deeply in our souls who we are, what we are really like, what we have done, and what is ours in our union with Christ because of His grace.

How can a father and mother help establish their children in the ways of God if they themselves do not have a thorough understanding of sound Biblical doctrine? How can older believers and pastors and Bible teachers carefully pass the baton of truth to subsequent generations in life's relay race if they do not have a firm grasp on the baton themselves? How can Christians build up one another in the faith today—when fierce hurricane winds of false teaching are blowing against God's people—if they do not possess the strategic building stones of sound doctrine?

Norm Wakefield has served you wonderfully in his book, *Anchored in Christ*. It is a gift to you, and an excellent expression of God's grace. Out of his passion to know Biblical truth (sound doctrine) accurately, to live that truth in his own life faithfully, and to minister that same truth effectively, he has written from his heart to your heart. How different that is from just passing knowledge from his head to your head, a purely mental exercise. This book is not an academic approach like a scholarly work. Norm presents the truth simply from God's Word, explaining Biblical truth with Scriptural references. He shares truth made sensible for daily living, as doctrine was meant to be. This is not a book for mere casual reading, however. It is easy to understand, but it should be read with your Bible nearby and pen in hand for underlining, notations, pondering and digesting. We must love God with our minds as well as our hearts. Like good, healthy, solid food, *Anchored in Christ* will nourish your soul, change your thinking, and wonderfully affect the way you live—all for God's glory.

I have known Norm and his precious family for many years. I have witnessed his passion for the truth and his passion to share the truth across America because of his deep concern for the condition of the church. He knows this condition well because he has crisscrossed our country for years ministering in conferences and churches. He has witnessed and felt among Christians the great need for sound doctrine that is so necessary if they are to be anchored in Christ.

Meditation on God's Word accompanied with prayer for revelation leads to transformation for God's glory. This book is an excellent tool to help you. Take it, read, think, contemplate, pray, and digest. You will be renewed in your mind and therefore be transformed in your life (Romans 12:2).

Jerald (Jerry) R. White, Jr.

Introduction

Foundations are important! We know how vital foundations are in childhood, in business, in a culture, or in a building, but do we understand the importance of a true and strong spiritual foundation? Everyone recognizes the importance of the formative years in childrearing. If the child is trained well in the early years of life, he will enjoy the blessings of such training through his entire life. On the other hand, if bad habits were established while he was young, decades may pass before he overcomes those character flaws. In the meantime, his life will be filled with frustration and trials. The early training of children, or the lack thereof, will ripple in a significant manner throughout their lives.

The business world provides another example of the importance of foundations. People can go along fine for a while as they seek to establish a new business, but as the months and years roll on, they find themselves overwhelmed by consequences from poor planning in the initial stages of development. I've seen companies fold because they failed to test and develop their product wisely. Other businesses fail because they didn't have a clear foundational mission and vision statement. It should not surprise anyone when a corporation goes bankrupt because its executives were not held accountable to a foundational standard. Precautionary measures should have been installed in the operation of the corporation in its initial stages. In business, the foundational development is vital.

In an even broader illustration, a culture's foundation dictates its strengths and weaknesses. The strength of a family is vitally related to the strength of the marriage that produced it. If marriages are falling apart on a large scale in a culture or society, we should not be surprised by the increase in poverty, teen pregnancies, abortion, teen suicide, and lower educational performance. More importantly, as an increasingly large number of families become dysfunctional, we should expect fewer qualified, trustworthy, and righteous leaders to rise up to lead the culture back to sound foundations. If the foundational unit of society—marriage and family—is not secure, righteous, and protected, then forthcoming generations will suffer tremendous grief and pain.

But the best picture of the importance of foundations is illustrated by the field of building construction. The foundation is the most important aspect of a structure. If you've done remodeling work on a house that was not square or level, you know the builder must work with the state of the foundation, from the floor to the roof. If it is skewed, the things built on top of it will not fit quite right. Tension and frustration may result. Later, the occupants must live with the problems produced by the foundation.

In a region that suffers earthquakes, the foundations of buildings are of great concern. Perhaps you recall, as I do, seeing news coverage of the earthquake damage in San Francisco and Northridge, California, and in Turkey and Japan. Images come to mind of collapsed buildings, buckled roads, pancaked freeways, and selfless rescuers searching for survivors.

For many, the violent jolts of an earthquake are analogous to what they experience spiritually on a daily basis. And the aftershocks continue to rock their structures. Some have found their faith able to withstand the shaking, but others are buried beneath the rubble of a defective faith, crying for help.

If you can relate to this, then you know how important spiritual foundations are in life. Foundations anchor the soul to the unshakable. It is my prayer that this book will be as effective as a rescuer when he breaks through to a trapped victim of a terrible earthquake. I trust God will pull you up, bring healing, clean off the faulty foundation, and build a new, strong foundation for faith that can withstand every shockwave that comes.

There may be others who don't feel at all shaken or in danger of a spiritual, structural collapse of faith; yet their foundations are weak and vulnerable, much like a building that survives the small temblors, but hasn't been tested by the "big one." If inspected carefully, these structures show that their foundations do not satisfy God's building codes.

You may be one of those who have the foresight to prepare for the future. You long to be anchored in solid rock. I hope this volume may anchor you in Christ, thus providing an unshakable security and faith, no matter what magnitude of spiritual "earthquake" may occur.

The old hymn, *The Church's One Foundation*, states a great truth. "The church's one foundation is Jesus Christ, her Lord." We must be anchored in Jesus and His Word. The Word of the Lord is eternal, and so this book is filled with scripture. I hope that after you have finished it, your Bible will never be the same to you. And by God's grace, neither will your responses to the shakings in your life.

Can you imagine the owners of buildings that have toppled in an earthquake reconstructing new structures on the same foundations? Wisdom requires a complete destruction of the old foundation and the establishment of a new, firmer foundation. Those new buildings need to be anchored more deeply and securely.

That same wisdom may be applied to the person whose faith has suffered collapse during a moral or spiritual earthquake. Before we construct a building that brings glory to God, there may need to be some demolition work. This may be hard to acknowledge. But the evidence is obvious in the church today in the United States: many spiritual buildings are swaying, cracking, and crumbling due to relentless quakes and aftershocks of trials and temptations.

We all know some, if not many, who lie buried beneath the rubble of what was supposed to be a house of faith. Why are many in the church today so shallow, sensual, powerless, and like the world? Why does the church resort to worldly marketing philosophies and methods to fill its pews?

We must put our foundation to the test: what is the basis for our faith? The conflict we feel because of the events of our lives is a spiritual *fault* in the foundation that is a nemesis to faith. The fruit of the Spirit of God is contrasted with the deeds of the flesh (Galatians 5:19-24). We are supposed to live in the love, peace, joy, and power of Jesus Christ. When we don't, it is right to ask, "Why?"

Are you spiritually hungry and do you desire to be holy? Are you tired of not being what the Bible says you ought to be? Tired of committing, recommitting, and rededicating, only to have your faith shaken by the next quake? Perhaps you're on the verge of despair. You're buried beneath the rubble and feel that if someone doesn't rescue you quickly, you might as well give up and die.

Despair comes from not understanding God and His ways, and our faith shakes when the events of life don't match with our understanding of God. But there's a *reason* why so many have a vulnerable faith. The problem doesn't lie in God's powerlessness to save or in a lack of sincerity and desire to have a house of faith glorifying to God. More than likely, it has to do with the foundation. Perhaps we are not securely anchored in the Solid Rock. Maybe we've been building on sand instead of stone.

Through this book we will re-examine and reconsider foundational scriptures—scriptures introduced during childhood or one's first exposure to the gospel presentation. Sadly, many of the verses used in modern evangelism have been extracted from their context and used to accomplish an end for which the verses were not written. They have been abused and misused.

The result has been tragic! Millions of professing Christians and many who have fallen away from the church have spiritual foundations built on half-truths and error. Consequently, they drift like a ship without an anchor. Their lifestyles reveal all-too-little evidence of the presence of the living Lord Jesus Christ. Many people sincerely believe they are Christians bound for glory but instead are deceived and bound for eternal destruction. Someone has cried, "Peace, peace" when there is no basis for peace! One reason for this is the many popular scripture verses that have been abused and misused.

In the first part of this book, we will re-examine some foundational scriptures. The result may be quite shaking! You may feel like your basis for faith has been demolished. Earthquakes test the foundation until all that remains is that which cannot be shaken. The truths of God's Word will be like a rescuer pulling you out of the rubble. Rebuilding can be uncomfortable. It takes time, effort, study, and patience. But it is worth it! And please understand that my motive is love for both the truth and you when I say, *if your basis for faith can be demolished, it needs to be*. Wrong use and interpretation of scripture cannot anchor your soul in Jesus. So, we'll put those scriptures back in their contexts, and then begin to rebuild the foundation.

Understanding who and what God is, God's purposes for creation, the fall of man, and sin form the core of the second section. If our ideas about God are askew, we'll find ourselves in error regarding man and sin. Quite often a person's faith fails because of the sin he sees in himself and in others. Why has God allowed sin? Why does He allow men to do terrible things to innocent people? Do we have an answer to the thousands and millions who die because of natural disasters? What about unanswered prayer? When we have a firm foundation regarding God and His purposes, these kinds of questions don't stumble us.

The third part of this book is dedicated to how God works in preparing His people for salvation. We'll investigate effective ways to present the scriptures and the gospel. One chapter will specifically address the evangelization of our children. How do we lead our children to Christ so they can be anchored in Him?

I trust the Lord to make your study both refreshing and stimulating. I hope your faith and your love for Jesus Christ will be renewed. Additionally, I think you'll find your mind and heart stimulated to investigate the scriptures more diligently. And when you have finished reading, I pray you'll stand before God and face life well anchored in the Lord Jesus Christ and His Word.

Part 1

Abused Scriptures

One

Joshua 24:15

*And if it is disagreeable in your sight to serve the Lord,
choose for yourselves today whom you will serve:
whether the gods which your fathers served which
were beyond the River, or the gods of the Amorites
in whose land you are living; but as for me and my
house, we will serve the Lord.*

A portion of Joshua 24:15 may be one of the most popular quotations from the Bible. Portions of it adorn Christian homes all across our country. Many families have, "Choose you this day whom you will serve" engraved or embossed on a plaque in their family rooms, entry ways, or bedrooms. Most evangelists would consider their gospel presentation deficient if they didn't quote part of this verse as an appeal to choose for Christ.

Have you ever questioned the idea of accepting Christ or choosing Jesus as Lord and Savior as the way of salvation? Perhaps you would be surprised to discover such an idea distorts the truth about salvation and how it is acquired. It is important to recognize (contrary to the popular interpretation of this verse) that salvation doesn't come because an individual chooses to accept Christ. More importantly, this verse doesn't teach that each man has a free will with which he may choose to accept or reject Christ.

It is significant to note that the whole verse is usually not printed or given in most evangelistic presentations. The truncated version can be misleading. Indeed, if the verse is examined within its immediate context, we find it teaches just the opposite of what it appears to teach when we only consider, "Choose you this day whom you will serve... as for me and my house, we will serve the Lord." There's much more to this passage of scripture.

Before we examine the passage, it is also helpful to consider the reasoning behind its current popular presentation. The *false* assumption is that if God holds a person responsible for obedience, then he must naturally have the freedom of will to obey. But this is not the case. Although man does have the physical ability to obey, he doesn't naturally have the spiritual freedom of will to make a choice resulting in salvation. The truth is that apart from union with Jesus Christ and the ensuing work of the Holy Spirit in one's heart, a command to obey can only reveal a person's hostility toward God and his inability to please God in the flesh.

Therefore, pulling this verse out of its context may lead someone to think his *choice* is the foundation for his relationship with God. He may think his destiny depends upon his decision. Furthermore, if that is true, then the logical conclusion is that the power source for his continuing to live the Christian life is his *choice*. But that teaching will not stand the test of God's Word or the reality of life. In fact, it leads to a shakable faith. Let's think about what happens when we receive a command from God.

The Power Source

Have you ever considered what a command from God reveals? When God makes a command, it exposes man's heart condition. If a person can obey, it shows the power of God at work in his heart. On the other hand, if he cannot obey, it reveals his will still lies in bondage to a darkened heart. Here's an example we can easily understand. When parents express their desires to their son, the condition and direction of the son's heart is revealed by his response. If his heart is toward the parents, obedience will follow. But if not, then a conflict will arise.

Here is what was happening in Joshua 24. Joshua's challenge to the nation of Israel created a situation designed to reveal the heart condition of that generation. His last recorded sermon to the nation of Israel preceded their occupation of the Promised Land. As we look at these verses in their context, we find that Joshua tested the fathers of

Israel by giving them some choices. But they aren't the choices implied in most gospel presentations. He first gave the command, then offered some alternative choices.

> *Now, therefore, fear the Lord and serve Him in sincerity and truth; and put away the gods which your fathers served beyond the River and in Egypt, and serve the Lord. And if it is disagreeable in your sight to serve the Lord, choose for yourselves today whom you will serve: whether the gods which your fathers served which were beyond the River, or the gods of the Amorites in whose land you are living; but as for me and my house, we will serve the Lord (Joshua 24:14-15).*

The Israelites were commanded to fear the Lord and serve Him. That is the obvious first choice. But it may be surprising to notice that "Choose whom you will serve" is not only referring to the Lord, but to various idols. Even more surprising might be the realization that Joshua didn't think they could choose God and walk that choice out faithfully!

> *And the people answered and said, "Far be it from us that we should forsake the Lord to serve other gods; for the Lord our God is He who brought us and our fathers up out of the land of Egypt, from the house of bondage, and who did these great signs in our sight and preserved us through all the way in which we went and among all the peoples through whose midst we passed. And the Lord drove out from before us all the peoples, even the Amorites who lived in the land. We also will serve the Lord, for He is our God."*

> *Then Joshua said to the people, "You will not be able to serve the Lord, for He is a holy God. He is a jealous God; He will not forgive your transgression or your sins" (Joshua 24:16-19).*

Joshua saw their spiritual inability to choose for God. He knew they would not and could not choose to serve God, but they *could* choose which idol they would serve.

> *"If you forsake the Lord and serve foreign gods, then He will turn and do you harm and consume you after He has done good to you." And the people said to Joshua, "No, but we will serve the Lord" (Joshua 24:20-21).*

But they were spiritually blind. They wrongly concluded that if given the choice between God and idols, they could choose to serve God. Notice carefully Joshua's response.

A Surprising Reply

> *And Joshua said to the people, "You are witnesses against yourselves that you have chosen for yourselves the Lord, to serve Him." And they said, "We are witnesses" (Joshua 24:22).*

Have you ever heard this warning by an evangelist to those who would choose for Christ? Joshua declared that they witnessed against themselves and would not serve God. So he sealed their testimony with a command.

> *Now therefore, put away the foreign gods which are in your midst, and incline your hearts to the Lord, the God of Israel. And the people said to Joshua, "We will serve the Lord our God and we will obey His voice."*
>
> *So Joshua made a covenant with the people that day, and made for them a statute and an ordinance in Shechem. And Joshua wrote these words in the book of the law of God; and he took a large stone and set it up there under the oak that was by the sanctuary of the Lord.*
>
> *And Joshua said to all the people, "Behold, this stone shall be for a witness against us, for it has heard all the words of the Lord which He spoke to us; thus it shall be for a witness against you, lest you deny your God" (Joshua 24:23-27).*

As you read on to the end of the book of Joshua and into the first chapters of Judges, Joshua's words were verified. As long as Joshua and his generation were around, the people worshiped and obeyed God. But as soon as they died, the people turned to idols. We see the same testimony today. As long as there is a strong spiritual leader present, those who don't have the Spirit of God assume a form of godliness. But when the godly influence is removed, their true powerlessness and lack of spiritual life is exposed in their apostasy.

In reality, these verses teach that even though *man has a responsibility* to worship God with his whole heart, *he does not have the spiritual freedom of will* to do so. Natural man, although he knows God's laws, is helpless without the Spirit of God to enable him to obey.

This conclusion drawn from these verses may be confirmed in numerous passages. Romans 7:15-8:3 accentuates this doctrine. Paul summarized this section of his letter with the following:

> *For the law of the Spirit of life in Christ Jesus has set you free from the law of sin and of death. For what the Law could not*

do, weak as it was through the flesh, God did: sending His own Son in the likeness of sinful flesh and as an offering for sin, He condemned sin in the flesh (Romans 8:2-3).

Responsibility Does Not Imply Freedom of Will

The important point for doctrinal foundational purposes is this: *responsibility does not imply freedom of will.* In fact, if we tell people to believe when they do not have the Spirit of God at work in their hearts, their attempts at being responsible for believing will only prove they *cannot* believe. For instance, telling them to have an unshakable faith will reveal their shakable faith. The powerlessness of the flesh will be unveiled just as it was in Israel.

Telling people to choose to believe puts them in a position for God to witness against them when they choose to obey. I can hear someone reacting, "But the Bible tells us, 'Believe on the Lord Jesus Christ and thou shalt be saved.'" Please think carefully about what I'm saying. I'm not saying we shouldn't tell people they *must* believe on the Lord Jesus Christ in order to be saved. I'm saying we shouldn't tell them they *can choose to believe.* A person can't just choose to believe. The person's choice to follow Jesus proceeds from Spirit-born faith in the heart. We'll talk about this later in the chapters on John 3:16 and Romans 10:9-13. For now, consider the importance of telling the truth to a person about his powerlessness to submit to Christ and about his need for a Savior. God's Word testifies that man is dead in his sin and does not have the ability to choose to do good by God's standards. Romans 3:11-12 confirms this teaching:

> *As it is written, "There is none righteous, not even one; there is none who understands, there is none who seeks for God; all have turned aside, together they have become useless; there is none who does good, there is not even one."*

So, using Joshua 24:15 to teach that man has a free will is using it to teach the opposite of what the passage actually emphasizes. Your faith will have a more secure base if you build with this truth: *man is not able to choose for God without the enabling work of God's Spirit.* An unshakable faith is not based upon man's ability to choose (and isn't the emphasis in most manmade religions always on *man's* glory?), but on God's Spirit working to produce fruit for *God's* glory. The fruit of the Spirit of God when the gospel is presented anchors faith in the work of God through Jesus Christ by the Holy Spirit, not in one's ability to choose correctly!

Two

John 1:12

But as many as received Him, to them He gave the right to become children of God, even to those who believe in His name.

Another very popular evangelistic verse is John 1:12. Often pulled out of its context, this verse also is frequently used in evangelical tracts to teach that a man must choose to accept Christ so he may be saved. We must be careful not to read into this verse something that is not there.

Using this verse without its context, evangelists often tell people there is something they must do before they can be saved—they must receive or accept Jesus. As with Joshua 24:15, the implication is that man has a free will because the Bible teaches that one must believe in Jesus and accept Him. These ideas then become weak foundation stones in the new convert's faith.

Let's look not only at verse 12 but also at verse 13, which completes the sentence and gives us the context. First, you'll notice that the words "accept" and "choose" are not in these verses.

Is "Received" the Same as "Accepted"?

But as many as received Him, to them He gave the right to become children of God, even to those who believe in His name, who were born not of blood, nor of the will of the flesh, nor of the will of man, but of God (John 1:12-13).

These two verses actually teach what Joshua 24 taught: man cannot and will not believe without a work of God in his heart. We cannot interpret "receive" to mean "accept with a free will" because verse 13 eliminates that possibility. Believing and being granted the power to become a child of God occur only by the will and power of God, not by the free will and power of man. A passage in John 6 also confirms this interpretation.

They said therefore to Him, "What shall we do, that we may work the works of God?" (John 6:28).

Jesus didn't answer this question. The answer He gave revealed *how* they would get spiritual food—by God's power, not their own.

Jesus answered and said to them, "This is the work of God, that you believe in Him whom He has sent" (John 6:29).

Jesus further testified that these people who came to Him were unbelieving. But how is this work of God accomplished?

Eternal Life Comes Because God Wills It

*No one can come to Me, **unless the Father who sent Me draws him**; and I will raise him up on the last day (John 6:44).*

*For He says to Moses, "I will have mercy on whom I have mercy, and I will have compassion on whom I have compassion." **So then it does not depend on the man who wills** or the man who runs, but on God who has mercy (Romans 9:15-16).*

Notice in the following verse that those who believe are those who already have eternal life. Note the order. Which comes first, eternal life or faith?

Truly, truly, I say to you, he who believes has eternal life (John 6:47).

Those who have been given eternal life believe because God has willed it and worked faith into their hearts. John 1:12-13 (see above) confirm the truth of Hebrews 11:1, "Faith is the assurance of things hoped for, the conviction [*evidence*] of things not seen." Since no one can believe and obey God unless God has first chosen him and performed a work of transformation in his heart, then the presence of an active faith indicates that God has already given eternal life to him—that is, God has given him the power to become His child. He received Christ as a gift of grace from God, which empowered him to become a child of God.

Not Everyone Can Receive

In contrast to those who receive the Son, Jesus commented about those who cannot receive the Spirit of the Son of God (not *will* not, but *cannot*).

> *If you love Me, you will keep My commandments. And I will ask the Father, and He will give you another Helper, that He may be with you forever; that is the Spirit of truth, whom the* **world cannot receive**, *because it does not behold Him or know Him, but you know Him because He abides with you, and will be in you (John 14:15-17).*

Same author. Same book. Same word as John 1:12—"receive." The beloved disciple recorded that Jesus apparently understood the distinct difference between those of the world and those who were children of God. Those of the world do not have the ability to receive the Spirit of God. But the children of God do receive Him. This point emphasizes that the Apostle John did not consider "receiving the Son" to be a matter of man's will, but a matter of God's will.

You Believe Because You Received

This is foundational to anchoring your faith in Jesus Christ. If you believe in the Lord Jesus Christ, you do so because God has given Jesus to you and you to Him. He has become everything you need for life in God, both now and forever. Note how 1 Corinthians 1:29-31 affirms this interpretation.

> *... that no man should boast before God. But* **by His doing you are in Christ Jesus**, *who became to us wisdom from God, and righteousness and sanctification, and redemption, that, just as it is written, "Let him who boasts, boast in the Lord."*

I have heard some teach that their free will choice operates within them apart from God's power (and it must, to call it "free"). They believe that God looked down through the corridors of all time and saw which men would choose for Christ and which ones would not, and then gave Christ to those who would. If one thinks that the apostle understood man to have a free will, then we should consider another inconsistency. If God ordained that no man should glory in His presence, why would He establish a way of salvation (namely, free will) that unavoidably enables man to share His glory? To have done so would allow man to glory in His presence because the man chose of his own free will apart from God. However, salvation based upon the power of God alone, not the free will of man, is what anchors one in Jesus Christ.

Is Our Will Ever Free?

Perhaps we need to redefine *free will*. We are all born in bondage to spiritual darkness. It is God who works in us through the power of His Word and Spirit to release our wills from the power of spiritual blindness and bondage. After the regenerating work of God, our wills are freed from slavery to sin. But our wills still are not free! According to Romans 6:17-18, the will is committed *by God* to righteousness.

> *But thanks be to God that though you were slaves of sin, you became obedient from the heart to that form of teaching **to which you were committed**, and having been freed from sin, **you became slaves of righteousness**.*

When we chose Christ, we did so by an act of our wills; however, our decision resulted from the will and power of God first working in us by His Spirit. When we were born again by God's Spirit, God produced faith in our hearts. That same God-given faith cleansed our hearts from an evil conscience and then working through love, moved us to trust and follow Christ. To Him be the praise and the glory forevermore! This revelation causes us to glorify God in our salvation. It also forms the basis for an unshakable faith because we know that God loved us even while we were His enemies. This assures us that if God is for us, no one, not even ourselves, can be against us.

Therefore, the foundation upon which the house of faith is built is God Himself. He saved us in Christ. If we try to build God's house (our faith) on the foundation of man's power to choose (which is the basic tenet of humanism), we can expect the house to crumble in the day of trials and judgment. If we base our lives on the firm foundation of God's power and will, then our lives, both here and in eternity, will be to the praise of His glorious grace. This is the lesson taught in John 1:12-13.

Three

John 3:16

For God so loved the world, that He gave His only begotten Son, that whoever believes in Him should not perish, but have eternal life.

What a tremendous truth! Do you think there is another verse of scripture more popular than this one? We see it on placards at professional ballgames, on billboards, and just about anywhere the gospel is presented. What can possibly be wrong with the way this verse is used in the church today?

As we look into the truths expressed by this most-favorite scripture, I hope you will conclude as I have that a significant part of the church today has misunderstood the message of John 3:16 and is using it in ways that God never intended. At the close of this chapter, we will compare the actual truths expressed by John with the modern abuse of the verse, but for the most part I want to focus on John's purpose for including the story of Nicodemus in his gospel narrative—that is, what Jesus was teaching about faith, how the Holy Spirit works in salvation, God's motivation in saving His people, and the extent of God's redemptive plan.

The great scope of God's love, His wonderful provision in His Son, and the promise of eternal life all reside in this glorious verse of scripture. But even so, we can mislead others if we don't include with it the rest of the story. If we don't consider the intent of the gospel writer, John, when he featured Jesus' encounter with Nicodemus, we might not make the important distinction between two very different kinds of faith: flesh-born faith and Spirit-born faith. If we are to become people of faith, we must recognize the qualities of both kinds of faith. Otherwise, we may be easily deceived and discouraged. This distinction was John's intent.

Have you ever felt you needed a shot of faith in the arm? Perhaps you've had times where you felt you just didn't believe enough. Maybe you've wondered why certain things didn't happen when you thought you did believe and trust God.

To understand what John was teaching when he wrote that "whoever believes in Him should not perish," it is helpful to begin reading in John 2:23. We see in the end of Chapter 2 people who believed in Jesus because of the signs He performed. But the kind of faith that comes by seeing signs is not the kind of faith to which Jesus gives Himself. Apparently that kind of faith is not saving faith. With this in mind, we are ready to see Jesus' meeting with Nicodemus in its proper perspective.

There Is a Kind of Faith Born of Flesh

They believed because they saw in the fleash.

Now when He was in Jerusalem at the Passover, during the feast, many believed in His name, beholding His signs, which He was doing (John 2:23).

The first thing to notice from the last verses of Chapter 2 is that many believed because of the signs they saw Jesus doing. The verses following verse 23 in Chapter 2 indicate that Jesus discerned this faith to be not the work of His Father and the Holy Spirit. This kind of faith is a faith born of the flesh—the natural man under the dominion of sin. Notice what John records about Jesus' response to this faith:

He, knows the hearts of men.

But Jesus, on His part, was not entrusting Himself to them, for He knew all men, and because He did not need anyone to bear witness concerning man, for He Himself knew what was in man (John 2:24-25).

Throughout the gospels we notice that Jesus would not entrust Himself to just anyone who said he believed. He understood there is a kind of faith that is not saving faith. There is a faith, not born of God, but generated by seeing signs. This kind of faith enables a man to follow a teacher or a philosophy, but it is not saving faith. It is the same kind of faith unconverted children of regenerate parents might possess. These children see God working in their parents and in their church, and that work is undeniable, so they believe. By itself, however, this belief is not saving faith.

Finding examples of this kind of faith is not difficult. I believe it is the same kind of faith exemplified by Simon the magician, recorded in Acts 8:13. Simon had been baptized and was "continuing on with Philip." But Peter apparently did not believe Simon had a saving faith, for he exclaimed, "May your silver perish with you!" (Acts 8:20). Judas Iscariot also portrayed this kind of faith. In fact, even the demons are said to believe (James 2:19), but I don't think anyone would believe the demons are regenerated! I think this kind of faith is the kind required of the children of elders, as stated in Titus 1:6. But most important to us as we consider the context of John 3:16 is that Nicodemus exemplified this kind of faith.

In John Piper's book *Future Grace*, we find some enlightening commentary on these verses.

> There is a warning here: this "believing" may not be saving faith. It is based on "beholding his signs." True faith can come through seeing the miracles of Jesus. But the danger is that some people were being carried away by the mere power of Jesus and its potential for overthrowing the Romans. Jesus rejected this kind of enthusiasm.

> So when John says "many believed in His name" (2:23) because they saw the signs He was doing, we are alerted to the fact this "believing" may be a persuasion based on His power that does not go to the heart of who He is. This is, in fact, what seems to be the case with these believers.[1]

Bible Commentator Leon Morris also wrote about these "believers":

> John is speaking of men who had made an outward profession, but in this particular case it did not go very deep.[2]

John continued his gospel by reporting Jesus' response to this sign-generated faith. He gave an example in Nicodemus. Certainly you have noticed in your reading of the gospels how Jesus tested his listeners by speaking to them in parables or through analogies. This was what He did with Nicodemus, and this is why John's recording of this encounter is significant. Jesus tested him to see if His Father was at work. The way Jesus often tested people was by making statements that could be understood only by the Spirit's revelation. When people understood these statements, then Jesus knew they were children of God. Notice what happened in

John's account of Jesus' encounter with Nicodemus:

> *Now there was a man of the Pharisees, named Nicodemus,*
> *a ruler of the Jews; this man came to Him by night, and said*
> *to Him, "Rabbi, we know that You have come from God as a*
> *teacher; for no one can do these signs that You do unless God is*
> *with him" (John 3:1-2).*

We can see from this declaration what men such as Nicodemus and the "believers" in John 2 believed. They believed God was with Jesus, but that belief is apparently not the same as saving faith.

> *Jesus answered and said to him, "Truly, truly, I say to you,*
> *unless one is born again, he cannot see the kingdom of God"*
> *(John 3:3).*

If Nicodemus had received revelation from God, I think Jesus would have encouraged him that he had been born again. But there had been no work of the Spirit. Nicodemus could not see the kingdom of God in Jesus or in himself.

This first kind of faith precedes the saving kind of faith created by the Holy Spirit. Once again, we notice that it is based on signs. Jesus did not recognize it as a work of God. It is a natural kind of faith, which sees but doesn't perceive the truth. It hears, but doesn't understand. John observed *many* who had this kind of faith. Many have the same kind of faith today.

Do you recognize this kind of faith in anyone? Is this the kind of faith your children have in God and in Jesus Christ? Here are the characteristics of natural faith:

- It is based on signs.

- It is born by natural means.

- It cannot see and understand the spiritual realities of the Kingdom of God.

- It is a form of faith, so a person who has it says he believes.

People who have flesh-born faith usually experience confusion and frustration when it comes to living the Christian life. It is not uncommon for children who have natural faith to become disillusioned with Christianity and the faith of their parents. They have been told they are saved because they believe; yet they don't have the power of God in their lives or the power to love and forgive others, or to obey God.

How does this happen? Could it be they were not taught the difference between natural-born faith and Spirit-born faith? If you detect this kind of faith in someone, may I suggest you not try to *convince* them of their lack. Let the Holy Spirit do the convincing! Simply show them the truth about natural-born faith and Spirit-born faith. You might use the examples I've already mentioned of the first kind of faith (the demons in James 2, Simon in Acts 8, Demas in 2 Timothy 4:10). Perhaps you can think of other examples and discuss with them how someone might feel and think about his relationship with God if he had only the natural-born faith. How might discovering the possibility of saving faith yet to come bring hope to someone who has tried to believe but has constantly experienced powerlessness?

Have you ever wondered what kind of faith *is* saving faith? We've all known people who profess to believe in God, but quite frankly, their lifestyles and values don't seem much different from those who don't admit to any kind of faith in God. In the third chapter of John's gospel, we learn about a kind of faith birthed by the Spirit of God. Jesus told Nicodemus, a leader of the Pharisees, that one must be "born again" to see the kingdom of God. Nicodemus revealed in his response his lack of understanding of spiritual things. Then Jesus proceeded to teach Nicodemus about...

A Kind of Faith Created by the Holy Spirit

Nicodemus said to Him, "How can a man be born when he is old? He cannot enter a second time into his mother's womb and be born, can he?"

Jesus answered, "Truly, truly, I say to you, unless one is born of water and the Spirit, he cannot enter into the kingdom of God. That which is born of the flesh is flesh, and that which is born of the Spirit is spirit. Do not marvel that I said to you, 'You must be born again.' The wind blows where it wishes and you hear the sound of it, but do not know where it comes from and where it is going; so is everyone who is born of the Spirit."

Nicodemus answered and said to Him, "How can these things be?"

Jesus answered and said to him, "Are you the teacher of Israel, and do not understand these things? Truly, truly, I say to you, we speak that which we know, and bear witness of that which we have seen; and you do not receive our witness" (John 3:4-11).

If Nicodemus had received faith through revelation by the Holy Spirit, then he would have received Jesus' witness. But it is clear Nicodemus had no clue about what Jesus was speaking. You can almost see the consternation on the face of this brilliant Jewish scholar. He couldn't deny God was with Jesus, but he was still spiritually blind and without understanding.

In a little while we will contemplate briefly the characteristics of saving faith described in this passage, in order to help us distinguish the difference between flesh-born faith and Spirit-born faith. In the meantime let's continue exploring how and why this verse is abused in the church today.

Jesus Introduced a New Redemptive Paradigm

Reading this conversation between Jesus and Nicodemus from our American, middle-class, multi-cultural, internationalist mindset perhaps clouds the significance of their words. Not only did Jesus explain the necessity of the new birth to Nicodemus, but He also described *the way the Spirit works*—and it's probably not the way Nicodemus thought. The Spirit blows where *He* wishes, saving all kinds of people by His transforming power, not according to their race or heritage or religious works.

Where did *Nicodemus* think the Spirit of God worked? More specifically, which nation or people did Nicodemus think the Spirit of God rested upon? And most importantly for us, what did these things have to do with John's purpose for including this encounter in his gospel?

Remember that Jesus referred to Nicodemus as "the" teacher of Israel. This was no common man or small-fry among the leaders of Israel! This was a Pharisee of Pharisees, a teacher of teachers, and an ardent nationalist. How did Nicodemus think the Spirit of God worked?

Well, I can't say for sure, but if he had the typical, nationalist Jewish mindset, he more than likely thought the Spirit of God worked in a redemptive manner only among the Jews, and the Gentile world was on the outside when it came to God's redemptive promises. It was because of this commonly held belief that, when God began to save the Gentiles, He had to use a sign (speaking in tongues) to prove to the Jews that He *was* working among the Gentiles (Acts 10:44-47; 15:8-9).

I think John's purpose for including this story about Nicodemus in his gospel was to emphasize to his readers that *the Spirit of God was bringing redemption to non-Jews through Jesus Christ.* Who better represented the line of thinking about Jewish nationalism than "the teacher" of Israel? If *he* stood corrected by Jesus, then all Israel would benefit by hearing of this encounter! Furthermore, the story would serve the purpose of providing an impetus to the believing Jews to take the gospel to the Gentile world.

There is additional insight as we consider Nicodemus as "the teacher" of Israel. Jesus and Nicodemus probably were not strangers to one another, and it is likely much had transpired between them. Perhaps Nicodemus had known Jesus as a twelve-year-old when He came to the temple to listen and to ask penetrating questions (Luke 2:46). Certainly Nicodemus had heard Jesus teach at the temple many times. It is likely that Jesus had witnessed to him often through telling him "earthly things." And perhaps the witness Nicodemus did not receive was that the heart of God was going to extend to more than just the Jews.

> *If I told you earthly things and you do not believe, how shall you believe if I tell you heavenly things? And no one has ascended into heaven, but He who descended from heaven, even the Son of Man (John 3:12-13).*

Apparently Jesus had previously told Nicodemus He had come from heaven and so should have been able to tell him of heavenly things. But instead of doing so in this encounter, Jesus gave him another earthly analogy from their national history.

> *And as Moses lifted up the serpent in the wilderness, even so must the Son of Man be lifted up; that whoever believes may in Him have eternal life (John 3:14-15).*

The impact of this verse is multiplied when we consider what Jesus meant by these words to this Pharisee. Just as God had provided a means of salvation for Israel in the wilderness, so God was also providing a means of salvation for *anyone* who believes.

John Explained the New Paradigm

I wonder, if we had been there in the room with Jesus and Nicodemus, what we would have seen on the face of Nicodemus when Jesus said, "whoever believes may in Him have eternal life." Maybe Jesus saw the perplexed "cow-looking-at-a-new-gate" look in his eyes and knew He needed to explain. Or perhaps Nicodemus was so fixed in his notions about salvation that Jesus could tell he wasn't understanding the full scope of the word, "whoever." Although there is no way to tell from the story, the little word "for" at the beginning of verse 16 indicates that an explanatory statement is forthcoming.

So this raises some questions about verses 16 through 21: How do these verses explain Jesus' comment in verses 14 and 15? And what is it about Jesus' statement, "And *as* Moses lifted up the serpent in the wilderness, *even so* must the Son of Man be lifted up; that whoever believes may in Him have eternal life" that required explanation to John's readers? As we study this section of their conversation, we do well to keep in mind John's line of reason. First, Jesus told Nicodemus the new birth was a work of the Holy Spirit (verses 5 through 8). Second, Jesus told him he lacked understanding about the work of the Spirit of God (verses 10 through 12). What was it Nicodemus didn't understand, and what was it about Jesus' witness that Nicodemus did not receive?

I would like to suggest, Nicodemus didn't understand that the Spirit of God was going to blow among the Gentiles. And it is likely Nicodemus wouldn't have received such a prophecy. The "whoever" in verse 15 needed explaining. The Jewish readers John had in mind, like Nicodemus, would need to understand that the work of the Spirit of God was not limited to the Jews. His Gentile readers also would be encouraged to know that Jesus had prophesied the work of God's Spirit among them. They too could have eternal life and not perish.

There are two opinions about who was speaking in verses 16 through 21: Jesus, or John. We will consider both, beginning with the traditional view that Jesus was the speaker of the following words, and John was quoting Jesus when he wrote them down:

> *For God so loved the world, that He gave His only begotten Son, that whoever believes in Him shall not perish, but have eternal life. For God did not send the Son into the world to judge the world, but that the world might be saved through Him. And this is the judgment, that the light is come into the world, and men loved the darkness rather than the light; for their deeds were evil. For everyone who does evil hates the light, and does not come to the light, lest his deeds should be exposed. But he who practices the truth comes to the light, that his deeds may be manifested as having been wrought in God (John 3:16-21).*

If Jesus was the one who spoke these words to Nicodemus, we can imagine how convicted Nicodemus must have felt. Numerous times Jesus exposed the Pharisees' love for the approval of men. For instance, the Lord warned in the Sermon on the Mount not to practice "righteousness before men, to be noticed by them." The Apostle John provided another example of how the Pharisees sought men's approval when he wrote that many of the rulers believed, but they would not confess Christ because "they loved the approval of men rather than the approval of God" (John 12:38-43). If we keep in mind what Jesus said about the Pharisees throughout the gospels, we might have a clearer picture of what Jesus was communicating to Nicodemus on this night, if indeed He was actually the one who said all these things to him.

Men like Nicodemus were careful to maintain a squeaky-clean image. Pharisees were not the kind of men who admitted their faults and neediness. They certainly didn't think of their self-righteous, religious deeds as wicked and evil. In the minds of the Pharisees, the "Gentile dogs" were wicked and unworthy. It is not a stretch of the imagination to conclude that Jesus' remarks to Nicodemus were targeting national and spiritual pride and love for man's approval. These would also be characteristic of a fleshly kind of faith, which He had already distinguished from Spirit-born faith. If *a Gentile* could be born again without having kept all of the laws and without displaying religious zeal according to the Law, what did that say about Nicodemus' paradigm of salvation and righteousness? Jesus always went for the heart!

The second view of whose words are recorded in verses 16 through 21, however, seems more likely to me. Rather than Jesus having spoken them to Nicodemus, I think it was John who wrote them later in explanation of what Jesus had previously said. A few reasons support this idea. First, the perspective of verses 16 through 21 appears to be that of a third party. In verses 14 and 15, Jesus referred to Himself as the "Son of Man," a title He often used. If Jesus were the speaker, why didn't He continue using that title throughout the rest of the conversation? The reference to Him changes from "the Son of Man" to "the Son" in verses 16 through 18, and there is no reference from the first-person perspective in verses 16 through 21, as there had been in verses 3 through 15.

Second, if you read through the Gospel of John, in all but a couple of instances, when Jesus spoke of God, He referred to Him as "My Father." However, in these verses, the reference is to "God," which would have been natural for the author. Third, verses 16 through 21 sound more like a commentary written after the events occurred. The words are similar to those used in John's first epistle, which was written near the same time as his gospel. (For instance, compare John 3:16 and 18 with 1 John 4:9, and John 3:17 with 1 John 4:14.)

If John was the author of these verses and was not quoting Jesus, he was providing here a very important commentary on Jesus' encounter with Nicodemus: *The wind of the Holy Spirit is going to blow into the world among the Gentiles. Most importantly, God has the same redemptive plan for the world—motivated by the same love—as He had for Israel. And His redemptive plan is not exclusively for the Jews!* This would have been unbelievable to Nicodemus since he did not have the Spirit, as it also would have been to John's Jewish readers. Let's look at John 3:14-17:

> *As Moses lifted up the serpent in the wilderness, even so must the Son of Man be lifted up; so that whoever believes will in Him have eternal life. For God so loved the world, that He gave His only begotten Son, that whoever believes in Him shall not perish, but have eternal life. For God did not send the Son into the world to judge the world, but that the world might be saved through Him.*

Why were Nicodemus and the Jews unable to think that salvation would include the Gentiles? Because pride is blinding. Since the Pharisees boasted in their own works, they failed to notice the importance of God's Word to Israel about His love being the reason they were favored. The prophet Jeremiah wrote,

> *"The Lord appeared to him from afar, saying, 'I have loved you with an everlasting love; therefore I have drawn you with lovingkindness'"* (31:3).

And Malachi testified to Israel,

> *"'I have loved you,' says the Lord. But you say, 'How have You loved us?' 'Was not Esau Jacob's brother?' declares the Lord. 'Yet I have loved Jacob'"* (1:2).

In both cases God's messengers were declaring God's great love as His motivation for saving His people. If verse 16 is John's commentary, it reiterates the point Jesus made in verse 15 and thereby emphasizes it: *For just as God loved His people in the wilderness and provided a means of temporal salvation to them, even so He loved His people in the world and provided a means of eternal salvation to them.*

I don't know if it matters a great deal who spoke or wrote the words contained in verses 16 through 21; it is the truth of them that concerns us most. If we view these verses as the words of John, they emphasize more poignantly the sense of the preceding discourse, namely, that forgiveness of sins is available to the Gentile world on the basis of faith in Christ as a result of the new birth by the Spirit of God. It would have been a new paradigm of salvation for people like Nicodemus who put their confidence in their choices of religious service, discipline, and sacrifice.

The Same Is True Today

Those who take pride in their choosing to believe in God, who are yet strangers to saving faith, face the same need for humbling that was lacking in Nicodemus. They need to recognize that their only hope lies in what God has done on their behalf in Jesus Christ. How about you? If you are married, how about your spouse and children? What kind of faith do you and they have? If you have only the first kind of faith, you may rejoice in God that you have the prerequisite to saving faith, but I encourage you not to be satisfied with anything less than Spirit-born, saving faith. You may glorify God by declaring your natural-born faith to be nothing about which to boast or in which to be confident.

If you now see the vanity of the first kind of faith, you may be on the doorstep to the second kind of faith. Will you renounce your self-righteousness and instead hope in the promise of God for those who believe in Jesus Christ, trusting not in *your own choice* to believe, but in *His work* that opened your heart to believe?

Those who have saving faith recognize its presence as something the Holy Spirit has produced in them. They recognize it as the fulfilled promise of eternal life that comes through Jesus Christ alone. They no longer hope in or rely on whatever they have done to try to please God, to win His approval, or to secure their redemption. In short, those who have this second kind of faith boast in the Lord! When asked how they know they are saved, they say with the Apostle Paul,

> *If anyone else has a mind to put confidence in the flesh, I far more: circumcised the eighth day, of the nation of Israel, of the tribe of Benjamin, a Hebrew of Hebrews; as to the Law, a Pharisee; as to zeal, a persecutor of the church; as to the righteousness which is in the Law, found blameless. But whatever things were gain to me, those things I have counted*

as loss for the sake of Christ. More than that, I count all things
to be loss in view of the surpassing value of knowing Christ
Jesus my Lord, for whom I have suffered the loss of all things,
and count them but rubbish in order that I may gain Christ
(Philippians 3:4-8).

But by His doing [I am] in Christ Jesus, who became to [me]
wisdom from God, and righteousness and sanctification, and
redemption, that, just as it is written, "Let him who boasts,
boast in the Lord" (1 Corinthians 1:30-31).

Therefore, let us boast in the glorious work of our Father in and
through His Son, Jesus Christ! Let us anchor ourselves in Christ Jesus,
our Lord. Our faith in Jesus alone and His death for our sins *is* God's
sign to us that we are His, and this becomes a solid rock upon which to
stand when the storms of life rage around us.

Six Characteristics of Saving Faith

Now that we have looked more deeply at the kind of faith created
by the Holy Spirit and at the scope of God's redemptive plan, I'd like
to go on to consider the signs that show how saving faith is developing
in a person. These are often not visible as they are happening in other
people's lives, but you may recognize them in yourself. These signs are
evident in the Gospel of John, Chapter 3.

Saving Faith Has Eyes to See and Enter the Kingdom of God

Jesus answered and said to him, "Truly, truly, I say to you,
unless one is born again, he cannot see the kingdom of God."
Nicodemus said to Him, "How can a man be born when he is
old? He cannot enter a second time into his mother's womb
and be born, can he?" Jesus answered, "Truly, truly, I say to
you, unless one is born of water and the Spirit, he cannot enter
into the kingdom of God" (John 3:3, 5).

The first sign of Spirit-born faith is that you have a new ability to
act on your desire for God and His kingdom. That is, where once you
were not interested or you felt hopeless, now you will come, believe,
and repent. You see and enter the kingdom of God. Dallas Willard in
his book *Divine Conspiracy* defines God's kingdom as the range of His
effective will where what He wants done, gets done.[3]

Within the context of Jesus' statements in John 3, I think He was referring to the advancement of the rule and dominion of the King of the Universe in the hearts of men. This is what it means to "enter into the kingdom of God." Whereas the first kind of faith simply allows one to *acknowledge the signs of the kingdom's presence in the world*, it doesn't enable one to *see the kingdom in the soul and spirit*. But the second kind of faith opens one's eyes to God's work in his own heart and in the hearts of others.

When people are born again, they are aware of the work of God in their hearts, enabling them to believe. They can tell the difference between the kind of faith they had previously and the kind they now possess. Surely you have heard testimonies of people who believed in God's existence and knew of the work of Jesus Christ on the cross but were proud, hostile, and rebellious toward God. Then they had an encounter with God, which changed their hearts and attitudes. They were conquered by the love and power of God!

Saving Faith Is Anchored in the Word of God

The second sign of saving faith is that you begin to hear God's Word with open ears and to think differently because of what you hear, as the Holy Spirit applies the Word of God to your mind and brings about a change of heart (John 3:5-8).

God's Word is the means by which saving faith comes to men. Jesus taught this when He told and then explained His parable about the sower:

> *"Listen to this! Behold, the sower went out to sow; ... And as soon as He was alone, His followers ... began asking Him about the parables. ... And He said to them, "Do you not understand this parable? And how will you understand all the parables? The sower sows the word. And these are the ones who are beside the road where the word is sown; and ... Satan comes and takes away the word which has been sown in them. And ... these are the ones on whom seed was sown on the rocky places, who ... immediately receive it with joy; ... but are only temporary; then, when affliction or persecution arises because of the word, immediately they fall away. And others are the ones on whom seed was sown among the thorns; these are the ones who have heard the word, and the worries of the world, and the deceitfulness of riches, and the desires*

*for other things enter in and choke the word, and it becomes
unfruitful. And those are the ones on whom seed was sown on
the good soil; and they hear the word and accept it, and bear
fruit, thirty, sixty, and a hundredfold." (Mark 4:3-20).*

Later, Peter reinforced the truth that salvation comes through the
Word of God when he wrote,

*...for you have been born again not of seed which is perishable
but imperishable, that is, through the living and abiding word
of God (1 Peter 1:23).*

Jesus told His disciples about the experience of those who come
to Him. They hear and learn from the Father because no one comes
to Jesus for salvation without first being drawn by the Father's word
(John 6:44-45). We hear His word, the Spirit blows into our hearts and
we embrace the truth, and we repent and believe. This is the power of
the new birth. Just as no one has any power to bring about his own
natural (water) birth, even so no one has power to bring about his own
spiritual (new) birth. Saving faith is accomplished through the living
and powerful Word of God, applied by the Spirit.

Saving Faith Is a Work of the Holy Spirit

The third sign of saving faith is that you begin to behave differently
by the transforming power of the Holy Spirit, whereas before you were
powerless to change yourself. The Spirit uses the Word to accomplish
the new birth. In Romans 10:17 we read,

So faith comes from hearing, and hearing by the word
[rhema] *of Christ.*

W.E. Vine comments in his *Expository Dictionary of Old and New
Testament Words,*

The significance of rhema (as distinct from logos) is exemplified
in the injunction to take "the sword of the Spirit, which is the word
of God" (Ephesians 6:17); here the reference is not to the whole
Bible as such, but to the individual scripture which the Spirit
brings to our remembrance for use in time of need, a prerequisite
being the regular storing of the mind with Scripture.[4]

Saving faith results when the Holy Spirit takes a scripture and
reveals its specific, practical application to our lives. As Jesus said in

John 3:6, the Spirit gives birth to spirit, whereas the flesh can only produce natural fruit. Nothing is quite as powerful to change us as God's Word applied by the Spirit to our thinking and our actions.

The Spirit's work is unpredictable. We can't plan it or control it. When new birth happens to people, they are aware of the Spirit's presence and work but can't tell how it came to them. They only know they've been affected by His power, just as Jesus described to Nicodemus the way the Spirit comes:

> *"The wind blows where it wishes and you hear the sound of it, but do not know where it comes from and where it is going; so is everyone who is born of the Spirit" (John 3:8).*

Nicodemus clearly didn't understand what Jesus was talking about. John 3:9-10 reads,

> *"Nicodemus answered and said to Him, 'How can these things be?' Jesus answered and said to him, 'Are you the teacher of Israel, and do not understand these things?'"*

Remember the high position and reputation that Nicodemus enjoyed as a Pharisee. As a great Jew, his confidence before God lay in his works, done in the sight of men (his praying on street corners, his fasting, his public giving exercises). His hope was that the God of Israel was as impressed with his knowledge and deeds as he was.

In contrast to Nicodemus, the person who has saving faith places his confidence in the work of the Spirit of God in his heart and life. He experiences from his conversion a new relationship with God and His Son, Jesus, through the ministry and presence of the Holy Spirit.

Saving Faith Is Founded on the Work of God in Christ

The fourth sign of saving faith is that you develop a solid foundation based on the work of God in Christ. As we read John 3:14-15, we see that Jesus is speaking on behalf of His Father and is making an astonishing promise of salvation to those who believe in Him. Saving faith must be rooted in nothing less than this promise from God. The promise depends upon God's glorious work of redemption and deliverance through Jesus' substitutionary death. Because we know that God will not lie to us, His promises regarding Jesus' death and resurrection bring hope. God's promises regarding Jesus' death and resurrection bring hope. Hope is a powerful dynamic, producing faith in the heart of one who receives the promises (see Colossians 1:3-5). Without promises, no hope exists. And without hope, there can be no faith.

With this in mind, we can understand what Jesus was revealing to Nicodemus that gives us an example of this aspect of saving faith. He gave the *foundation* for the promise of eternal life—God lifting up His own Son! The definitive sign of Spirit-born faith is that *it focuses on God and gives glory to God*. The mistake many people make today is thinking the foundation for the promise of eternal life is *a person's own choice or decision to believe in Christ*. What distinguishes saving faith from natural faith is that it doesn't rest in the work of man (choosing to believe), but in the work of God (Jesus' death and resurrection).

This is the analogy provided in the testimony about the serpent being lifted up in the wilderness. In that event, God demonstrated the way He would bring about eternal salvation for His people. First, He revealed His wrath. Then He sent forth His promise as a means by which faith could be born and the Spirit could work. In His conversation with Nicodemus, Jesus simply reiterated that truth: eternal life can't be received without faith, and saving faith can't be born without a promise.

Saving Faith Rests in God's Love

The fifth sign of Spirit-born faith is that you rest in God's love for you (John 3:16), and you stop thinking God loves you because you love him.

Many people's faith is anchored in themselves rather than in God's love. Without realizing it, they rest their faith in *their* love for God because they were told that God loves them so much, they ought to love Him in return. However, placing their faith in their own ability to love God is like building a house on shifting sand. When storm winds blow in life, if one's love for God is cold or wavering, one's faith is liable to be gone with the wind. Therefore, saving faith stands firmly on the fact of God's love *for us* revealed in Jesus Christ, not our love *for Him*.

Saving Faith Glorifies God

Sign number six stands out to me as an easy test when I am trying to discern true faith. Saving faith wants all the glory to go to God for anything done which is good. It is not self-exalting, smug, impatient, frustrated, or merciless toward others who don't "perform" so well.

And this is the judgment, that the light is come into the world, and men loved the darkness rather than the light; for their deeds were evil. For everyone who does evil hates the light, and does not come to the light, lest his deeds should be exposed. But he who practices the truth comes to the light, that his deeds may be manifested as having been wrought in God (John 3:19-21).

John struck at the heart of his Jewish readers—the Nicodemuses, the people who have taken pride in their having "believed" (but by the power of their flesh), who have gone to great pains not to let others see their sins and their weaknesses. But his words also strike at the heart of every subsequent reader of his gospel who has the same kind of faith as Nicodemus had. Just what would it have "cost" Nicodemus to believe in Jesus? It would have cost him his position, his coveted praise from men, and his sense of worthiness before God.

Since salvation results from a Spirit-born kind of faith and not from natural faith in signs and wonders, the fact that Nicodemus recognized Jesus' connection with God means very little. Nor does this Pharisee's prestigious position as "the teacher" of the Jews count for much. A lifetime of good deeds means nothing, if one has not been moved by the Spirit of God. This would have been a very hard pill for Nicodemus to swallow. And although the Bible does not tell us what the ultimate outcome was of this clandestine meeting with Jesus, we can hope that Nicodemus was eventually truly saved. If he was, then we can expect that, like the Apostle Paul, he became a humble man and confessed that all he had lived for was trash—dung, as Paul called it—compared to the faith that comes from the Holy Spirit. He would have "changed his garments" (no doubt having been required to leave his teaching position as a Pharisee), testifying that there is no glory in the works and faith of the natural man, and that the only thing that counted was the Spirit-produced faith in his heart toward Jesus Christ. If he did take such a course of action, then his soul truly became anchored in Jesus. A similar kind of Spirit-born humility and confession is what it "costs" every person who comes to saving faith in Christ.

People in every time in history and from every religion want to justify themselves before God and glorify themselves before men. The only exceptions to this self-justification and -glorification are those who have been born again by the Spirit of God. When someone wants all the glory for his salvation to go to God, it clearly signifies the presence of saving, Spirit-born faith.

Can You See the Difference?

John 3:16 has been misused to convince people that God loves everyone and thus they should put their faith in Jesus. I hope you'll notice that this verse is not *prescriptive* (giving people something they can do to be saved) but is *descriptive* (expressing what Jesus meant when He told Nicodemus the Holy Spirit was going to blow wherever He wished). Has He blown in your life? In the lives of those you love?

> *The wind blows where it wishes and you hear the sound of it,*
> *but do not know where it comes from and where it is going; so*
> *is everyone who is born of the Spirit (John 3:8).*

We have seen throughout this passage that Jesus presented a new paradigm to Nicodemus with regard to the work of the Holy Spirit: He was going to blow amongst the Gentiles, revealing God's love for them. How grateful many of us can be for this wonderful love of God, which has given the promises of God also to us who were,

> *"Separate from Christ, excluded from the commonwealth of Israel, and strangers to the covenants of promise, having no hope and without God in the world, but now in Christ Jesus... have been brought near by the blood of Christ" (Ephesians 2:12-13).*

The table on the following page deals with four commonly misunderstood topics arising from John 3. It compares John's message (the actual teaching of the passage) with the frequently encountered, modern-day abuses of this scripture.

Topic	Meaning of the Passage	Modern Misunderstanding
Nature and Object of God's Love	God loves the world the same way that He loved Israel. Just as He provided a means of salvation through the serpent lifted up before the Jews, He has now provided a means of salvation through His Son, Jesus. Those who believe in the Son will be saved, but they believe because of the will of God and the divine work of the Holy Spirit in their hearts.	God loves the whole world *so much* that He sent Jesus to die for the sins of the whole world. He wishes that everyone would come to Him and choose to believe in His Son so that He could save us all, but the responsibility rests on us to make the right choice.
Work of the Holy Spirit	The Spirit moves as He wills, like the wind, coming to those whom God has chosen, producing faith and repentance in them. The work of the Spirit produces genuine faith, spiritual birth, and the peace of God.	The Holy Spirit comes whenever a person chooses to believe in Jesus and prays the sinner's prayer. The Spirit responds like the genie in Aladdin's lamp—and gives the person a sense of peace, happiness, and forgiveness.
Salvation	Salvation is initiated and completed by God. He grants repentance and new life to every one He has chosen, and then they believe. All glory goes to God.	Salvation is granted to anyone who decides to believe in Jesus and recites the sinner's prayer. John 3:16 is used to encourage people that God loves them so much that all they have to do is choose to believe and they will be saved.
Source of Love	Saving faith rests in God's love—love from God toward us in Christ revealed in His death for us and His love flowing through us to others by the Holy Spirit.	Saving faith rests on our love for God, which we ought to feel in response to His kindness to us. Since He loved us so much we need never be afraid if we don't have the consistent ability to love others.

I encourage you to take time to review these six signs of saving faith revealed in John 3 and consider your experience with God.

1. Saving faith has eyes to see and enter the Kingdom of God.

2. Saving faith comes by the Word of God.

3. Saving faith is a work of the Holy Spirit.

4. Saving faith is founded on the work of God in Christ.

5. Saving faith rests in God's love.

6. Saving faith glorifies God.

Four

Acts 2:38

*And Peter said to them, "Repent, and let each of
you be baptized in the name of Jesus Christ for the
forgiveness of your sins; and you shall receive the gift
of the Holy Spirit."*

In this chapter and the next, we'll look at two passages of scripture
from the book of Acts that are often used to tell people how to
become Christians. If these verses (2:38 and 16:31) are taken out of
their context, they appear to be telling people they must *do something*
in order to be saved. However, if left in their context, we see that the
key to understanding what these people were told lies in understanding
the particular situations they were in. The misuse of these scriptures
doesn't come so much from the *misinterpretation* of the specific
verses as from the *misapplication* of them.

In both cases, the Spirit of God obviously had worked in the hearts
of the hearers. There were indications that God had granted repentance
and faith. These passages teach us that when the Spirit of God is at
work, people repent and believe. When there is evidence that God is
granting repentance and faith, that is the time to give a new believer
the promises from Scripture about forgiveness, the Holy Spirit, and
eternal life. Is it right to take these verses out of their contexts and
consider them the rule or standard for evangelism? Many have done
so. It is not right, and for a good reason.

The Book of Acts is a historical record of the days after Jesus ascended into heaven and gave His Spirit to the church. The book is perhaps best thought of as the acts of the Holy Spirit in the birth of the church. It is not a teaching book like the letters of Paul are, so it serves a different purpose. As we read it, we are observers, learning how the Spirit of God worked and led men to speak and act in various circumstances. We may discover certain principles underlying those words and actions, but wisdom forbids our concluding that things are always to be done the way we read they were done in Acts.

Let's see the significance of what Peter told his hearers as it relates to the historic Day of Pentecost. Try to put yourself into this scene from Acts 2:4-8.

God Gets Their Attention

And they were all filled with the Holy Spirit and began to speak with other tongues, as the Spirit was giving them utterance.

Now there were Jews living in Jerusalem, devout men, from every nation under heaven. And when this sound occurred, the multitude came together, and were bewildered, because they were each one hearing them speak in his own language. And they were amazed and marveled, saying, "Why, are not all these who are speaking Galileans? And how is it that we each hear them in our own language to which we were born?" (Acts 2:4-8).

To begin with, we see God did something to get the attention of the people. When the Holy Spirit was first sent, the apostles proclaimed the gospel in Aramaic, their native language. Then a miracle took place—the people from every nation under heaven heard the gospel in their own native tongues! Peter proclaimed to this large crowd that they were witnessing the fulfillment of God's promise, made through the prophet Joel. We read of their amazement and response in verses 12 through 21:

And they all continued in amazement and great perplexity, saying to one another, "What does this mean?" But others were mocking and saying, "They are full of sweet wine."

But Peter, taking his stand with the eleven, raised his voice and declared to them: "Men of Judea, and all you who live in Jerusalem, let this be known to you, and give heed to my words. For these men are not drunk, as you suppose, for it is only the third hour of the day; but this is what was spoken of through the prophet Joel:

'And it shall be in the last days,' God says, 'that I will pour forth of My Spirit upon all mankind; and your sons and your daughters shall prophesy, and your young men shall see visions, and your old men shall dream dreams; even upon My bondslaves, both men and women, I will in those days pour forth of My Spirit and they shall prophesy. And I will grant wonders in the sky above, and signs on the earth beneath, blood, and fire, and vapor of smoke. The sun shall be turned into darkness, and the moon into blood, before the great and glorious day of the Lord shall come. And it shall be, that everyone who calls on the name of the Lord shall be saved.'"

Peter Explains God's Sign

The typical evangelistic encounter rarely has the accompanying signs of Pentecost. We might imagine that Peter had the crowd's rapt attention. He explained what God was doing and, by the leading of the Holy Spirit, brought Jesus Christ into their minds.

Men of Israel, listen to these words: Jesus the Nazarene, a man attested to you by God with miracles and wonders and signs which God performed through Him in your midst, just as you yourselves know—this Man, delivered up by the predetermined plan and foreknowledge of God, you nailed to a cross by the hands of godless men and put Him to death. And God raised Him up again, putting an end to the agony of death, since it was impossible for Him to be held in its power (Acts 2:22-24).

At this point, you can imagine what conviction was wrought in the hearts of those whom God was converting! Peter drove home the significance of their having crucified Jesus: the One they had put to death was going to be their Judge! Peter clearly proclaimed God's sovereignty in Christ's crucifixion; however, that didn't leave the people unaccountable for their part in His death. What were they to do since God had raised Jesus from the dead and made Him Lord? The Lordship of Jesus Christ lies at the heart of the gospel. As Paul wrote to the Romans, it is faith in His resurrection and His Lordship that we confess when we are saved. That is why this part of Peter's sermon is vital to our understanding of evangelism.

> *This Jesus God raised up again, to which we are all witnesses. Therefore having been exalted to the right hand of God, and having received from the Father the promise of the Holy Spirit, He has poured forth this which you both see and hear. For it was not David who ascended into heaven, but he himself says: 'The Lord said to my Lord, "Sit at My right hand, until I make Thine enemies a footstool for Thy feet."'*

> *Therefore let all the house of Israel know for certain that God has made Him both Lord and Christ—this Jesus whom you crucified.*

The People Respond

> *Now when they heard this, they were pierced to the heart, and said to Peter and the rest of the apostles, "Brethren, what shall we do?" And Peter said to them, "Repent, and let each of you be baptized in the name of Jesus Christ for the forgiveness of your sins; and you shall receive the gift of the Holy Spirit"* (Acts 2:32-38).

God had obviously convicted these men that they were guilty of murdering God's appointed Messiah. The Spirit of the Lord was clearly blowing.

What was the effect of His blowing? They repented. Repentance has come to mean *a change of mind and conduct*. But it originates from two Greek words, *meta* meaning "after" and *noia* meaning "to perceive." Vine's *Expository Dictionary of Old and New Testament Words* indicates the word implies that a person changes his perception of something on the basis of what he observes.[5] *After watching the display of the Spirit's work at Pentecost, the Jews were thinking differently about who Jesus was and about their relationship to Him.* Before the day of Pentecost, they had believed Jesus was an impostor, a trouble-maker, a blasphemer, and *their enemy*. But as Peter spoke, by the grace of God, they saw differently.

That's not possible without the work of the Spirit of God. Peter knew that. When he saw they were pierced to the heart and were asking what they should do, Peter responded according to what he saw God doing. They were thinking again about who Jesus was and about their relationship to Him. So Peter gave the very timely instruction, "Repent and... be baptized." It is interesting that most gospel presentations today seldom include "be baptized" at the outset. Why did Peter feel led to include this in his message?

Baptism communicated the concept of identifying with Jesus and receiving a witness from God. The significance of this is that when they were baptized, they were being identified publicly with Jesus and with those who had repented and renounced their confidence in the ceremonies of Judaism.

So what conclusion can we draw from these verses regarding evangelism? It is important to know what the Spirit of God is doing in the heart of the hearer. A faith based solely upon the words of a preacher is a shakable faith, but one built upon the Word of the Spirit spoken to the heart can withstand any storm in life.

But what if the Spirit of God isn't speaking to the heart of a listener? Consider Jesus' encounter with the rich young ruler. Jesus didn't tell *him* to repent and be baptized. Instead, He commanded him to go, sell everything he had, give it to the poor, and come follow Him. Why don't we use this example in evangelistic presentations? Because it was a historical account that applied only to the rich young ruler. For the same reason, we must be careful not to think that Acts 2:38 should be universally applied in every evangelistic presentation.

If God is granting repentance, then it is timely to tell a person to repent. But we should not make sacred the particular way Peter talked with the crowd on that day. The most we should say about what happened is that the Spirit led Peter to encourage these hearers, *and them alone*, to repent and be baptized. The Spirit prepares people differently to hear the gospel message. In another situation the Spirit of God may lead His ambassadors to say something similar, yet different. We'll see an example of this truth in the next chapter, when we look at Acts 16:31.

Five

Acts 16:31

And they said, "Believe in the Lord Jesus, and you
shall be saved, you and your household."

We are living in a time when there is a great emphasis on evangelism and church growth, and when the numbers of nickels and noses measure the success and significance of ministries and preachers. In this unspiritual climate, many ministers feel a tremendous pressure to get "decisions for Christ." The evangelist, church staff, or preacher may be tempted to reduce the gospel to a formula. Some have even designed so-called "blueprints for salvation." The consequence of this type of evangelism is that many people expect mere compliance to a formula—raising their hand or walking down to the front of the church during an altar call or invitation—to result in their salvation.

Beware of Reducing the Gospel to a Short Formula

Perhaps no scripture lends itself to being treated as a formula more than this verse in the sixteenth chapter of Acts. This verse is also used in many evangelistic tracts and presentations. What is the problem with that? Remember what we learned in the last chapter as we considered Acts 2:38? Acts is a historical book and is simply telling some of the ways the Holy Spirit worked among the apostles in the places where they were bringing the gospel. The things we read there should not be used to formulate doctrine or to establish evangelistic methods.

In the context of the book, Acts 16:31 is a response by the Apostle Paul and Silas to a particular man (a jailer) after a specific incident (an earthquake) took place in Philippi. The verse is part of a larger story describing what happened in that city when Paul and Silas preached the gospel there. When they told the Philippian jailer to believe in the Lord Jesus and he would be saved, it was exactly the right thing to tell him because of what was happening in the jailer's life at that time. Paul and Silas were sensitive to what the Spirit of God was doing that night.

But applying this verse to everyone in every situation turns these verses into a short formula for salvation. Doing so may mislead some into thinking that *choosing to believe* is the basis for salvation. They may wrongly conclude, "If it's going to be, it's up to me." This kind of thinking won't hold anyone firm when the storm winds blow. When we are telling others about Christ, it's important to be attentive to God's Spirit so we know when He is working and when He is not.

D. Martyn Lloyd-Jones, arguably one of the foremost expository preachers of the last century, aptly described the importance of dealing correctly with verses like Acts 16:31 when he wrote,

> We are living in a time of trouble; many people are unhappy and face great problems. Some people cannot sleep; some are worried about money; others are anxious about their health and are afraid that they cannot get any help—their world is full of problems. And such people go to a Christian service and are told, "Come to Jesus and you will get all that you require." Now if you merely say to those people, "Confess with your mouth the Lord Jesus, and believe in your heart that God hath raised him from the dead," I say you are misleading them.
>
> If you merely say to them, "Believe on the Lord Jesus Christ and you will be saved," and then ask, "Do you believe on the Lord Jesus Christ?" and they say "Yes!", if you then reply, "You are saved," you are misleading them. We must "speak the word of the Lord" to them, "the word of God," as Paul and Silas did to the Philippian jailor and to his household. We must draw this thing out; we must expound it. They must not merely believe the story of Jesus, but must know its significance.[6]

How Can I Be Saved From This Situation?

A study on the word "salvation" gives us further insight into what was happening that night in the prison. The word translated "save" may also mean "deliver" or "preserve." To "save" or "deliver" best suits the situation in which the jailer found himself. The context also helps us determine how to interpret the word. It is likely that the first concern of the jailer at the moment he asked the question, "What must I do to be saved?" was to be *delivered* from the hands of his commander.

Consider the great confusion that earthquakes tend to create. The text suggests there was chaos in the compound in its immediate aftermath. The jailer's thoughts were probably not too clear. He had secured Paul and Silas in stocks, and now he was being hastily awakened because there was trouble. Who told him the news? What did they tell him? We are not sure, but we know he thought his prisoners were gone, and that meant his life was on the line. He and his family would be held responsible and probably would be executed because of the prisoners' escape.

Thus he was in a predicament where he feared death was imminent. At first he thought the prisoners for whom he was responsible had escaped. Then he learned that they were still in the prison! Were they going to take vengeance on him and his family? Would they then escape after all? Were they going to somehow bring great trouble on him before his commanders? This dilemma meant that he and his household faced certain and dire, if not fatal, consequences. So was he concerned about his soul's salvation? I don't think so. More than likely, he was simply in great fear for his life and perhaps the lives of his family.

The scriptures tell us how Paul and Silas came to be in the custody of the jailer.

> *And when they had inflicted many blows upon them, they threw them into prison, commanding the jailer to guard them securely; and he, having received such a command, threw them into the inner prison, and fastened their feet in the stocks"* (Acts 16:23-24).

According to archeological excavation in Philippi, the prison compound comprised a number of buildings surrounding a courtyard. The family of the jailer probably worked with him in cooking, feeding, and caring for the prisoners. The jailer and his family likely lived in a dwelling adjacent to the prison house. But whether near to it or far away, they apparently were able to sleep while Paul and Silas were singing and praying, and while the earth was shaking! Luke gives us details of the earthquake and the jailer's response:

> But about midnight Paul and Silas were praying and singing hymns of praise to God, and the prisoners were listening to them; and suddenly there came a great earthquake, so that the foundations of the prison house were shaken; and immediately all the doors were opened, and everyone's chains were unfastened. **And when the jailer had been roused out of sleep and had seen the prison doors opened, he drew his sword and was about to kill himself, supposing that the prisoners had escaped** (Acts 16:25-27).

Who roused him? And when was he roused? It was probably the members of his household who woke him. The word "when" suggests it was long enough after the earthquake for him to have convinced himself that his prisoners were long gone.

We know he was in terrible fear because he thought that his prisoners had escaped. Perhaps he figured that if he killed himself, it would appear that someone had overpowered him and released the prisoners. At least his honor would remain intact. Or maybe he determined it would be nobler to kill himself than be executed for negligence. How was he to be delivered out of such a predicament?

> But Paul cried out with a loud voice, saying, "Do yourself no harm, for we are all here!" And he called for lights and rushed in and, trembling with fear, he fell down before Paul and Silas, and after he brought them out, he said, "Sirs, what must I do to be saved?" (Acts 16:28-30).

The suicide was prevented when Paul shouted that no prisoners had escaped. This must have amazed the jailer. In the darkness and confusion, he probably could not see if anyone was still in the prison. If he did not feel the earthquake, then he wouldn't have known how long the doors had been open. He may have come out of his own quarters, seen the doors open, and assumed the worst. But upon hearing Paul's good news, he called for his family to bring lights.

Why did he fall in fear before Paul and Silas? He may have thought they held his life in their hands. He may well have been thinking in those first moments after being awakened that someone had freed the prisoners from the stocks, and now they were going to kill him. He would certainly have expected such retribution from typical prisoners.

Saved From the Vengeance of God, or of Man?

Considering all of the circumstances of that night, the jailer's request, "Sirs, what must I do to be saved?" could well have been asked in another sense than the evangelical context that is typically assumed by the modern church: "Sirs, what will it cost me to be saved from your hands?" Or perhaps he realized that he was in an even greater danger—death at the hands of Paul and Silas' God. If he was *their* enemy, then obviously he was *God's* enemy! If *they* could kill him, what might their *God* do to him?

But is there anything in the context suggesting the jailer had *spiritual* salvation in mind when he asked the question about being saved? No, not really. This is not a man who had demonstrated any interest in their message previous to the work of God in the earthquake.

Paul and Silas Spoke the Word of the Lord

When Paul and Silas admonished the jailer to believe in the Lord Jesus, it is also possible they were responding to a different question from the one the jailer was asking. They certainly were not going to miss this opportunity to be kind to a man who had persecuted them. *Clearly, Jesus had given them an opportunity to testify to the jailer.* Paul and Silas discerned the work of the Spirit of God and believed they should preach Christ and salvation to the jailer.

I think the jailer was surprised at their response. They didn't want money. They weren't interested in blackmail at all. They loved him.

> And they said, "Believe in the Lord Jesus, and you shall be saved, you and your household." And they spoke the word of the Lord to him, together with all who were in his house. And he took them that very hour of the night and washed their wounds, and immediately he was baptized, he and all his household. And he brought them into his house and set food before them, and rejoiced greatly, having believed in God with his whole household (Acts 16:31-34).

Verse 32 should not be overlooked. Paul obviously didn't have a formula in mind when "they spoke the word of the Lord to him, together with all who were in his house." We don't know exactly what gospel presentation Paul and Silas gave, but we can be sure it contained the great truths found in Paul's epistles. The historical accounts in Acts are summaries of events. Luke, the author, wasn't concerned about the full content of the gospel message given, in most cases. When we read, "they spoke the word of the Lord," we can know from Paul's letters that his gospel involved the Lordship of Jesus Christ over all things. We can also safely assume the resurrection and its significance were central to Paul's message. Both Lordship and the resurrection are central to saving faith, as mentioned in Romans 10:9-10.

Through the events of that night, God had taught the jailer to fear God more than men. The jailer's care for his prisoners' wounds confirmed that God had in fact granted him repentance and faith. Much like in the events of Pentecost, the working of the Spirit of God was evident in this story.

A Formulaic Gospel Opens the Door to a Counterfeit Experience

Sadly, many people have fallen victim to unscriptural evangelistic methods and messages. They were perhaps under the pressure of the devil's "stress program" of great trials or calamities and therefore vulnerable to a message lacking the full gospel truths. It is dangerous to think that "believe on the Lord Jesus Christ and you shall be saved" was Paul's entire gospel message. This idea misses the miracle of salvation and reduces the gospel to a powerless formula. Any "recipe" for evangelism is misleading and opens the door for a counterfeit experience of Christ if the Spirit has not been genuinely working in the heart of the listener. A person who has simply "made a decision for Christ" or followed a "formula" prayer may not have experienced the true salvation of Christ at all.

However, while some "salvation" experiences may in fact be counterfeit, I don't want to scare you with this thought. If you first believed in Jesus because someone shared Acts 16:31 or another verse like it with you, and you have since seen genuine and consistent change in your life by the power of God, do not be afraid. You can be sure that you are truly saved, the Spirit of God has worked in your heart, and God is glorifying Himself through you.

What Can We Learn?

Learning the full truth of God's Word from this passage may help many who have been held in bondage and hopelessness due to "zeal for God, but not according to knowledge," as the Apostle Paul wrote about the Jews in Romans 10. What truths does God *intend* for us to learn through these verses in Acts 16? They teach us that when the Spirit of God has brought someone to fear God more than man, then he is ready to be told to believe on the Lord Jesus Christ. That's the time to tell him what God accomplished in Christ. Does this appropriate fear of God describe your life? Then do not fear. If it does *not* describe your life, I urge you to pray and ask God to teach you to fear Him more than any man.

Another lesson here is that an evangelist must be in tune with what the Spirit of God is doing in the heart of the hearer. We should not view these verses as teaching that one must "choose to believe" as a condition for salvation. Nor should we draw the conclusion that since Paul told *that* jailer to believe on Jesus, then *everyone's* salvation depends upon what he does with his free will: accept or reject Christ. Such a conclusion produces a faulty foundation and a shakable faith. Instead, here is the key to evangelism that results in believers who are anchored in Christ: Keep in step with the Spirit of God, and teach the whole truth about the Lordship of Jesus Christ and its significance.

How About You?

Perhaps you are one of those who have suffered the delusion of thinking that because you raised your hand to give mental assent to Jesus, then you were born again. If you are, you know what I'm talking about when I speak of the frustration of trying to live the Christian life without power or a new nature, and with false ideas about God, sin, and salvation. You've probably wondered about Jesus' promise that the truth will set you free. If you don't feel free, it's because what you heard wasn't the full truth! The problem hasn't been Jesus and His unfaithfulness in keeping His promises, but rather the faulty foundation laid by zealous ministers who, like the Jews, served others, but not according to knowledge.

As you continue to read and study, you'll be amazed at how scriptures will come to mind that have never made sense to you before but now do. Also, there are other verses like Acts 16:31 that may be part of your foundation and have caused confusion. We'll study most of those verses in this first section of the book. Read on with expectation. The Holy Spirit is rebuilding your foundation, anchoring you in Christ, and He will teach you.

Six

Romans 10:9-10, 13

*... That if you confess with your mouth Jesus as Lord,
and believe in your heart that God raised Him from
the dead, you shall be saved; for with the heart man
believes, resulting in righteousness, and with the mouth
he confesses, resulting in salvation.... For "Whoever will
call upon the name of the Lord will be saved."*

I was attending an evangelistic meeting in Southern California with thousands of believers and seekers. The message that evening was biblical and the worship was lively and moving. However, what took place during the altar call alarmed me. The evangelist made an emotional appeal for the unbelieving listeners to stand if they didn't want to go to hell and wanted to join God's "forever family." If I recall correctly, he offered them the opportunity to make their eternal destiny sure, based on the verses above. He led them to repeat a prayer confessing Jesus as Lord and acknowledging they believed in Him for the forgiveness of their sins. As they said "amen," the crowd erupted in applause and the evangelist praised them for making the most important decision of their lives. They were now a part of God's family.

Although I was comforted by the idea that God's Spirit was at work in some and by the sincere love and passion of the evangelist, I was troubled by several things: First, the misuse of scripture to encourage them to pray with him. Second, the wrong idea that these people's salvation depended on what *they* did rather than on what *God* did.

Third, the tragic result in some cases of people *thinking they were saved* from the wrath of God when they *were not born again* by God's Spirit. Fourth, the frustration those poor unregenerate souls would experience as they attempted to live the Christian life without the Holy Spirit. Fifth, the unbiblical example that many of these thousands would surely follow as they would repeat the process to others, imitating the evangelist's methods.

Those are some of the alarming results of what has been called "decisional regeneration"—the idea that the Holy Spirit regenerates (or saves) someone when he or she makes a "decision" for Christ. This practice usually consists of a person's accepting Christ as his or her Savior by praying "the sinner's prayer" or inviting Christ into the heart.

A *Brief* History of Decisional Regeneration

You might be surprised to discover that this method of salvation, whereby one invites Christ into his or her heart, has no biblical foundation whatsoever. In fact, the idea of "decisional regeneration" is historically a new idea. Indeed, it didn't become popular until the 1800s. Charles Finney, an evangelist of the Second Great Awakening in the United States, was primarily responsible for advancing this method. Since then, leading people to make a decision for Christ by inviting Him into their hearts has become the popular, accepted, and even indisputable method of evangelism.

An Unscriptural Method

I hope no one is terribly shaken by this information, although I can understand how one might be. You might be thinking, "This can't be true! When I was saved, I asked Jesus into my heart. If what you're saying is true, then I must not be saved!"

No, I am not suggesting that. What I am stating is that the idea of decisional regeneration and *salvation as a result of inviting Christ into one's heart* is not a biblical idea. However, the misuse and misinterpretation of Romans 10:9 and 13 has not prevented God from saving many. His power to save isn't dependent upon the perfect presentation of the evangelist. Isn't that encouraging? But it doesn't mean we shouldn't seek to be as accurate as we can be in our message and presentation.

Don't Confuse Cause and Effect

We've been learning in previous chapters that individuals who think they were saved by inviting Christ into their hearts were not regenerated *because* they prayed the sinner's prayer. Rather, they prayed the prayer because *they already had been regenerated by God's Spirit.* If you are one who responded to an invitation to receive Christ, and you were truly born again when you did so, then your response *was evidence of a work of the Holy Spirit* in your heart that He had been doing before you ever heard the invitation. You probably would have done *anything* (within reason) that you had been asked to do. Why? Because the preliminary work had been done, and faith was then born in you at that moment when you heard God's Word. You may have a misunderstanding about how you were saved because of the way the gospel was presented to you. If you were born again through a method such as the one I mentioned above, then don't worry. Your heart is now right with God, but your mind wasn't taught according to truth. Your mind may need to be renewed.

We want to be careful not to validate a particular method simply because God gave new birth at the time the scriptures were misused and misinterpreted. We can see the danger of such logic if we consider the testimony of a friend of mine who was saved while he was under the influence of alcohol. God spoke to his heart while he was in the midst of a drunken stupor. Should he therefore conclude that God works powerfully when people are drinking alcohol? I think we would all agree he should not!

Some may respond, "So what's the big deal, then? If God can save regardless of what methods are used, apparently it is okay to use some *creativity* when it comes to evangelism and the gospel presentation." On the contrary, if we believe the Bible is the standard for our faith and practice, then we must agree that God's grace doesn't give us license to do or think whatever we wish. Truth matters. That was the very accusation Paul raised against his countrymen. They had a false zeal—a zeal, but not according to knowledge (Romans 10:2). We don't have the privilege of being creative with ideas when it comes to salvation. If we want God's power and anointing to be on our lives and our message, then our zeal must be according to knowledge (or truth).

If we believe in the sufficiency of scripture, then we should agree we are not free to add to what God has revealed in His Word. Of course, we also don't want to take away from His Word. Indeed, we want to say what God says so we can stand with confidence before Him and others as we proclaim the good news of the gospel.

If we think we are free to use our creativity when it comes to the gospel and salvation, then we throw away our confidence before God. How can we be sure God won't allow Satan to enter in and counterfeit the experience of "accepting Christ" with a flood of good emotions that are not really based on the Holy Spirit's work? Certainly it is possible if we ignore truth. Although *you* may have truly been born again when you heard about inviting Christ into your heart, there have been multitudes of people who were not born again but were instead deluded. The tragedy is that they think they are *saved* because they prayed such a prayer of invitation. Furthermore, they live powerless, Christ-less lives and profane His great name. What hope do they have if they think they have *tried* Jesus, and He didn't work for them? They have nothing solid upon which to anchor when the storms of life strike. They have no real hope unless they come to see the truth!

Is Faith Something *We* Must Do?

To answer this, it is important for us to study these two verses in Romans 10. Paul wrote,

> ... *That if you confess with your mouth Jesus as Lord, and believe in your heart that God raised Him from the dead, you shall be saved;*

> ... *For "Whoever will call upon the name of the Lord will be saved."*

The context of this passage was Paul's concern for the Jews, his fellow countrymen, who had sought to be right with God on the basis of their own power to choose to obey His law. His point up to this place in the book of Romans had been that the law does not have the power to save; in fact, the law actually proves man does not have the ability to save himself. Sin holds him in bondage to his own self-interests. This is important contextual information as we interpret Chapter 10. We want to guard against an interpretation that suggests another "work of the flesh"—something we must do—in order to be saved.

Many today have the idea that believing in God is solely a choice of the will. If this is true, then faith is a work of man rather than a work of God. As we learned in the last chapter, an evangelist who thinks this way will essentially reduce "faith" to a prayer of invitation anyone can recite. A work of the Spirit of God in the heart is not even considered important, let alone essential.

Let's look at this idea point by point. Telling someone he may be saved if he will *choose to believe* is actually giving him a law. There is value in knowing what God requires. However, if the Holy Spirit is not regenerating the person's spirit, the only thing this "law" can do is show the weakness of the flesh and the power of sin to hold a person in bondage to his own self-interests. If God the Father is not speaking to a person's heart at the same time as the evangelist is calling him to faith, then telling him he has to choose to believe will only reveal that he does not have the ability by the power of his will to convert his heart (Romans 7:14-24). We observe this inability of the will whenever the gospel is presented and the hearers do not respond to the call of the evangelist. (Later we will consider those who do respond to the evangelist's call even though there has been no saving work of the Spirit.)

Back to Chapters 4 Through 9

To gain a clearer understanding of Paul's message up to Romans 10:9, 10, and 13, let's backtrack to Romans Chapter 4. Here we notice that the apostle tackles the Jews' wrong understanding about how they could obtain righteousness. Contrary to the popular opinion held among Paul's countrymen, Abraham wasn't justified before God on the basis of his works, but via faith (4:2-3). The rest of the chapter explains why justification comes by faith and not by works of the law.

Chapter 5 then reveals the solid rock of Christ upon which believers stand. Paul showed that we gain assurance before God only by the great truth that God justified His people through the righteous work of His Son, which is the reason that grace reigns over sin. All of Chapter 5 contrasts *grace* (the effect of God's covenant with Abraham) with *law* (the effect of God's covenant with Moses).

As he led his readers through this idea, Paul stated (in Romans 5:20) that the law only increases transgressions, and grace super-abounds wherever sin abounds. Being an ex-Pharisee, he knew these statements were going to raise some questions. Therefore in Chapters 6 through 7, Paul inserted a parenthetical section answering the questions about grace reigning over sin and the purpose of the law. In Chapter 8, Paul continued his thrilling assertion that the work of God in justifying sinners by faith has delivered them once and for all from all condemnation and fear of separation from God.

Chapter 9 further unfolds God's plan of salvation by faith and not by confidence in man's willpower to choose and obtain righteousness on his own without a work of the Holy Spirit. Paul grieved over the ignorance and failure of his brothers in the flesh as they tried to obtain God's righteousness through their religious works. Did their misunderstanding mean God had failed to fulfill His promises to His people? Absolutely not! Paul spent the entire chapter defending God's plan and purpose in justifying both a remnant of Israel and the Gentiles *by faith*. But further explanation was needed to answer the question, "How is it that the Jews—who sought righteousness—*didn't* obtain it, and the Gentiles—who weren't seeking it—*have* obtained it?"

The Jews Thought They Had to *Do* Something

Chapter 10 begins with Paul expressing true zeal: he is zealous for his brothers in the flesh to know and receive the truth about the gospel. However, they have a major problem: *false* zeal. They display zeal, but not according to the true knowledge of what God's Word says when it comes to having righteousness before God. I fear that may be the same problem many evangelists have today. Paul establishes the context of the chapter, and indeed the whole book, by stating this in Romans 10:4:

> *For Christ is the end of the law for righteousness to everyone who believes.*

We must be careful not to insert subconsciously "everyone who *chooses* to believe" where it says only "believes." If we do that, we will entirely miss Paul's point. The Jews' problem was that they felt they had to do something to obtain God's righteousness. That's what Paul meant here by the phrase "the end of the law for [obtaining] righteousness." He explained the idea further in verses 6 through 7 when he wrote that the righteousness based on faith doesn't speak about great things to be done by a man so he may be saved, such as trying to ascend into heaven or trying to raise Jesus from the dead. Both feats are impossible for any human being. In other words, if a person is going to try to fulfill what God requires by his own effort and willpower, he might as well try to ascend into heaven or resurrect Jesus from the dead!

God Has Made Salvation Simple and Available to Both Jew and Gentile

Instead of putting salvation beyond our reach, God has made salvation simple and available to both Jew and Gentile by justifying His people via faith.

> But what does it say? "The word is near you, in your mouth and in your heart"—that is, the word of faith which we are preaching, that if you confess with your mouth Jesus as Lord, and believe in your heart that God raised Him from the dead, you shall be saved (Romans 10:8-9).

What does it mean, "to confess with your mouth"? The word "confess" comes from two Greek words, *homo* combined with *logeo*, which together mean, "to say the same as." Before one can say the same thing another says, the one confessing must first hear and know what to confess. *And that is the key to saving faith.* It is not something someone can create on his or her own. It requires a work of God whereby God Himself speaks to the heart and produces faith in Christ. The following verses confirm this interpretation:

> For with the heart man believes, resulting in righteousness, and with the mouth he confesses, resulting in salvation (Romans 10:10).

> "No one can come to Me, unless the Father who sent Me draws him; and I will raise him up on the last day. It is written in the prophets, 'And they shall all be taught of God.' Everyone who has heard and learned from the Father, comes to Me."

> ... And He was saying, "For this reason I have said to you, that no one can come to Me, unless it has been granted him from the Father" (John 6:44-45, 65).

Notice first that Romans 10:10 tells us faith is a condition of the heart, not a choice of the will. One might argue that the will is a part of the heart, and therefore plays an active role in salvation. But two verses clearly refute such an idea. John 1:13 states that we are born again by God's will and power, neither by the will of the flesh nor by the will of man. Second, Paul wrote in Romans 9:16 that salvation "does not depend on the man who wills or the man who runs, but on God who has mercy." So although the will may be active in *working out* one's salvation, it should not be considered as the *originator* of faith.

Second, Jesus' remarks in John 6 teach us that before someone can come to Him and believe on Him, he must be taught by the Father. When a man confesses (Romans 10:10), he is simply agreeing with what he has heard God speak within his own heart. And when God speaks to the heart, that man or woman *believes* without any effort or choice of the will.

Who Are the "Whoevers"?

For the Scripture says, "Whoever believes in Him will not be disappointed." For there is no distinction between Jew and Greek; for the same Lord is Lord of all, abounding in riches for all who call upon Him; for "Whoever will call upon the name of the Lord will be saved" (Romans 10:11-13).

Who are the "whoevers"? Did Paul mean either *anyone* or *everyone*? No, he meant neither of these. The "whoevers" are those to whom God has spoken, and therefore they believe in their hearts.

*How then shall they call upon Him in whom they have not believed? And how shall they believe **in Him whom they have not heard**? And how shall they hear without a preacher? (Romans 10:14).*

I highlighted the words above on purpose because versions of the Bible differ in their rendering of verse 14. For instance, the King James Version reads, "And how shall they believe in him *of whom* they have not heard?" And Today's English Version is translated, "And how can they believe, if *they have not heard the message?*"

But the New American Standard Bible says, "And how shall they believe *in Him whom they have not heard?*" There may be some debate about which translation is accurate. However, there is a big difference between hearing about Jesus and *hearing* Jesus firsthand. This translation makes us ask, *how can someone believe who has not actually heard Jesus speak to him?* Saving faith cannot come as a result of just hearing *about* Jesus; one must actually have a personal encounter with God where he hears the word of the Lord. If that is what Paul meant, then apparently he knew some of his readers would think faith comes through hearing the preacher, without need for God Himself to reveal truth to the heart. So he posed the question, "How shall they hear without a preacher?" It almost seems like he was leading his readers on with this series of questions. He anticipated that their response to each question would be, "Right!" Remember the three questions in verse 14 (above)? Then Paul goes on:

And how shall they preach unless they are sent? Just as it is written, "How beautiful are the feet of those who bring glad tidings of good things!" (Romans 10:15).

But watch carefully what the Scriptures say regarding the people's response to the ministry of the preachers. They give an interesting answer to that last question. After quoting the Old Testament verse regarding the blessing of God on the preachers whom He sends, Paul wrote, "However"—and cited another passage in Isaiah about the results when preachers are sent but the Holy Spirit isn't speaking to hearts: The hearers do not believe!

*However, **they did not all heed** the glad tidings; for Isaiah says, "Lord, **who has believed** our report?" So faith comes from hearing, and hearing by the word of Christ (Romans 10:16-17).*

If we agree with the New American Standard Bible's translation, the last question raised in verse 15 leads to the conclusion in verse 17 that God *must speak to each person who is to be born again by faith.*

On the other hand, if we accept the King James Version translation, then apparently Paul *purposely intended* for the argument to fall apart in order to make his point. Here is the line of reason: Calling upon Jesus requires believing in Him. Believing in Him requires hearing of Him. Hearing of Him requires a preacher—right? Wrong! Again, verse 16 makes it clear that people often do not listen to preachers! Because this is so, Paul continues, we must conclude that believing comes by hearing, and *hearing comes by the word of God.* Not the word of God through the preacher, which is often ineffective, but through the Holy Spirit, which is always effective wherever He wants it to be. In verse 17, the Greek word for "word" is *rhema.* W.E. Vine explains this:

> In connection with [both *logos* and *rhema*], the phrase "the word of the Lord" ... is used of a direct revelation given by Christ of the gospel; in this respect it is the message from the Lord, delivered with His authority and made effective by His power.[7]

It is true that we need preachers. They present the Scriptures to the *minds* of their listeners. But that presentation cannot produce faith, which resides in the *heart.* We tend to think preaching is *all* unbelievers need. Apparently the Romans also thought so, and Paul was leading his readers to understand that such a belief or conclusion is wrong. Saving faith does not come by merely hearing the gospel message *about* Jesus. Preaching Christ does not necessarily result in salvation (or else everyone who hears would be saved). Faith only comes when the Holy Spirit takes the word of Christ and speaks to the heart.

Faith—A God-Created Condition of Heart

What shall we conclude? We see that faith is a condition of heart, created by the word of Jesus Christ spoken to the heart. Hearing comes by the word of God spoken by Jesus Christ and applied by the Holy Spirit. Those who hear this way will call upon the name of the Lord and be saved.

I think it is important to note that Paul's idea of "calling upon the name of the Lord" bears no resemblance to the idea of "inviting Christ into your heart." Calling upon the name of the Lord means crying out to Him for mercy because of His promises. A person cries out for mercy when he has been convinced and convicted of his sin and then has received faith in the promises of God by the power of the Holy Spirit.

Romans 10:20 seals the point:

> *"And Isaiah is very bold and says, 'I was found by those who sought Me not; I became manifest to those who did not ask for Me.'"*

How did these Old Testament saints find God? It wasn't by their asking Jesus into their hearts. God reveals Himself to whomever He wishes. And when He chooses to reveal Himself, He needs only to speak through His Word and by His Spirit, and one believes.

These verses teach that when God speaks to the heart of a person, he or she will believe and call upon the name of the Lord. Although God has appointed men to preach, their preaching, without the Holy Spirit's work, produces no redemptive fruit. We are assured that when we preach, God will powerfully save those He has chosen to save. We preach. God speaks. Faith is born. The sinner runs to God on the basis of that faith. God saves, to the glory of His grace.

You Live How You Think You Began

On such truth, your faith is anchored in the solid rock of Jesus Christ. But if a person does not understand this truth, he may think he became a Christian because he chose to believe. And if he thinks *his choice* is how he got into the kingdom, then he'll probably think he is also to live in the kingdom *by his choices.* Here is the problem with this idea: If someone chooses one day, by his own will, to walk with Jesus, what happens if he chooses another day, by his own will, *not* to walk with Jesus? Or what happens if life gets too hard with persecutions or tribulations of all sorts, and his "choice for Christ" is dependent on his will? What if he is weak and he denies Christ? Because his soul may shake in trying times, he has nothing solid and immovable on which to anchor himself. There is no basis for rest or peace for his soul.

Jesus stressed the importance of His *Father's* choice when He told His disciples that even *His own* choice of them did not mean they were all saved, because one of them was a devil (John 6:65, 70). He also plainly stated in John 15:16 that *we have not chosen Him, but He has chosen us.* And Paul clearly asserts in 1 Corinthians 1:30-31 that it is

> *"By His doing* [we] *are in Christ Jesus, who became to us wisdom from God, and righteousness and sanctification, and redemption, that, just as it is written, 'Let him who boasts, boast in the Lord.'"*

So when Paul wrote in Colossians 2:6, "As you therefore have received Christ Jesus the Lord, so walk in Him," he was emphasizing that you received Christ by grace, trusting in the power of God, and so you may confidently continue to walk in the same way. Though Paul wrote it as an instruction, I think it has application as a warning—that we should not fall into thinking we walk in Christ by the power of our free will alone.

I do not mean by that statement that we don't make choices to follow Jesus. We do, but we do not rely on them for our standing with God. Nor do we think we are saved because *we* chose to believe in the first place. If we rely on that mistaken supposition, then we will fall either into despair or pride, depending on whether we feel like a failure or a success. We must make choices, but we should never forget that we are saved *and kept* by the grace and power of God through the faith *He* has authored and is perfecting in us (Hebrews 12:2a).

Consider the testimony of one woman who came to see the importance of right thinking about faith. She wrote,

> "If we think we must 'choose' Christ, then we must also 'choose' everything from that first step forward. This creates a very shakable faith when I consider my own demonstrated inconsistencies in making the 'right' choices and when I look

at 'believers' who later seem to 'choose' not to follow any more. But knowing that God chose me and spoke to my heart has taken away my fear that some trial may come to me where I will not be strong enough to 'choose' to walk in Christ through it. I used to be so afraid that because I chose Him, it was my responsibility to cling to Him through every storm of life. I had no assurance that *He held me* or that He loved me, so I was always trying to prove to Him, myself, and everyone else how much I loved Him. I did this to wipe out my fear of some spiritual tidal wave that would disengage me from Him. Bible verses to the contrary were of no help. The underlying and overruling 'truth' in my life was that I chose Him and would have to 'keep up my faith' through my last day on earth. Therefore the idea that believers might have to pass through the tribulation was more than I could bear. 'The Rapture' was my greatest assurance of eternal safety."

Can you relate to her? If a person *says* she chooses to believe, that doesn't necessarily mean she is righteous before God. She may be, but not because she chose to believe! My friend found her faith to be very shakable because of the wrong interpretation of these verses in Romans, along with other verses. She thought she began by generating enough faith in Christ to pray to receive Christ. Thus she felt *she* had to continue to generate God-pleasing faith until the day she died. There's no peace in a faith originating from the flesh.

Our Confidence Is in God's Choice

This truth is important for this reason: if you know that you were born into the kingdom because God chose you and has spoken to your heart, then you know you are in relationship with Him via His grace (God's working His will in your life). As a result, you will seek to *continue* to live in relationship with Him on a daily basis, trusting in God's grace. You'll look to Him as your teacher, guide, and source of faith to live your life.

This kind of relationship provides a sturdy base upon which to build a life with God. It also is foundational to joyful and Spirit-led evangelism. The Spirit never intended for Romans 10:9-10 and 13 to persuade people to choose to believe in Jesus as their Savior. Bringing people to faith in Jesus is God's jurisdiction. Our responsibility is to preach not only the *facts* that Jesus Christ is Lord and God has raised Him from the dead, but also to teach the *significance* of those facts.

Dr. D. Martyn Lloyd-Jones explained in his commentary on Romans 10:9-10 why it is important to understand this passage correctly. He said,

"I believe that this misunderstanding [thinking that all a person must do is choose to say he believes that Jesus is Lord and has been raised from the dead] is responsible for many of our troubles in the Christian church. *I am sure it is responsible for most of the problems among evangelical people.*"[8] [Emphasis added.]

He illustrated in that chapter the misunderstanding people have who cite the simple statements recorded by Luke in the book of Acts. Lloyd-Jones continued,

Apostolic preaching did give the facts, but it never stopped at the mere recital of those facts; it always went on to give their meaning and significance... So... I would remind you of this all-important point, and it is something which we must never forget as we read the Scriptures, and particularly a book like the book of Acts. What you have there is not a full report; it is not a complete and exhaustive account; it is not a shorthand note of every word uttered by the preacher; it is not a tape-recording! These are just summaries, synopses, given in the briefest possible form, and our business, therefore, is to realize that and to understand something of the fullness of their content.

Now all this is important, especially today, for many reasons. We are living in a time when there is a great emphasis on evangelism, and when pressure is brought upon preachers to get "decisions." And it is just at that point that all this becomes important. Men and women must know what they are deciding about, and why they should decide. Now the danger is that, in the anxiety to bring people to salvation, too little content may be given, so that if people merely say, "Yes" to something that is said to them, then all is thought to be well.[9]

The point I wish to stress is that sound theology should dictate our evangelism so that sound foundations may be established in the hearts of those we evangelize and disciple. Just as we do, they need a Solid Rock upon which to stand. Romans 10:9-10 and 13 were not written so we could isolate them and use them in a gospel presentation to lead people to make decisions for Christ. Paul wrote those verses to inform his readers of the content of saving faith and to teach them that such faith comes from God and not themselves. I recommend D. Martyn Lloyd-Jones' commentary on Chapter 10 of Romans for an extensive explanation of the content of saving faith.

These verses are not the only ones used to promote the idea of decisional regeneration. In Chapter 7 we will look at another one commonly used.

Seven

---

1 Timothy 2:4

Who desires all men to be saved and to come to the knowledge of the truth.

There was a time in my life when I struggled with any idea about God that could not be understood by unbelievers. I found myself uncomfortable with any concept of God that would make people feel helpless or unworthy. My zeal for seeing people saved and the joy I received from witnessing influenced my understanding of what the Bible says. One of the verses with which I encouraged people was 1 Timothy 2:4. On the surface, it seems to say what everyone would like to think about God: He wishes He could save everyone—every single person.

Later, as I began to think through the influence of humanistic philosophy upon Scripture interpretation, I reinvestigated this passage. I realized that other verses such as those we've discussed had been taken out of context and used to encourage people to "choose for Christ" in the power of the flesh. This caused me to take another look at everything I had been taught.

Many Christians feel they must present to others a God who loves everyone and wants to save everyone. Such a message makes them feel like they are wanted, which has an emotional appeal. God is sometimes presented as "having a big empty spot in His heart which only *you* can fill." Doesn't that make you feel important? It might, but is it true?

A common understanding of 1 Timothy 2:4 is that God desires for every man to be saved, without exception. It is often used to convince unbelievers of God's great desire for them to become His children. But is this what Paul intended to convey when he wrote this first letter to Timothy?

Many arguments refute the popular view of 1 Timothy 2:4 that God wants to save all men without exception, but in this chapter I'd like to focus on four of them:

1. The context of this verse (kings and authorities have the power to make life either peaceful or terrible for believers, so don't neglect to pray for them, as well as for others).

2. The Greek word used in the phrase "all men" (God is saving *all kinds* of men).

3. God's sovereignty requires that no one can thwart His will (He saves all whom He wishes to save).

4. God has determined to destroy (not save) some men.

The Context Is Prayer on Behalf of Men

The immediate context of 1 Timothy 2:4 is most important in interpreting verse 4. Paul urged Christians to pray on behalf of "all men," and he pointed out particularly kings and all who are in authority. Those who had civil authority over believers at this time were persecuting, abusing, and killing them. So why did Paul urge these Christians to pray for such men? In verse 2 Paul answered that question. Let's look at verses 2 and 4 in their context.

> *First of all, then, I urge that entreaties and prayers, petitions and thanksgivings, be made on behalf of **all** men, for kings and all who are in authority, in order **that we may lead a tranquil and quiet life in all godliness and dignity.** This is good and acceptable in the sight of God our Savior, **who desires all men to be saved and to come to the knowledge of the truth.** For there is one God, and one mediator also between God and men, the man Christ Jesus, who gave Himself as a ransom for all, the testimony borne at the proper time (1 Timothy 2:1-6).*

What does verse 4 teach us from its context? First, that God works in the lives of men, so we should pray for them, with thanksgiving.

Second, men in authority have power to make life for those they rule over either difficult or peaceful. So Christians ought not to forget about rulers in their prayers. As a result of God's work in the lives of civic leaders, Christians "may lead tranquil and quiet lives in all godliness and dignity."

In the previous chapter, Paul had recalled his own days as a leader among the Pharisees, persecuting Christians. But God saved him and made him an example of the magnitude of His grace. This was probably in his mind as he encouraged Timothy to teach his flock to pray for the abusive civil rulers over them, calling such prayer "good and acceptable" in God's sight. Using 1 Timothy 2:2 and 4 to encourage someone that God desires to save him, particularly, misses Paul's intended point.

The Greek Word for "All"

Understanding the word Paul used for "all" (as in "all men") helps us understand what he had in mind when he wrote this passage. Although his intention could be discerned from only the context, an additional study of the word "all" confirms the contextual interpretation.

The root Greek word for "all" in this passage—that is, specifically in the phrases "on behalf of *all* men," "who desires *all* men to be saved"—is the word *pas*. *Vine's Expository Dictionary of New Testament Words* states the following about *pas*:

> When used without the articles, it means, "every kind or variety." When used with the article, it means "whole or the totality of persons or things referred to."[10]

The word "all" used in verses 1 through 4 has no article, so it means "all kinds," not "every one without exception." Therefore, these verses are telling us to pray for *all kinds* of men, even men in authority, since God desires to save *all kinds of men*, and to bring them to a knowledge of the truth. This interpretation makes perfect sense in the context, as well as with the rest of Scripture.

What God Desires, He Accomplishes

Next, let's examine verse 4 in light of some other places in God's Word that shed light on His intentions for the salvation of men. Several scriptures testify that God accomplishes everything He wishes. This must include the salvation of men. Read the verses below and consider what it means for God to be sovereign. Do you think it is possible for Him to *desire* all men to be saved, but then for Him to "submit" His own will to the will of men, so that His own desire is unfulfilled?

> *But our God is in the heavens;* **He does whatever He pleases** *(Psalm 115:3).*

> *"Remember the former things long past, for I am God, and there is no other; I am God, and there is no one like me, declaring the end from the beginning and from ancient times things which have not been done, saying, '***My purpose will be established, and I will accomplish all My good pleasure***'" (Isaiah 46:9-10).*

> *For* **the LORD of hosts has planned, and who can frustrate it**? *And as for His stretched-out hand, who can turn it back (Isaiah 14:27)?*

> *So then* **He has mercy on whom He desires**, *and* **He hardens whom He desires** *(Romans 9:18).*

Although the context of each of these verses has its own historical setting, there is no reason to believe the truth declared in them isn't timeless for every situation. If when he wrote his first letter to Timothy Paul actually had in mind that God wishes to save all men without exception, then we find ourselves with a problem: *Why* isn't He saving all men? Is He too weak? Does man's will have power over God's will? And if man's will has power over God's will, then who in actuality is sovereign? This kind of thinking only leads us into further absurdities and difficulties.

The scriptures above assure us that *whatever God desires, He accomplishes*. He is not wringing His hands in sadness or distress over all those who will not come to Him. God has neither desired nor intended to save all men, or else they would all be saved. Who can frustrate His plans? Isaiah 14:27 clearly implies the answer to that question: No one! Rather, God desires to save *all kinds of men without distinction*—Jews and Gentiles, male and female, rich and poor, kings and subjects, etc.

God Has Determined to Destroy Some Men

Finally, God's Word explicitly teaches His plan for the destruction of many. Here are two examples:

But the present heavens and earth by His word are being reserved for fire, kept for the day of judgment and destruction of ungodly men (2 Peter 3:7).

... dealing out retribution to those who do not know God and to those who do not obey the gospel of our Lord Jesus. These will pay the penalty of eternal destruction, away from the presence of the Lord and from the glory of His power, when He comes to be glorified in His saints on that day, and to be marveled at among all who have believed—for our testimony to you was believed (2 Thessalonians 1:8-10).

If God desires for all men to be saved, and He accomplishes all He desires, then why would He be planning for the destruction of some men? This thinking is insensible.

Some who read this may think, "Maybe God is not actually going to destroy the wicked." If He were not, then the references about God's wrath, eternal destruction, the outer darkness, and more severe judgment for one city than another—just to name a few—are meaningless. God's Word affirms that *God wills to destroy the wicked.* I know this doesn't sit well with those who want to encourage unbelievers that God loves them and has a wonderful plan for their lives. It doesn't sit well with people who love mercy and don't like the idea of anyone being eternally separated from God. But it is what God has declared.

Our faith must be anchored in a mighty God who can save whomever He wishes—a God who is big enough to defend His own character before men. Without realizing it, we "put God on trial" when we bristle at the idea of His creating some creatures for a purpose other than to save them. The Word of God is clear and explicit. If we're to be anchored in the Solid Rock in the storms of life, we must stand on the entire counsel of the Word of God—even if we don't understand it, or it opens the door for unbelievers to accuse God and us of being unfair and unloving.

This whole idea about God's never intending to save everyone may "torque your theological grid" quite a bit. We all have a set of theological and philosophical ideas that we believe to be true. As we evaluate the events of our lives, we look at those events through this system of ideas. This is our grid. If your grid doesn't view all the events of life as under the complete control of God, then it is out of line with biblical truth. The Bible presents a reliable picture of what it means for God to be sovereign over *all* of His creation. As we continue through this book, that picture will become clearer and more focused.

If you feel the same way that I felt years ago—uncomfortable with any concept of God that would make people feel helpless or unworthy—I urge you to continue working through the ideas in the rest of this book. Look up the scripture references; keep reading much of God's Word for a fresh exposure of His revelation about Himself, His purposes, and His ways; and pray for the Holy Spirit to give you understanding and ways to communicate the truth without being offensive.

There is another aspect of the common view of 1 Timothy 2:4 that I would like to address. That is the stress it puts on believers to tell everyone they meet about Jesus. Have you ever been out at some event or in a conversation with someone where you *didn't* present the gospel or God's plan of salvation, and later you felt guilty about it? Have you worried that someone may have lost his last chance to be saved because you didn't tell him about Jesus? I have actually heard people say, "If he dies and goes to hell, it will be my fault!"

If you have ever felt that way, then consider this weakness in your foundation: You have been taught that God is unhappy with you for not doing your part to wrangle your circumstances into "witnessing opportunities," and so a sinner went to hell because of your unwillingness or inability to "speak up for Christ." What a guilt trip this idea has put on the church!

The result for many is fear, both for others and for their own relationship with God. They worry that God is displeased with them, because they have been told that *He* desires all men without exception to be saved and to come to the knowledge of the truth. So if they are not witnessing of Christ everywhere they go, they feel like a failure, or really deficient in their faith, or unloving toward others, or some other such thing that God is not speaking to them. I believe this idea underlies much of Christians' thinking and causes a great deal of condemnation in the church. So God's people try harder to allay their fears about God's displeasure by becoming busier with "kingdom work"—yet they don't want to simply spend time with their Savior. Does this describe you? My hope in writing this book is to deliver you from such unfounded fears.

God has given us the responsibility and the privilege of sharing Christ with others, and He provides many opportunities for us to do so. But this sharing should be natural, loving, and led by the Holy Spirit, not contrived or forced out of a sense of "Christian duty." God is not relying on us to approach "all men" with some form of gospel presentation because "He wishes for all men to be saved." God is saving men as

He wishes: sometimes through the bold and delighted testimonies of His children to unbelievers, and sometimes through more quiet and unnoticed means. We will talk much more about these things in the chapter on "*Evangelism God's Way.*" The important thing to remember for now is what we talked about in Chapter 5: be sensitive to the leading of God's Spirit and to what He may be doing in the hearts of the people we encounter.

As we take one last look at 1 Timothy 2:4, here are our options about what it means:

1. God *desires* to save all men, but He is too weak to accomplish such a work.

2. He *desires* to save all men, but He has turned over His sovereignty to men in the arena of salvation. He has submitted His own will to the will of men, and their desires sometimes overrule His. Therefore, He is not actually sovereign.

3. He *is* sovereign over *all* of His creation, He accomplishes *everything* He desires, and He is saving all whom He wishes to save. He *never intended* to save all men.

Which revelation of God do you see in the Bible? I hope the answer is obvious.

At the risk of offending God's enemies, we boldly declare God's ability to save everyone He wishes to save. *The faith produced in the heart of anyone is a testimony to God's unfailing power to save all whom He has given to His Son, Jesus Christ* (John 6:37 and 39). God is saving *all kinds* of men. That's why we pray to God for the salvation of kings and those in authority!

In Chapter 4 of this same letter from Paul to Timothy, we find another verse that *appears* to say God is the Savior of all men. We'll look at that one next.

Eight

---

1 Timothy 4:10

For it is for this we labor and strive, because we have fixed our hope on the living God, who is the Savior of all men, especially of believers.

Another passage of scripture easily misunderstood if taken out of context is 1 Timothy 4:10. The theme of Chapter 4 is the deliverance and preservation of the saints during the time of apostasy from the church. Part of Paul's purpose in writing this letter to Timothy was to tackle the problem of false teaching, which was common in the early church. The questions Paul addressed in this chapter were, "How are believers to be protected from falling away? How are they to live and persevere to the end?" Notice that he was not informing Timothy about how people may be eternally saved. Rather, his focus was on matters of this present life.

Paul *appeared* to be saying that God is the *Savior of all men without exception*. One might use this verse to direct people to Jesus as the *only Savior for men*, but this was not Paul's point. 1 Timothy 4:10 raises the question, "Is God eternally saving all men?" The phrase, "especially of believers" adds a puzzling consideration if we think the verse is referring to eternal salvation. Don't you agree? Why did he say that? Again, as with many of the verses we have already considered, the context is the key. Let's look at it.

Watch Out for Trusting in Disciplines

> *But the Spirit explicitly says that in later times some will fall away from the faith, paying attention to deceitful spirits and doctrines of demons, by means of the hypocrisy of liars seared in their own conscience as with a branding iron,* **men who forbid marriage and advocate abstaining from foods**, *which God has created to be gratefully shared in by those who believe and know the truth (1 Timothy 4:1-3).*

Paul tackled the problem of people being led astray by men who emphasize outward actions and bodily disciplines. The church faces this difficulty today, doesn't it? He continued in verses 4 through 8,

> *For everything created by God is good, and nothing is to be rejected, if it is received with gratitude; for it is sanctified by means of the word of God and prayer. In pointing out these things to the brethren, you will be a good servant of Christ Jesus, constantly nourished on the words of the faith and of the sound doctrine which you have been following. But have nothing to do with worldly fables fit only for old women. On the other hand,* **discipline yourself for the purpose of godliness**; *for bodily discipline is only of little profit, but* **godliness is profitable for all things, since it holds promise for the present life and also for the life to come**.

Godliness Is the Key to Preservation

In these verses, Paul contrasted bodily discipline and godly discipline as they relate to preservation *in this present life*. He encouraged Timothy to emphasize training in godliness because of the promises of God. Having communicated that, he wrote,

> *It is a trustworthy statement deserving full acceptance. For it is for this we labor and strive, because we have fixed our hope on the living God, who is the Savior of all men, especially of believers (1 Timothy 4:9-10).*

The first important word needing to be clarified is the word "Savior." According to *Strong's Exhaustive Concordance of the Bible*, this Greek word can also be translated "deliverer" or "preserver."[11]

When a word has several possible translations, a basic rule for determining the writer's most probable intention is to consider its use in a sentence. Because this chapter's context is *this present life*, I think Paul was communicating that God is the *preserver* of all men. He wanted Timothy to put his hope in God, who preserves everyone in life, but especially believers. As a pastor, Timothy could trust God to *preserve* the members of his flock and protect them from falling away.

The second word needing attention is the little word, "all." As we learned in the previous chapter, the form of the word and its context indicates a reference to *different kinds of men*, not all men without exception (see page 61). Therefore, we should understand that Paul was declaring God to be the preserver of *all kinds* of men: those who rely on bodily disciplines, but especially those who believe and trust in God.

The following verses verify such an interpretation. Paul encouraged Timothy to pay careful attention to himself and his teaching since it would insure the preservation of him and his flock. As with the word "Savior" in verse 10, the word "salvation" in verse 16 is best understood to mean "preservation."

> *Prescribe and teach these things. Take pains with these things; be absorbed in them, so that your progress may be evident to all. Pay close attention to yourself and to your teaching; persevere in these things; for as you do this you will insure salvation* [preservation] *both for yourself and for those who hear you (1 Timothy 4:11-16).*

Verse 10 teaches us that God alone is the preserver of life for all men. He keeps those who think commitment to bodily exercise and disciplines is the way to live in this present life, but He especially keeps believers who exercise themselves in godliness and trust in God alone. Paul never taught that God eternally saves all men; such an idea can be clearly refuted by numerous scriptures. In this passage, he gave Timothy advice about the best way to safeguard his flock from the destructive heresies that focused on commitments to bodily disciplines. His purpose was to teach them to exercise themselves in godliness.

Knowing that God will keep until the very end all those who are His children anchors our faith in bedrock truth. What a confidence to have for anyone who shepherds the flock of God! If he leads the people to exercise themselves in godliness, they will be protected against the apostasy taking place in the church today. On the other hand, if we interpret this verse to mean that God wants to save everyone, then our faith is going to be shakable, for God has obviously not kept His Word. Such an interpretation raises many questions. If His desire is to save everyone but He hasn't done so, what confidence can we have in His Word as it applies *to us*? We might live in fear of falling away from our own salvation. Furthermore, what confidence can we give someone else to whom we are witnessing? How are we to explain to them the many people who have professed Christ, yet have not persevered to the end? Has God failed? If He has, then what assurance can we have that we will live eternally with Him? We have none other than our own ability to persevere, and that is no anchor at all!

God has given us a wonderful ground of confidence in these verses. We who have believed in Christ will be preserved to the end. God will keep us! He will protect us! To God be the glory!

Nine

Titus 2:11

*For the grace of God has appeared, bringing salvation
to all men...*

Have you ever seen the bumper stickers that say, "Jesus: He died for
the opportunity" or "Give Jesus a chance"? Titus 2:11 is often cited
to teach this idea: *God has given an opportunity for salvation to all
men without exception, and being saved depends only upon whether or
not one chooses to be saved.* Is this what Paul meant? Was he referring
to the grace of eternal salvation? Or was he writing about a different
type of grace? Was he saying that God has brought eternal salvation to
all men through the death and resurrection of Jesus Christ? Or, as we
saw with the words commonly translated "Savior" and "salvation" in 1
Timothy 4:10, does the alternate translation "preservation" better fit
the context of this verse?

We have learned in previous chapters the importance of finding the
context of a verse to help us determine its meaning. So again, if we look
at the context of this verse and then use the rest of Scripture to give
confirmation, we may expect to arrive at the truth Paul had in mind.

Just as Timothy needed advice regarding how to pastor a flock that
was being exposed to various heresies and wrong doctrine, Titus also
needed similar counsel. Apparently the church in Crete was experiencing
a problem with men who were posing as Christians but were troubling
others by their deeds and heretical teaching that included disputes about
the Law (Titus 1:9, 16, and 3:9). Chapter 1 described the troublemakers

and set the stage for Paul's assertion in Titus 2:11 that "the grace of God had appeared, bringing salvation." Chapter 2 included instructions for different types of believers about how to lead godly lives. In Chapter 3, Paul continued to exhort Titus about how to instruct the righteous but "reject" and "shun" any factious and perverted men who would not receive his warnings.

In the first verses of Chapter 1, Paul reminded Titus of his responsibility to appoint elders over the flock in Crete, men who could exhort and refute these men who were rebellious and ignorant of God's grace.

Not Everyone Knows of God's Grace

*For there are many rebellious men, empty talkers and deceivers, especially those of the circumcision, **who must be silenced** because they are upsetting whole families, teaching things they should not teach, for the sake of sordid gain. One of themselves, a prophet of their own, said, "Cretans are always liars, evil beasts, lazy gluttons." This testimony is true. For this cause **reprove them severely**, that they may be sound in the faith, not paying attention to Jewish myths and commandments of men who turn away from the truth (Titus 1:10-14).*

Notice that this passage is quite similar to what we found in 1 Timothy 4:3, where people who professed to know God and lived among the true believers were introducing heresies and advocating "preservation" based upon living an ascetic lifestyle. Within the church Titus was shepherding, these same kinds of false teachers were upsetting whole families. What was Titus to do in such a situation? Paul continued:

Sound Doctrine Is Important

*To the pure, all things are pure; but to those who are defiled and unbelieving, nothing is pure, but both their mind and their conscience are defiled. They profess to know God, but by their deeds they deny Him, being detestable and disobedient, and worthless for any good deed. **But as for you, speak the things which are fitting for sound doctrine** (Titus 1:15-2:1).*

Just as Paul encouraged Timothy to attend to sound doctrine, so he advised Titus to teach specific things "fitting for sound doctrine" to certain groups of people. In these following verses, notice what kinds of people Paul was instructing Titus to address. This counsel in Chapter 2 concerns the believers whom Titus was shepherding—those who were being "upset."

> **Older men** *are to be temperate, dignified, sensible, sound in faith, in love, in perseverance.* **Older women** *likewise are to be reverent in their behavior, not malicious gossips, nor enslaved to much wine, teaching what is good, that they may encourage the* **young women** *to love their husbands, to love their children, to be sensible, pure, workers at home, kind, being subject to their own husbands, that the word of God may not be dishonored.*
>
> *Likewise urge the* **young men** *to be sensible; in all things show yourself to be an example of good deeds, with purity in doctrine, dignified, sound in speech which is beyond reproach, in order that the opponent may be put to shame, having nothing bad to say about us. Urge* **bondslaves** *to be subject to their own masters in everything, to be well-pleasing, not argumentative, not pilfering, but showing all good faith, that they may adorn the doctrine of God our Savior in every respect (Titus 2:2-10).*

With verse 10, we come to the end of the specific instructions to these groups of people. Next, in verse 11—the verse in question here—he told them why they ought to live this way and why this kind of living would preserve them in the face of false teaching: *For the grace of God has appeared, bringing salvation to all men.* What did Paul mean by this?

Does it seem to you that in this discourse Paul was instructing Titus to encourage *unbelievers* about God's provision to save them? As Paul addressed the problem of legalistic agitators among the flock of God, was this statement about the grace of God bringing salvation to all men a rabbit trail about eternal life, thrown into the middle of instructions about how to live in the present world? Did Paul mean that God *is* saving all men, or even that He desires to save all men? By the context, it doesn't appear so. But then what else could he have meant? Let's look at the important words in verse 11 and correlate their meanings to the context of the epistle.

What Grace Appeared?

The first word we need to consider in this verse is "grace." Paul was urging Titus to teach the true believers in Crete how to live before God *in this present life,* in contrast to the professing believers, defined in Chapter 1, who were not living godly lives. He was not advising Titus to teach anyone about God's gift of eternal salvation. In this verse, the most suitable definition of "grace" is "the power to do what is right"— that is, *grace for living to the glory of God.*

Some confusion may arise in the minds of many who have memorized these verses in the King James Version. In my opinion, this translation of verse 11 is unfortunate and misleading: "For the grace of God that bringeth salvation hath appeared to all men." We know that the grace for right living has *not appeared to all men* because there is so much unrighteousness in the world. It is obvious from Chapter 1 that the grace of God had not appeared to those who were straying from the truth. No, those men wouldn't have seen God's grace at all in Paul's instructions.

Some People Are Blinded

The King James Version conveys the idea in Titus 2:11 that "God's gift of eternal salvation has appeared to all men." But this contradicts other scriptures that refer to unbelieving men who are blinded to the truth. These other verses tell us that some men are blind because God has actually made them blind to fulfill His purposes in the world. They may not remain blind forever, but whether they see the truth or not, God is working out His eternal will in them:

> *But though He had performed so many signs before them, yet they were not believing in Him; that the word of Isaiah the prophet might be fulfilled, which he spoke, "Lord, who has believed our report? And to whom has the arm of the Lord been revealed?" For this cause* **they could not believe,** *for Isaiah said again,* **"He has blinded their eyes, and He hardened their heart; lest they see with their eyes, and perceive with their heart, and be converted, and I heal them"** *(John 12:37-40).*

> *... just as it is written, "God gave them a spirit of stupor, eyes to see not and ears to hear not, down to this very day" (Romans 11:8).*

They do not know, nor do they understand, for He has smeared over their eyes so that they cannot see and their hearts so that they cannot comprehend (Isaiah 44:18).

Yet to this day the LORD has not given you a heart to know, nor eyes to see, nor ears to hear (Deuteronomy 29:4).

The Apostle Paul teaches us that Satan also blinds the minds of men. But when men do see the truth about Christ, God is the One who gives them sight:

*And even if our gospel is veiled, it is veiled to those who are perishing, in whose case **the god of this world has blinded the minds of the unbelieving, that they might not see the light of the gospel of the glory of Christ**, who is the image of God. For we do not preach ourselves but Christ Jesus as Lord, and ourselves as your bond-servants for Jesus' sake. For **God, who said, "Light shall shine out of darkness," is the One who has shone in our hearts to give the light of the knowledge of the glory of God in the face of Christ**. But we have this treasure in earthen vessels, that the surpassing greatness of the power may be of God and not from ourselves (2 Corinthians 4:3-7).*

So depending on His purposes, God either blinds eyes and hardens hearts, or He shines in hearts to give light. These passages clearly show that the eternal saving grace of God has obviously not appeared to all people. In fact, some *cannot* see it because God has determined they *will not* see it. For this reason, we cannot consider it a possibility that Paul had in mind God's *eternal saving grace* as the grace which has appeared to all men.

The Word "All" Is Important Again

The second word we must interpret carefully in Titus 2:11 is the word "all." As we learned in 1 Timothy 2:4 and 4:10, we should question whether Paul's meaning of that word in this verse was "every one without exception," or "all kinds of men." Again, the Greek word for "all" is *pas* without an article (see the explanation in Chapter 7). Therefore, since Paul used this specific construction, and since the verses preceding this one mention different kinds of individuals, we may safely assume Paul had in mind *various kinds of individuals* to whom the grace of God has been manifested.

God Has Given a Way for Our Preservation

And when this grace appears, it brings with it salvation. This now raises more questions. Did Paul mean *eternal salvation*? Or was he speaking of a *temporal deliverance* from some dangerous situation? Or did he have in mind the idea of *preservation through some trial*?

His meaning becomes clear in verse 12. The grace of God has appeared through specific instruction, which has come to us who believe—to the church, to the people who have ears to hear. I think Paul had "sound doctrine" in mind when he used the word "grace." He referred to it in verse 1 of Chapter 2: "... teach the things which are fitting for sound doctrine." Then giving specific "sound doctrine" for Timothy to teach to his people, Paul said, "For the grace of God has appeared." And here is the summary of all that previous teaching: The grace of God has appeared,

> *Instructing us to deny ungodliness and worldly desires...*

We notice this contrasts with the character of those who were causing problems. They were "liars, evil beasts, and lazy gluttons" (Titus 1:12). Furthermore, the grace of God comes to us as we...

> *... live sensibly, righteously, and godly in the present age, looking for the blessed hope and the appearing of the glory of our great God and Savior, Christ Jesus; who gave Himself for us...*

He did not say that Christ gave Himself for every man, but for us—believers.

> *... that He might redeem us from every lawless deed and purify for Himself a people for His own possession, zealous for good deeds (Titus 2:12-14).*

How Christians live in this present age concerned Paul. If Titus taught his people to live for God's glory in this present age, while looking forward to their inheritance, they would be saved, or delivered, from these rebels, empty-talkers, and deceivers. Thus the true meaning of Titus 2:11 as Paul intended it is this:

> This power to live rightly (grace) was the deliverance (salvation) God was bringing to the various kinds of believers (all) within the church at Crete.

However, when verse 11 is pulled out of its context, it appears to teach that God wants every single person to be saved. Taken out of context, the verse even seems to suggest universalism—the idea that God is saving everyone—which we know is unbiblical. But when considered in its context, we find instead the glorious truth that the key to enduring in this life is to deny ungodliness and worldly desires and to live sensibly, righteously, and godly while looking to the day when the Lord Jesus will deliver us out of this age. This was the teaching Titus was to emphasize.

If we wrongly conclude that God has given eternal saving grace to everyone, and it is up to them to choose to exercise it, our faith can only founder in disillusionment and disappointment. Just look at all the people God wants to save who refuse Him! What's going on here? The evangelist is disappointed when he sees all the people who lose out on salvation because they refuse to make the "right choice." And the unbeliever is disappointed when he tries to follow the formula of the evangelist in choosing to believe but doesn't find the power to live the Christian life.

But if we believe that God is preserving His sheep in the face of false teaching, heresy, and other worldly troubles, we have great confidence. He intends for our faith to persevere to the end. He has given His people grace through instructions in how to live once they have been regenerated by God's Spirit. Our faith has a wonderful hope because it is grounded in the unshakable purposes of God for His people. This hope is further established when we know God's plan for us at the end of the age: the appearing of the glory of our great God and Savior, Christ Jesus (Titus 2:13). This was Paul's purpose for Titus 2:11.

In the next two chapters we'll move on to the second letter of the Apostle Peter. This epistle contains two scriptures that often trouble Christians, and so they deserve a closer look. The first has to do with the idea of our eternal security in salvation, and the second is another verse that I'm sure has already come to your mind if you've been taught that God wants to save everyone.

Ten

---

2 Peter 2:1

*But false prophets also arose among the people, just
as there will also be false teachers among you, who
will secretly introduce destructive heresies, even
denying the Master who bought them, bringing swift
destruction upon themselves.*

Two passages in 2 Peter require special examination. First, we
will look at 2 Peter 2:1. This is not a verse commonly misused
in evangelism, but sometimes it is erroneously used to suggest that
people who have truly been saved may still fall out of the hand of God
and lose their salvation if they are seduced by destructive heresies.
This verse appears to say false teachers, teaching destructive heresies,
were denying the Lord Jesus who bought them. The verse begs two
questions: "Can someone for whom Jesus died ultimately be lost and
destroyed?" And "If even the teachers whom God calls can fall into
destructive heresies and be lost after Jesus saved them, what hope do I
have as a common sheep to not do even worse than they, and ultimately
lose my salvation?"

Accuracy with the text is important, as is caution that we not bring
a preconceived speculation into the interpretation, so let's ask some
other questions. As we've learned with the other verses we've studied
so far, we begin with, "What is the context of 2 Peter 2:1? To whom
was Peter writing?" In verse 1 of Chapter 1, we see Peter's salutation to
fellow believers.

A Contrast in Kinds of Believers

Simon Peter, a bondservant and apostle of Jesus Christ, to those who have received a faith of the same kind as ours, by the righteousness of our God and Savior, Jesus Christ.

Peter implies here that there are those who have another kind of faith—a faith they did not receive from Jesus Christ—which is based upon sensuality. John mentioned this shakable, non-saving kind of faith when he wrote of some who believed in Jesus because of the signs they saw Him do. We distinguished between these two kinds of faith in the chapter on John 3:16. These "believers" introduced to us in John 2 were like some of the 5,000 who we read about in John 6, who after being fed by Jesus, wanted to make Him king. They thought they believed in Him. They had a *kind* of faith, but not the kind of faith born by the Spirit of God. So the context is that there were two kinds of "believers" among these people to whom Peter was writing. The sensual "believers" are the ones of whom Peter was warning his readers in Chapter 2, verse 1. Then he continued his warning:

And many will follow their sensuality, and because of them the way of the truth will be maligned; and in their greed they will exploit you with false words; their judgment from long ago is not idle, and their destruction is not asleep (2 Peter 2:2-3).

Tragically, there are people who "use" Jesus for personal gain. If they exploit Jesus, they will also exploit their fellow men. In their greediness to gain a reputation or a sense of significance in this world, they teach what is false. These "ministers" fashion their messages around what will attract people. For these, the only standard of measure for their methods is that they bring in the people and keep them satisfied. Their concern isn't sound doctrine. Their goal is to use people to achieve their own ends. Does this look and sound familiar? We have in our time the same kinds of people as Peter was warning about in his day.

First-Hand Experience

Here is another question: Why was this message of warning so important to Peter? Consider his history as a disciple of Jesus. I think Peter knew quite well about these kinds of false teachers and what motivated them. He had been like them! Perhaps this warning sprang from His own experience when he rebuked Jesus. Do you remember the encounter described in Matthew 16:21-28? Jesus had prophesied

He was going to be crucified. Immediately Peter took exception to Jesus' statement and told his Lord that He was wrong about the prophecy.

What motivated Peter's rebuke? Jesus told Peter he had his mind set on the things of man and not the things of God. Perhaps it was Peter's greed for glory as a member of the Messiah's "inner circle," that motivated him to "exploit" Jesus that day. The Son of God responded with, "Get thee behind Me, Satan." What a shock that must have been to Peter! Surely he learned from that experience. Later, as he wrote this epistle, Peter said of these false teachers that greed was their motivation. If the spirit of Satan, working through false teachers, would exploit the Savior, it would even more surely exploit the people who followed Him.

Can Jesus Lose Anyone He's Redeemed?

Now the questions come to mind, "Who were these false teachers? Were they really men whom Christ had redeemed?" As we go back and look at verse 1 of Chapter 2, we notice these false prophets rose up *among the people*. Peter did not say they were part of the body of Christ. He didn't say they were saved. In fact, later in the chapter he indicated they were obviously *not* saved. He simply warned of false teachers who would rise up among the believers. What was the danger? They would secretly introduce error, "even denying the Master who bought them."

This phrase is perhaps the most important one in the whole verse. "The Master who bought them" sounds synonymous with "Christ who redeemed them." But is it? Dr. Richard Belcher, in his book *A Journey in Grace*, brought to light an important observation about the word "Master" in this verse. The term used here for "Lord" (KJV) or "Master" (NASB) is not the term commonly used to refer to the Lord Jesus Christ. The Greek word *kurios* is the title for "Lord" most commonly used to refer to Him. But in this verse Peter used the Greek word *despotes*. This term in the New Testament usually refers to God as the "Sovereign Master over all," but sometimes it refers to men as the masters of servants. In Jude it refers to God's sovereignty over all things, as opposed to His lordship.[12]

It is important to note that Peter also used the common word *kurios* in this same chapter, so he obviously understood the difference between the two terms and intended to communicate a distinction in persons— verse 1 referring to God as the Sovereign Master over all, and verses 9, 11, and 20 referring to Jesus as "the Lord." Because Peter used both terms, therefore, it seems almost certain that the "Master" Peter had in mind in verse 1 of Chapter 2 refers to God, the Father, who owns all persons and things in creation.

The other term in this important phrase is the word "bought." Belcher again clarifies this word well. In every case where this word is used in the New Testament, it refers to

> "... a complete purchase which puts the buyer in ownership and possession of the object, and it never speaks of a potential purchase such as suggested in a general atonement."[13]

God, Sovereign Over All, Never Loses Those Whom He Saves

Understanding the meanings of these two words gives us very helpful guidance. "Lord" or "Master" in 2 Peter 2:1 wasn't a reference to Christ as the Redeemer of men, but to God and His sovereign ownership and authority over all men, including these false teachers. This interpretation of the verse makes the most sense. It also resolves the difficulty that otherwise arises if we view the phrase "the Master who bought them" as meaning that Christ redeemed these men who later became false teachers and denied Him.

Both the Old and New Testaments clearly teach that God is the owner of all He has made. The Psalmist, David, wrote, "The earth is the Lord's, and all it contains, the world, and those who dwell in it" (Psalm 24:1). In the New Testament the Apostle Paul quoted David, "... for the earth is the Lord's, and all it contains" (1 Corinthians 10:26). So the whole world is owned and sustained by God, including those who deny Him even as they claim to be Christians.

The rest of 2 Peter 2 also confirms the interpretation that "the Master who bought them" is *God who owns them.* Peter informed his readers that God would not let these false teachers escape judgment. He assured them that God would destroy these teachers. They were creatures of instinct, born to be captured and killed, and were like a dog that returns to its vomit. In other words, Peter made a definite distinction between the spiritual conditions of these false teachers and of the righteous whom God is able to rescue and preserve. In his mind it was clear: the Spirit of God had never regenerated these false teachers, and therefore God would judge and destroy them.

Throughout the rest of Scripture, I can find no place teaching that the Lord Jesus' purchase of His people resulted in such a catastrophe as some think these verses teach. A couple of passages suffice to make this point clear:

> All that the Father gives Me shall come to Me, and the one who comes to Me I will certainly not cast out. For I have come down from heaven, not to do My own will, but the will of Him who sent Me. And this is the will of Him who sent Me, **that of all that He has given Me I lose nothing**, but raise it up on the last day (John 6:37-39).

> My sheep hear My voice, and I know them, and they follow Me; and I give eternal life to them, **and they shall never perish**; and no one shall snatch them out of My hand. My Father, who has given them to Me, is greater than all; and **no one is able to snatch them out of the Father's hand**. I and the Father are one (John 10:27-30).

These passages leave no room for the possibility that the Lord Jesus will ever lose one for whom He died. God has given Jesus to His people to be their Redeemer. And redeem them He will, for indeed, He does the will of God always. If Jesus bought them through suffering His Father's wrath against them in their place, then there can be no more danger of destruction or wrath. In constrast, Peter was sure about the fate of these false teachers: they would be destroyed.

It seems most accurate, then, to conclude that Peter was not saying these false teachers were once saved and then fell away. In reality, they never were saved. Like the false prophets in Old Testament times, they rose up in the midst of the people and sought to lead God's people astray. Eight verses after Peter's declaration that these men were bringing swift destruction upon themselves, he asserted that God is able to rescue His people from temptation. If Peter believed God is able to save from destruction those for whom He died, why would he think that Christ died for these false teachers but wasn't able ultimately to save them?

From this passage in 2 Peter we learn we must be on the alert for false teachers who will appear to be a part of us. Some men, greedy for their own gain, will preach a sensual gospel and use sensual methods. We should not be surprised when many follow them. However, we may be confident that God is able to rescue us from being sucked in by their false teaching, sensuality, and unprincipled methods. Their error will not shake our faith if our foundation is firmly anchored in Jesus.

Eleven

2 Peter 3:9

*The Lord is not slow about His promise, as some count
slowness, but is patient toward you, not wishing for
any to perish but for all to come to repentance.*

This verse doesn't appear very troublesome on the surface, does it?
Christians often use 2 Peter 3:9 to convince unbelievers that God
wishes for everyone without exception to come to repentance and not
perish. But this erroneous idea falls short of the truth when tested
with Scripture.

Perhaps you've heard this verse used to portray God as one whose
heart is breaking from rejection by men. This portrayal suggests that
if people only knew how much God wanted them to repent and not
perish, perhaps they would repent. Such a message does appeal to the
self-seeking and self-exalting nature of unbelievers. One of human
nature's greatest desires is to feel significant. But if we use this verse to
make people feel like God "wants" them and "needs" them, we will be
misusing God's Word. As we look more closely at this passage, we find
that Peter had something entirely different in mind. He did not write
this letter for unbelievers. His purpose for writing this chapter was to
assure *believers* about God's care *for them* until the return of Jesus
Christ, and to encourage them to live holy lives.

2 Peter 3:9 is often misunderstood in the church today for two
reasons. First, most Christians believe God loves all people equally.
We will look closely at this idea later when we consider God's purpose

in creation. Second, many Christians apparently don't know how to study God's Word to understand the context or find the writer's line of reason. Consequently, having drawn a faulty conclusion about its meaning, they present this verse (and others like it) outside of both its context and the author's line of reason.

So let's look at the general context of the book of 2 Peter and at his reasoning as it develops. To whom is he writing? Believers. "To those who have received a faith of the same kind as ours" (1:1). Why? Because "there will also be false teachers among you" (2:1). Therefore, Peter says, "Beloved, I am stirring up your sincere mind by way of reminder" (3:1). He is speaking to the church. And of what is he reminding them?

• To develop godly character in the midst of darkness (Chapter 1).

• That God's judgment against those who promote their false opinions (destructive heresies) is active as He keeps them chained in darkness for the day of punishment (Chapter 2).

• That God is preserving the righteous in the midst of the wicked (Chapter 2).

• That God is patient toward the beloved, and they need to be diligently on their guard and growing in the grace and knowledge of Jesus Christ before His return on the Day of the Lord (Chapter 3).

Why Hasn't Jesus Returned as He Said He Would?

Now more specifically, beginning in verse 1 of Chapter 3, we discover that Peter was answering the question some among them had raised about why the Lord Jesus had not returned as He had promised (verses 3 through 4). Keeping in mind this line of reason guides us in interpreting verse 9, which must give a clear answer to this question. Let's get into the flow of Peter's thoughts:

> *This is now, beloved, the second letter I am writing to you in which I am stirring up your sincere mind by way of reminder, that you should remember the words spoken beforehand by the holy prophets and the commandment of the Lord and Savior spoken by your apostles. Know this first of all, that **in the last days mockers will come** with their mocking, following after their own lusts, and **saying, "Where is the promise of His coming?** For ever since the fathers fell asleep, all continues just as it was from the beginning of creation" (2 Peter 3:1-4).*

It is helpful to consider also the mockers' line of reason: *Why hasn't Jesus come and set up His kingdom on earth? He hasn't come as He said he would. Look, everything is still the same as it was from the beginning. There's still suffering. Wickedness and ungodly men abound all the more.* Although Peter doesn't state this, the implication from verse 7 is that these men concluded: *Therefore, we may live as we like.* But Peter noted their ignorance of what God had recorded in the Scriptures. He continued:

> *For when they maintain this, it escapes their notice that by the word of God the heavens existed long ago and the earth was formed out of water and by water, through which the world at that time was destroyed, being flooded with water.* **But the present heavens and earth by His word are being reserved for fire, kept for the day of judgment and destruction of ungodly men** (2 Peter 3:5-7).

We notice here a clear statement of God's purpose for preserving the heaven and earth—that it may become the destruction site of ungodly men. Does God wish for everyone without exception to be saved from destruction? If He does, then why did He by His Word reserve the present heavens and earth for the purpose of destruction, and why did He plan for the destruction of ungodly men?

Let's return to the question of why Jesus has not yet set up His kingdom here on earth. Peter continued in verses 8 and 9:

> *But do not let this one fact escape your notice, beloved...*

Peter Was Writing to Believers

It is significant to notice that Peter specifically addressed the children of God as the "beloved" of God. He pointed out one fact that had escaped the notice of these mockers, but should not escape the notice of God's people:

> *... that with the Lord one day is as a thousand years, and a thousand years as one day.*

God's timing differs from ours.

> *The Lord is not slow about His promise...*

His promise to set up His kingdom will be fulfilled.

... as some count slowness, but is patient toward you...

Who is the "you" God is patient toward? The "you" can only refer to the "beloved of God," not to the ungodly men and the mockers. Grammar rules instruct us that a pronoun refers to its nearest antecedent. In this case, the antecedent is "the beloved." So why hasn't Jesus set up His kingdom yet? Because He is patient toward those God has given Him.

God Doesn't Wish for Any of His Beloved to Perish

... not wishing for any to perish...

The antecedent rule applies again: "not wishing for any *of you* to perish." Peter was not referring to every human. He had already stated that God has planned the destruction of the ungodly, whom we may call the "unbeloved." As for the beloved, He doesn't wish for them to perish,

... but for all to come to repentance.

All of whom? The antecedent *still* applies: "all of *you*"—the beloved of God. His reference now is necessarily broader, encompassing the whole church, until the "Day of the Lord" (2 Peter 3:10). So Peter was teaching that when the last one whom God has given to Jesus has "been loved" and has come to repentance through the working of God's Spirit, Jesus will return and set up His kingdom. He will not come a year or a day sooner!

The moment the last soul comes to repentance, then the Father will turn to His Son, seated at His right hand, and perhaps say something along this line, "The time has come for the great wedding ceremony. I have made Thine enemies a footstool for Thy feet. Sound the trumpets! With the holy angels and the saints above, obtain Your inheritance!" And the Lord Jesus will rise and come again to earth. His beloved who have died will come with Him, and His beloved who are alive will rise to meet Him (1 Thessalonians 4:15-17). Then this present heaven and earth will be judged, and the ungodly men who flee from His presence will be destroyed with it (Revelation 20:11-15).

Jesus Will Return When the Last One is Saved!

That's why Jesus tarries. The last of the elect has yet to repent. More time is needed. He has vowed He will lose not a single one and He will raise each one up on the last day (John 6:39-40). Therefore, He is patient toward us who are His beloved.

This is the only interpretation of verse 9 that makes sense within Peter's line of reason. God has promised judgment for the wicked. For Peter to tell us this and then to say Jesus has not come again because He doesn't want anyone to perish is both inconsistent and nonsensical.

It is amazing that much of the church today believes God is not "getting what He desires," especially regarding the salvation of souls. This presents a picture of God wringing His hands and lamenting, "Oh, I *wish* they would come to Me!" We contemplated this idea in Chapter 7, but this kind of thinking is so prevalent in the church today that it bears repeating here. Is it possible that God wants souls to be saved but must endure their not being saved because He has subjected His own will to the "free will" of men? May it never be! His Word tells us this is *not* possible but, rather, God does what He pleases (Psalm 115:3 and 135:6), He will accomplish all His good pleasure (Isaiah 46:10), and no one can thwart His purposes (Job 42:2). Therefore, whomever He wants to save will be saved. In correlation, if He has purposed to destroy the wicked (Revelation 21:5-8), then it is not possible for *this* purpose to be thwarted, either. He cannot wish both to destroy the wicked *and* to save them.

Therefore, since God is being patient toward those who are His until we all have come to repentance, Peter concluded that we ought to conduct ourselves in holiness and godliness, looking forward to the great day of the Lord when He comes to set up His kingdom on a new earth where righteousness dwells.

Does this fit your understanding of God? Upon what is your faith anchored? Is it built upon the sand of man's ability to choose, or is it anchored into the rock, the firm foundation of God, who is powerful to save all whom He has set His affections upon? We should make it our aim to present to others the true God as He is revealed in the Scriptures. And what do the Scriptures show Him to be? A God who wishes to save but cannot? Or One who promises to save and does?

We must not be afraid of the truth, even if it appears to be unpalatable to people who think God ought to want to save everyone. The truth is that God is just and holy. He ought to want to *destroy* all of us—and some of mankind, He will. The amazing thing is this: a holy, just God has made a way through His Son, Jesus Christ, to redeem a people out of this world—a people who were really not of this world—a people created in Christ Jesus from before the foundation of the earth. They were a people from every tribe, tongue, people, and nation. To the praise of His glorious grace, He has called you His beloved. Aren't you glad He waited to bring judgment upon the earth until He brought you under the power of His love? Such love and power provide an anchor for our souls in Jesus Christ.

Twelve

---

1 John 1:9

*If we confess our sins, He is faithful and righteous
to forgive us our sins and to cleanse us from all
unrighteousness.*

This verse is often used to inform unsaved people that if they would only confess they were sinners, Jesus would forgive them, and they could be saved. This notion has led to the use of the "sinner's prayer," whereby a Christian leads a willing person in a prayer confessing that he is a sinner. Then on the basis of this verse, the sinner is encouraged to "take it by faith" that his sins are forgiven.

Written to Believers

I don't think this is what the Apostle John had in mind. First of all, it is evident he was not writing his epistle to the unsaved. He wrote it to a community of believers. As with so many of the other verses we've studied, using this verse as an evangelistic tool is inconsistent with its context and its intended purpose. Secondly, God does not forgive *because* a person confesses his sins. If we look carefully at 1 John 1:9, we see that John did not say forgiveness is contingent upon confession. *That would mean that the basis of forgiveness is something we do instead of what God did in Jesus Christ.*

Believers Know Their Sins Are Forgiven

Instead, this verse is an encouragement to *believers who already know their sins are forgiven*. Those who receive encouragement from this verse already know they have an Advocate with the Father, even Jesus Christ, the righteous. These know they have a propitiation for sins in the atoning sacrifice of Jesus. But what happens when we use this verse to try to convince unbelievers that all they must do is "say the words" and God will forgive their sins? These people are left doubting that anything really happened when they "prayed" because the Spirit of God has not spoken the truth of that prayer to their hearts. We can certainly say John was teaching the importance of confession for those of us who trust in Christ. By it we gain a clear conscience. We are assured that if we confess our sins, our sins *have been forgiven* us.

Here's another way of phrasing 1 John 1:9 through 10:

Since we know He is faithful to forgive our sins and to cleanse us from all unrighteousness, then let us confess our sins. If we don't confess our sins, we make Him a liar, and His word is not in us. He has said we are sinners, so let us confirm His word by confessing it when we sin. We need not be afraid of condemnation.

This is a glorious comfort to us who believe. Believers are the ones for whom John intended it. It may be appropriate to tell an unbeliever he should pray and confess his sins to God. However, I wouldn't recommend using this verse to support the idea. It is a misuse of this scripture to promise someone who is wicked and selfish that if he confesses he is a sinner, God will forgive him his sin. It may result in someone praying a prayer from a selfish motive rather than by the work of the Holy Spirit in his heart. He may not be truly converted and may think he is a Christian because he admitted he is a sinner. Consequently, he might even become resistant to the full gospel—that is, repentance, obedience, and discipleship—since he believes he is saved. Another tragic result may be that, because he will continue in sin, he will give unbelievers another reason to malign and mock Jesus Christ. Perhaps millions have been deceived into thinking they are forgiven, although they have no witness in their spirits from God that they are forgiven. This is tragic.

The good news of the gospel is that through the atonement of Jesus Christ, all those who come to God through faith in Christ are forgiven their sins. Believers need not come to God asking for forgiveness with the thought that God *will* forgive if they ask Him to. Believers come knowing they already *are* forgiven because of the faith God has granted them in their hearts. They confess their sins as the Lord convicts them because they need their consciences cleansed of the guilt. They *thank* Him because they know they *are* forgiven through the atoning blood of Christ.

The Fellowship of Confession

I have seen two problems afflicting believers because of their misunderstanding of 1 John 1:9. The first is that some believers fall into a pattern of confession motivated by fear. Their relationship with God is dominated by guilt. Thinking they were first forgiven *because* they prayed and asked God to forgive them, they worry that they must always be "prayed up" and have no unconfessed sins hanging over their heads. If calamities come upon them, they blame their own failure to maintain a "paid up confession account" with God. *"I wouldn't have been in this car wreck if only I'd been more diligent about confessing my sins..."* They may also wrongly accuse other believers. I know of one woman who was deeply hurt by Christians telling her that she must have had "unconfessed sin" in her life, or else her son would not have been born with cystic fibrosis.

What causes Christians to think like this? Misunderstanding 1 John 1:9, they confess and repent out of *fear*. This fear sometimes leads to perfectionism. And perfectionism leads either to pride in oneself and intolerance toward others (if one "performs" well), or else (if he doesn't) to a sense of personal failure.

The second problem I've seen is that some believers rarely confess their sins at all. They are unaware of the gift God has given them of continual confession and repentance. They think they have already done all that was required of them on the day they "accepted the Lord," and any further confessions are unnecessary. They have a kind of "been there, done that" attitude toward confession. Thinking of 1 John 1:9 as an evangelistic tool, they neglect confession of their own sins on a continual basis, and so they miss out on the dual blessings of fellowship with God and a clear conscience.

Not for Evangelistic Use

Another common problem arises because 1 John 1:9 is incorrectly used as a promise in evangelism. This abuse leads people to believe they are forgiven *because* they prayed a prayer of confession. If asked why they think they are Christians, they may reply that they know they are because God's Word says if they confess they are sinners, He promises forgiveness. Perhaps they may feel certain that they are Christians because they have invited Christ into their hearts.

Although these people may be genuinely born by the Spirit of God, their explanation of the process of salvation may mislead others. Additionally, since they think *they* initiated God's forgiveness by their prayer rather than that *God* initiated it by His grace, they will probably lack the basis for a deeper appreciation of God's glorious grace toward them. The correct response to the question is this: they know they are Christians because God has given them faith in the Lord Jesus Christ that their sins are forgiven.

There may be some readers who are troubled with these things. Perhaps at the time you believe you were converted, you prayed just such a prayer. If you did, the question is, do you continue to confess and repent before God because you know God is faithful to forgive? If you do, then you probably were born again by God's Spirit. You were not saved *on the basis of praying the sinner's prayer*, but on the basis of Christ's work on the cross. You believed His death is applied to you because God gave you the faith to believe it. Your salvation did not come because of your confession, but your confession of sin came because God's Spirit was applying salvation to your heart! That is the purpose of 1 John 1:9—a glorious verse to give confidence and encouragement to those who believe.

In the next chapter we will look at how John continued to provide a solid foundation for faith in the second chapter of his first letter.

Thirteen

---

1 John 2:2

And He Himself is the propitiation for our sins; and not for ours only, but also for those of the whole world.

How do we know our sins are forgiven and God's promise of cleansing will be fulfilled as we confess our sins before the Lord? 1 John 2:1 and 2 give us tremendous assurance when we sin or when we feel accused by the enemy of our souls. Jesus is our Advocate before the Father, and He has made propitiation for our sins! Are these terms unfamiliar to you? They are glorious in their significance for believers!

First of all, what is an advocate? *Merriam-Webster Online* defines *advocate* as "one that pleads the cause of another before a tribunal or judicial court."[14] Noah Webster's *1828 American Dictionary of the English Language* defines it as "one who defends, vindicates, or espouses a cause, by argument."[15] So Jesus pleads our cause and defends us before the throne of God. We are *not guilty* by virtue of His atonement on our behalf.

Secondly, what is a *propitiation*? The term means *the appeasement of wrath by the payment of a ransom or sacrifice.* It is a form of the word used to refer to the "mercy seat" in the tabernacle. The shedding of Jesus' blood satisfied God's justice on behalf of all for whom God sent Him. There is no wrath left in God for those who have been justified by His Son's propitiation. The debt has been *entirely* paid.

Did Jesus Die for Everyone in the World?

So what did John mean when he wrote that Jesus is the propitiation not only for our sins but also for those of the whole world? At first glance, the verse seems to indicate that Jesus died for everyone in the whole world. But when we examine what John wrote in his gospel, and compare it with other scriptures, it becomes apparent John had something else in mind when he wrote this verse.

First, we want to take into account John's audience. John was one of the apostles whose ministry targeted the Jews. Both his gospel and his letters reveal his great desire to communicate to the Jews God's gracious gift of His Son for their salvation. But the scope of God's provision of mercy in Christ exceeded what most of his readers expected—it was for the Gentiles also. He sent His Son to be the Savior of *the world*. The question is, "What is *the world*?"

"The Whole World" Refers to Non-Jews

We discussed in the chapter on John 3:16 how Jesus addressed the nationalistic mentality of the Jews when He spoke with Nicodemus. John's audience in this epistle was also Jewish, and we need to keep that in mind. Just as Nicodemus did not expect to hear that the grace of God would extend to Gentiles, so these Jewish converts were still grappling with the same idea. In the first chapter of this epistle, John used the pronouns "we, our, and us," clearly referring to those first eyewitnesses of Jesus' life and ministry. They were all of Jewish descent. Therefore, when he used the pronoun "our" again in Chapter 2 ("He Himself is the propitiation for *our* sins"), we should reasonably expect that he was using the word in the same way as he did in Chapter 1—as referring to believing Jews.

Also, knowing that this idea of Gentiles being included in salvation was a theme in John's gospel, we should not be surprised to find the same theme introduced in this letter. It seems best to assume the apostle was implying that Jesus was not only the propitiation for the sins of "us" Jews, but also for "them" who were non-Jews. If this was John's meaning, then "the world" does not refer to *every single person in the world* but to *those whom God has given to His Son throughout the whole world*. There are a number of reasons to accept this interpretation.

We Don't Believe in Universalism

First, we can eliminate the notion that Jesus was the propitiation for *every single person in the world* because we already have seen that God has planned for the destruction of some. The erroneous belief that the blood Jesus shed covers everyone so all will ultimately be saved is called *universalism*. We know from previous verses we've studied that God has no intention of saving every one in the whole world.

God's Atoning Power Is Absolute and Unlimited

Second, we can reject the idea that the atonement extends to everyone but is only *effective* to save those who choose to believe in Jesus. Why? Because God's power in the atonement is *absolute* and *unlimited* to effectively fulfill His intended purposes. Remember that in all things, God fulfills all His own desires. God saves every single one whom He has decided to save. Any other idea is inconsistent with what is revealed in the rest of Scripture. If we reject this idea, we are essentially saying God is not all-powerful, and His will can be defeated by the will of man.

Jesus' Blood Wasn't Wasted

Furthermore, if the blood of Jesus were merely *available* to every single person but not *effective* to actually save everyone, then some of the blood of Jesus has been "wasted" on those for whom it was "available" but never "applied." The Scriptures declare we are saved by "the precious blood of the Lamb" (1 Peter 1:18-19). God would never "waste" His Son's blood on people who would never want it. God did not send Jesus to die merely to "give everyone an opportunity to believe."

God's Word Explicitly Limits Salvation to God's People

Fourth, numerous scriptures explicitly refer to Christ's dying for "His people." For instance, in Matthew 1:21 we read, "And she will bear a Son; and you shall call His name Jesus, for it is He who will save *His people* from their sins." The angel did not say He would save *everyone*, but He would save those who were *His*. This is another reason to accept that John was teaching in 1 John 2:2 that Jesus was the propitiation for only those His Father had given Him. Jesus stated the same thing in John 6 and John 10:

*All that the Father gives Me shall come to Me, and the
one who comes to Me I will certainly not cast out. For I have
come down from heaven, not to do My own will, but the will of
Him who sent Me. And this is the will of Him who sent Me, that
of all that He has given Me, I lose nothing, but raise it up
on the last day (John 6:37-39).*

*My sheep hear My voice, and I know them, and they follow
Me; and I give eternal life to them, and they shall never
perish; and no one shall snatch them out of My hand. My Father,
who has given them to Me, is greater than all; and no one is able
to snatch them out of the Father's hand (John 10:27-29).*

These verses indicate the *effectiveness* of Jesus' propitiation for
those who are His. So, if Jesus were the propitiation for the sins of *every*
single person in the world, then there would be no wrath left in God for
any single person in the world. That's how powerful the atoning sacrifice
of Jesus was. But the notion that there is no wrath left in God for anyone
in the world is refuted by all the scriptures portraying God's wrath and
indignation toward the unbelieving and disobedient. References to hell
and an eternal retribution are too numerous to ignore. Thus we are led
to look for a different interpretation.

No Scriptures Explicitly Teach That Jesus Died for Everyone

A fifth reason to accept this interpretation is the absence of
scriptures indicating explicitly that Christ died for every single person.
Some perhaps may cite John 3:16, 1 Timothy 2:4, 1 Timothy 4:10, or
Titus 2:11; but we have already shown that those scriptures do not teach
a universal atonement. In fact, we could turn to many other scriptures
where He reveals that unrepentant men have no union or part in Christ's
atonement for sin.

Jesus Is the Only Means of Propitiation for Anyone

The interpretation harmonizing with all the Scriptures is this: John
was saying that not only the Jews but also all of God's people who are
in the world have no other means of propitiation than Jesus Christ.
The phrase *not of ours only* referred to John and his Jewish brethren.
Again, the phrase *but also for those of the whole world* included all
the saints who were of other tribes and nations. John encouraged the

believers that Jesus Christ is God's only means of propitiation *in the world*; and if they have believed on Jesus, then they have an Advocate and a propitiation for their sins, along with everyone else in the world who has believed.

This interpretation has no scriptural conflict. However, some of us have an inherent sense that God should treat everyone equally. When we are told that He chooses to save some and not others, that is offensive to our sense of fairness. But if we are to be firmly anchored in Christ, we cannot let our own thinking and desires be our authority. We must stand upon the entire counsel of God.

From our examination of what the Apostle John wrote in his gospel and in his letters, we can conclude from Scripture that Jesus died for those whom God gave Him. The idea that Jesus died for every single person in the world is anchored in man's desires and in the wrong interpretation of God's Word. However, we may confidently say that Jesus is the only means of salvation God has provided to the whole world. With this we have no argument, and our faith is firmly anchored on a solid foundation.

Fourteen

Revelation 3:20

Behold, I stand at the door and knock; if anyone hears
My voice and opens the door, I will come in to him,
and will dine with him, and he with Me.

From this verse, a faulty method of evangelism has arisen which has gained such popularity that to question it is almost equal to questioning the existence of God or the truth of the Bible. The false teaching arising from the misuse of Revelation 3:20 works powerfully against anchoring the faith of believers into Christ Himself.

The erroneous teaching is that a person must invite Jesus into his heart to be saved. Based upon this verse, pulled out of its context, an evangelist may lead a willing unbeliever in a sinner's prayer that includes inviting Christ to keep His promise and enter in. Whether this person has heard Jesus Christ speak to him or not, the "new convert" is told he is a Christian because "God would not lie." If Jesus said He would come in, and this person opened the door and asked Him in, then he can take it by faith that Jesus *did* come in.

Errant Evangelistic Methods Produce Horrendous Results

This idea of how someone is saved has produced horrendous results: the contemporary visible church as a whole is lukewarm, and Jesus said He would spit such believers out of His mouth (Revelation 3:16) These are strong words! In this chapter we will look at not only the misapplied promise of verse 20 but also the reason Jesus gave that rebuke. Seeing the lukewarm condition of the church today should cause us to examine our own place within it.

The faith of the majority of people attending evangelical churches today is built upon the erroneous notion that salvation comes *because* they invited Jesus into their hearts. We've seen in previous chapters that this kind of faith *may* come from signs they have seen, or from a desire to get out of trouble or have a better life, or from any number of motivations *other* than to "know God and Jesus Christ" through humble repentance and a desire to please Him (John 17:3, Ephesians 5:3-10). Though God surely has called many who have prayed to receive Jesus into a life that is pleasing to Him, others who are trusting in a self-generated faith are just as surely destined to fall away when times get tough.

The evangelism methods that encourage unbelievers to believe what God has not spoken to them may effectively provide the stage for the great apostasy described in the Scriptures, when millions of unregenerate, deceived people will fall away from the visible church in time of persecution and trial.

Today, even without persecution, there is a different kind of mass exodus of people leaving many churches! However, in contrast to those whose faith has not come from God, these people are born again and hungry for God's glory. There are hundreds of home churches being planted annually in the United States consisting of families escaping the worldliness infiltrating their former spiritual homes. I know of five such assemblies in my own local community! The parents with whom I've spoken are concerned that they cannot find families with Christ-centered values and faith with whom they may fellowship. Furthermore, their passion for separation from the world's ways is considered archaic and divisive by the mainstream and evangelical churches.

I'm not suggesting that all of the modern churches are corrupt or that we cannot find Godly fellowship unless we join home churches. We must always be sensitive to how God is leading us in our decisions to belong to or leave specific fellowships. We must be very careful not to reject a fellowship in a spirit of divisiveness or because of personal conflicts with other members or the leadership. But it has been my experience that many churches today have abandoned the true gospel in favor of modern marketing methods and shallow, seeker-friendly messages that are meant to attract the largest possible audience rather than to feed the sheep of God. It is in those situations that the sheep are often being led by Christ to form home fellowships.

Hallelujah for God's Grace!

I'm also not asserting that all who have prayed the sinner's prayer and invited Christ into their hearts are unregenerate. God's grace covers a multitude of mistakes on our part. Without a doubt, the Spirit of God had already prepared some for regeneration when this kind of invitation was given to pray and ask Jesus to come into their hearts. Perhaps it was so with you. You would have done anything an evangelist required of you because your heart had already been changed and you were ready to come to know Christ. You may have been told to invite Christ into your heart, so you did. But it was not the prayer of invitation that saved you. Your heart is firmly founded upon the Lord Jesus Christ as your Cornerstone, but perhaps your *thinking* has been anchored on the crumbly foundation of free will and humanism.

At first, you may think this sounds heretical. But I urge you to be a Berean, and study this passage of Scripture thoroughly and honestly with me as you rethink what this passage actually teaches. Let's read Revelation 3:14-20 and note the facts.

The Letter Was Addressed to Believers

> *And to the angel of the church in Laodicea write: The Amen, the faithful and true Witness, the Beginning of the creation of God, says this...*

Jesus did not address the lost, the unsaved, or the unregenerate. He instructed John to write to the lukewarm *church* of Laodicea.

> *I know your deeds, that you are neither cold nor hot; I would that you were cold or hot. So because you are lukewarm, and neither hot nor cold, I will spit you out of My mouth (14-16).*

Lukewarm water results from mixing cold with hot. In the church, the true regenerate believers (the hot) have been mixed with the unregenerate but professing believers (the cold). The Laodicean church, perhaps in order to reach out to the world and create an environment conducive to a worldly mind, compromised holiness. Perhaps they became so *seeker-sensitive* that they compromised their *Spirit-sensitivity*. Whatever the cause, the effect was that the church had undergone an influx of "cold water," lowering the spiritual temperature of all its members—so much so that the church as a whole, living by worldly standards, thought it was doing great. They thought they were in need of nothing because they were so successful. John continued:

Because you say, "I am rich, and have become wealthy, and have need of nothing," and you do not know that you are wretched and miserable and poor and blind and naked, I advise you to buy from Me gold refined by fire, that you may become rich, and white garments, that you may clothe yourself, and that the shame of your nakedness may not be revealed; and eye salve to anoint your eyes, that you may see. Those whom I love, I reprove and discipline; be zealous therefore, and repent (17-19).

These verses indicate whom the Spirit of the Lord addressed. He didn't offer fellowship to the cold. He didn't offer fellowship to the unbelieving church members. He spoke to those He loved—the only ones who have ears to hear. These were His people, His children, at whose door the Lord Jesus stood and knocked. Then He said to them,

Behold...

Only God's people can behold the Lord Jesus at the door. The unsaved do not have eyes to see Him.

Jesus Offered Deeper Communion to Believers

Behold, I stand at the door and knock; if anyone hears My voice and opens the door, I will come in to him, and will dine with him, and he with Me (verse 20).

In this passage Jesus was speaking to His people who had been influenced by the sensuality and unprincipled standards of the world that were infecting the church. His letter to this church was an invitation to holiness. It was not an offer of salvation. He invited them to deeper fellowship.

A person may be a Christian but lack deep fellowship with the Lord Jesus. It is the heart of the Lord Jesus to want deep communion with His people, and because of His grace and mercy, He comes to seek and to save His sheep when they go astray. But He will not reveal more of Himself—indeed, He cannot and maintain His integrity—if they mingle with the world and try to be acceptable to it. The Apostle Paul wrote in

Romans 8 that the Spirit Himself bears witness with our spirits that we are children of God. In this passage in Revelation, the same concept is presented, but in different words.

One of the consequences of living according to the world's standards is an inability to hear the Spirit of Truth. The Apostle John wrote in his first epistle about those who love the world and the things of the world: such love is not from the Father (1 John 2:15-16). Later, he warned of the spirit of antichrist who is in the world, and who is also the spirit of error. Those who listen to the world do not listen to the word of the apostles (1 John 4:3-6). It was this kind of worldliness that had infected the church in Laodicea and led them into error.

This Word Is Relevant to Today's Church

Do you see the same condition in the visible church today? In an effort to make God acceptable to the world, standards of holiness have been lowered in the name of evangelism and church growth. The result is a church that is distasteful to the Lord Jesus because it does not call its members to holiness and differs little from the world. Unbelieving members enjoy a "come as you are, stay as you are" atmosphere. Others outside of the church see its lukewarmness and have no respect for it. Jesus told us in the Sermon on the Mount what would be the world's response to a church that had lost its saltiness or effectiveness: "It is good for nothing except to be thrown out and trampled under foot by men" (Matthew 5:13). This is precisely how the world is responding to the lukewarm church today.

On a positive note, these verses should encourage you about Jesus' desire for deeper communion if you are His child! He longs to share His life with you and manifest His presence in your life. What a wonderful hope there is in knowing that your Lord and Savior is so near, all you have to do is look up. Do you feel lukewarm, complacent, and in need of renewal and refreshing? Take heart! He's at your door with a wonderful offer of fellowship.

> *"He who overcomes, I will grant to him to sit down with Me on My throne, as I also overcame and sat down with My Father on His throne. He who has an ear, let him hear what the Spirit says to the churches" (Revelation 3:21-22).*

Fifteen

Anchored in a Firm Foundation

The purpose behind our study thus far has been to clear the way for a new foundation. It's really not a new foundation, but an old one. Time-tested. Trial-tested. Bible-tested. A foundation anchored in Jesus Christ alone. Not Jesus Christ along with man's morality or fleshly efforts at believing. Not Jesus Christ along with man's power to choose, but Jesus Christ alone!

Perhaps what we have studied so far has raised questions regarding your own salvation or how a person is saved. I have hoped it would be so—but with good purpose. If the storms of life toss you about like a rag in the wind, then you need to question these things. The result of such questioning can only be a deeper knowledge of God's Word and a fresh encounter with the Lord Jesus Christ. I see no other hope for the church of our day but to go back and start from the beginning so that we might rebuild on a firm foundation. *We need revival!*

Better Now Than Later

With all due respect, if your faith has been built on the wrong interpretation of these verses we've studied in Part 1, or on the false teaching of God's Word, then your faith is vulnerable. Now is the time to find out, not when you stand before the Eternal Word of God in judgment. The Word that will judge us (John 12:48) will not be what we *thought* the Word says, but what it *really* says. For the church of God to be built on the truth, it will be necessary for the old foundation and its crumbling building to be torn down and cleared out of the way.

I know this is no quick, easy, painless task. Many may have to deal with a sense of betrayal by those who preached the gospel to them. Others may feel that to doubt the veracity of what they have been taught is like accusing sincere parents and ministers of being false teachers and liars.

May I encourage you that there is another way to respond? Like you, a minister or parent is a product of his education, the relationships he has had, the books he has read, the movies he has watched, the music he has listened to, and all the other influences to which he has been exposed. Have we not all, at one time or another, discovered we were wrong about something? When we did learn the truth, we realized we had not held to what was wrong for the purpose of propagating falsehood. More than likely, we were doing what seemed reasonable and right as far as we knew at the time. The same is true for many ministers and parents. Most freely gave what they had with sincere hearts.

How Does Wrong Teaching Get Started?

I wouldn't want you to think that most ministers knowingly mislead people. I don't think they do. But most seminary-trained ministers are heavily influenced by the particular theological persuasion and philosophies of the seminaries they attended. The Scriptures should be used to rightly teach the Word of God so the Spirit of God will work in peoples' hearts and draw them into the Kingdom of God. Sadly, many ministers are instead being trained to use the Scriptures as a marketing tool to persuade the maximum number of people to join their organizations. Most modern seminaries, pursuing the popular goal of "church growth," tend to equip ministers to build churches using sales-oriented methods that neglect the teaching of sound doctrine. I'm afraid some seminarians study to become successful ministers in the eyes of their peers and the community more than in the eyes of the Lord.

The "big membership numbers" goal is also reinforced when active ministers often ask each other questions such as, "How big is your church? Is your church growing (in numbers)? How many have you baptized this year (regardless of how many are genuinely converted)? Are you the *senior* pastor?" (This begs a further question of whether or not the pastor's church is *big* enough to have men serving *under* him.)

In contrast, I could count on one hand the number of times I've been asked, "How *holy* is your church? Is your church demonstrating that it is separate from the world? Is your church growing in love, faith, and hope in Jesus Christ? Are the converts in your church demonstrating the power of Jesus Christ in their lives? How are the husbands doing at loving their wives?" All of these questions refer to the fruit of sound teaching and the establishing of an unshakable faith in the lives of the members.

In our "user" generation, many have succumbed to using God's Word to fit their purposes rather than to conforming their doctrine and methods to the biblical standard. Instead of thinking and studying to see if what we have been taught really harmonizes with the Scriptures, many have just accepted what their teachers have said.

I wonder if the baby-boomer upbringing set the stage for this. With so many children in the education system, there wasn't time for questions and answers. Perhaps we were discouraged from thinking and asking questions, which would have delayed the achievement of the teacher's objectives. So after years of conditioning us to believe that regurgitation of facts is adequate training, we find ourselves doing the same thing in the church. We figure the Bible teacher, the pastor, or our parents ought to know the truth. If they say a verse means such-and-such, then they're probably right. Who am I to ask questions—even if what I hear doesn't make sense and contradicts the realities of life or other scriptures?

This is a striking truth: "If people don't think *for themselves* and know the facts *for themselves*, they can be controlled." The principle applies in many arenas, including political, educational, theological, and religious. And as a result, an entire generation may walk in darkness.

Be a Berean

The purpose of this book and the recorded audio series, *Unshakable Faith: Building a Firm Foundation*, is not to indict sincere, God-fearing ministers, parents, and Bible teachers. For years, I myself used these scriptures in the wrong way, not because I knew better or wanted to mislead others. I was doing the best I could with what I had been given. I had never heard them taught and interpreted any other way; I had only heard them used within the context of an evangelistic presentation. It wasn't until my life was falling apart and I lay in the rubble of my powerlessness that God began to turn my heart to examine my foundation.

I had heard that the truth sets us free. I had applied all the truth I had been taught as best I could, and yet I was not free. But I noticed I was not alone. There were millions of evangelicals around me in the same or worse predicament. We were not testimonies of God's power and grace. The question gnawed at me, "Could the reason we aren't free be that our foundation is not based firmly on the real truth of God's Word?"

This question launched me into an all-out investigation. Not that I doubted the sincerity and love of those who taught me, but perhaps I had not understood them, or perhaps they had been taught wrong things and were only repeating what they had been taught—just as I had done for 17 years.

As I read history and studied the Bible, commentaries, and the biblical languages, I began to discover what I have shared with you. What I have taught in this book is not new. It is essentially what has been called reformed theology, or the Doctrines of Grace. Many men believed and taught these truths prior to the twentieth century— including John Calvin, Martin Luther, John Knox, Jonathan Edwards, and many other great preachers of the past. We must be careful not to reject this theology because it is not what is taught in all the modern churches. We don't want to fall prey to the same dangerous attitude many liberal educators espouse with regard to truth and understanding of those who have gone before us. To them truth and reality are defined only by what is current and contemporary. They think that men and ideas of the past cannot be relevant.

Today, by the mercy of God, reformed theology is returning to the church. Christians are examining the modern church's teaching and seeing that the popular but unbiblical evangelical methods are leading to increasing worldliness in the church.

We want to be wise and not be like the shortsighted, willfully blind post-modernists of our day. Such an attitude is similar to what the Apostle Paul condemned when he wrote this to the Corinthians:

> *For we are not bold to class or compare ourselves with some of those who commend themselves; but when they measure themselves by themselves and compare themselves with themselves, they are without understanding (2 Corinthians 10:12).*

We can't afford to be careless when we're looking for something solid in which to anchor our souls and lives. You may have been taught error, and may even have passed it on. Most of the church appears to have been trained in error, and the leaders and their congregations pass it on. What I'm teaching now is not new, but old and being rediscovered.

As you read this book—or any book, for that matter—whether it seems right or off-base to you, do not measure your knowledge and understanding by the measure you have always used—elders and peers who may have been trained in error. Be a Berean, "examining the Scriptures daily, to see whether these things are so" (Acts 17:11).

If you will go back beyond our current generation's teaching, valuing the truths that men of God have previously discovered, you will find rich treasure indeed! And you will find that many questions troubling you today will be answered. This is my hope for all who read this book.

If a generation does not measure itself by a standard other than itself, it may easily think it is rich, wealthy, truthful, and without need. I hope we can learn from the bad example of Rehoboam, Solomon's son, who chose to listen to his peers and forsake the counsel of his father's elders. In 1 Kings 12:8 we see the foolishness of someone who anchored into the wrong words. "But he forsook the counsel of the elders which they had given him, and consulted with the young men who grew up with him and served him." Verse 13 says, "And the king answered the people harshly, for *he forsook the advice of the elders which they had given him*." What followed was divisiveness and destruction that affected Israel for a long time.

The purpose of this study is to provide tools with which God may build a firm foundation in the hearts of His people. I trust you'll find the remaining chapters helpful in answering many of the questions this first section has created. I encourage you to test everything you read by the entire counsel of God's Word. By the grace of God, you will understand and know your Bible and your Savior like never before. My prayer for you is that the Spirit of God will be your teacher, and He will bear witness to the truth, which will anchor you into nothing other than Jesus Christ, Himself.

In the next two parts of this book, I look forward to sharing with you how great and wonderful God's plan is in creation, to stand in awe with you in God's purposes for sin and the Fall, to bow in humble worship of God's objective in history, to rejoice with you in the glorious grace of God in Christ Jesus, through whom we have been called. In each chapter you'll find that everything ties into the Cornerstone given by God—this Cornerstone the builders rejected when they chose the false cornerstone of man's ability to choose God. When you have finished, I pray that your heart will see the heart of God in such a way that it will turn to your heavenly Father like never before. Perhaps the winds of revival may again blow across this great nation as we establish a firm foundation on Jesus Christ. May God's Spirit continue to minister to you as we consider in the following chapters the nature of God, His purposes, and His work in salvation.

Scriptures	Misuse or Error
Joshua 24:15	We are saved by our free-will choice to believe in and serve God.
John 1:12	We need to "accept the Lord" by our free will, and then He will save us.
John 3:16	God loves everyone and saves anyone who will choose to believe in Jesus.
Acts 2:38	We should expect salvation experiences just like those described in Acts, including speaking in other tongues and performing or experiencing signs and wonders.
Acts 16:31	We must simply choose to receive Christ by our own free will, and we will be saved.
Romans 10:9-10, 13	If we just confess that Jesus is Lord and call on His name, we will be saved.
1 Timothy 2:4	God wants to save everyone and wishes we all would choose to believe in Jesus.
1 Timothy 4:10	God wants to save everyone and wishes we all would choose to believe in Jesus.
Titus 2:11	God wants to save everyone and wishes we all would choose to believe in Jesus. God is saving all men (universalism).
2 Peter 2:1	We can lose our salvation if we are led astray and believe wrong doctrine. By our own sin, we can fall out of the hand of God.
2 Peter 3:9	God wants to save everyone and wishes we all would choose to believe in Jesus.
1 John 1:9	If we just pray the "sinner's prayer" and confess our sins, God will save us.
1 John 2:2	God wants to save everyone and wishes we all would choose to believe in Jesus.
Revelation 3:20	Jesus is knocking at the door of every person's heart, asking to come in to save us. If we just open the door, and accept the Lord by praying the sinner's prayer, He will save us.

Without the regenerative work of God in the heart, we are in bondage to sin and darkness and cannot "choose" God.

"Accepting the Lord" is an unbiblical idea. We are regenerated by the work of the Holy Spirit in our hearts, and we receive Christ and are made sons of God by His grace and power—not by free will.

Real faith is born of the Spirit of God. God loves both Jews and Gentiles alike and will send His Spirit to work in the Gentile world so they will believe in Christ and be saved.

The work of the Holy Spirit in the first century was unique, and while the Holy Spirit can work any way He wishes, we should not make the events described in Acts into a "formula" for salvation or expect specific signs and wonders as proof of salvation.

Salvation is the work of God and is wrought by the Spirit of God in the human heart. The evangelist should be sensitive to what God is doing in a person's heart and not simply offer a formula for "accepting Christ."

"Accepting the Lord" is an unbiblical idea. (See theme for John 1:12). We believe in Christ with saving faith, which comes not by simply hearing with our ears but by hearing the "rhema" of Christ in our hearts. This kind of hearing is the work of God, not the result of our decision.

God is sovereign. He chooses who will be saved and grants repentance and faith to His sheep. God is saving all kinds of people.

God is the preserver of life for all men. Leaders of flocks should pursue godly teaching and godly conduct for the sake of their flocks. God is sovereign over whom He saves and will keep (preserve) all whom He has chosen to save.

The grace of God has come through hearing the truth when God has given us ears to hear it and receive it. It comes to those who believe—by His grace. The truth is sound doctrine.

False teachers who never were true believers will fall away to destruction. God will keep His sheep, and they will never lose their salvation. We cannot fall out of the hand of God.

God has a timetable that will allow every person He has chosen to save to come to repentance and be saved. God is not trying to save everyone, and He is never defeated by the will of man.

The "sinner's prayer" is not a biblical idea. We are saved when God grants faith and repentance to us and we confess our sins because we know we are already forgiven through the finished work of Christ on the Cross.

Jesus is the only means of salvation provided by God for the world. God is saving every person He has chosen to save.

Jesus speaks to believers who have been influenced by the destructive beliefs of the world. He calls them to come to renewed holiness and fellowship with Him. He is not knocking at the door of the hearts of unbelievers, asking them to choose to believe in Him.

Part 2

God Revealed in the Scriptures

Sixteen

What Is God?

What we *think* about God influences the way we live our lives. What we *believe* about God causes our faith to rise or fall on a daily basis.

For faith to weather the most violent storms of life, it must be founded squarely upon the nature, character, and Being of God. A person's comprehension about God is like a fountain, out of which flows the rest of his understanding about man, sin, and salvation. If one errs in his doctrine regarding what and who God is, he will err in all the other important doctrines.

After my new birth at age 29, I hungered to know the truth about God. I was searching to discover how I had deceived myself for 17 years, thinking I was a Christian when I was not. Beginning at the root, I decided to first make sure my thoughts about God were on target. I acquired a number of systematic theology books and began to read and meditate on the Being of God. I was asking questions like, "What does it mean to be God? Who is the real God? Is He what and who I've been told He is in Sunday school and church?"

Becoming God-Centered in Our Thinking

One of the first things I discovered about my thinking about God was that it was extremely *man*-centered. I recall that many years earlier I had thought God was waiting for me to open the door of my heart and choose to accept Him. That kind of notion about God was reinforced weekly with almost every altar call I heard. He was portrayed as reacting to what man did or didn't do. Some preachers actually explained that God had limited Himself to the free will of mankind. He *wanted* to do great things in and through men, but *they* held the reins to the whole show. That perspective was not what I found in the theology books and in the writings of the great men of God in the Bible and in history. They portrayed *God* as the center of all things.

As I perused the Scriptures to see how God was presented, I was surprised to find that God wasn't at all like that. The Scriptures testify that God is living and acting in every event in history and is in complete control of all things—even Satan and evil. Scriptures like the ones below are very clear and resound with glory to God for His sovereignty:

> *For from Him and through Him and to Him are **all things**. To Him be the glory forever. Amen (Romans 11:36).*

> *Yet for us there is but one God, the Father, from whom are all things, and we exist for Him; and one Lord Jesus Christ, by whom are **all things**, and we exist through Him (1 Corinthians 8:6).*

> *For by Him **all things** were created, both in the heavens and on earth, visible and invisible, whether thrones or dominions or rulers or authorities—**all things** have been created by Him and for Him. And He is before **all things**, and in Him **all things** hold together (Colossians 1:16-17).*

The human race is by nature man-centered. We tend to think of God in human terms, don't we? We expect God's idea of fairness to be the same as ours. Often I hear people talk as if they expect God to have the same vision for life that they have—to make them happy and comfortable! Not only do our human limitations hinder us in our thinking about God, but also our minds have been terribly affected by the presence of sin in our souls.

If we wish to be sure about what God is and who He is, we should certainly give priority in our thinking to the Scriptures' recording of God's view of Himself. Read what God says about Himself, both to His own people and to Cyrus, King of Persia:

> *To whom would you liken Me, and make Me equal and compare Me, that we should be alike?... Remember the former things long past, for I am God, and there is no other; I am God, and there is no one like Me, declaring the end from the beginning and from ancient times things which have not*

been done, saying, "My purpose will be established, and I will accomplish all My good pleasure" (Isaiah 46:5, 9-10).

I am the Lord, and there is no other; besides Me there is no God. I will gird you, though you have not known Me; that men may know from the rising to the setting of the sun that there is no one besides Me. I am the Lord, and there is no other, the One forming light and creating darkness, causing well-being and creating calamity; I am the Lord who does all these (Isaiah 45:5-7).

Wow! What a God! There is no one like Him. We shouldn't think of Him in human terms with human limitations. He *causes well-being* and *creates calamity.* Is your idea of God big enough to recognize His sovereignty over all the affairs of history? Whatever He purposes, He accomplishes. He's not waiting for man's free will to make choices before He can act. If God wants something done, He will do it. Both light and darkness have a purpose in His plans.

Some have replied to this God-centered thinking by arguing that such an idea of God makes Him the author of sin. We'll discuss that particular issue in the section on God's purposes for sin and the fall of man. But for now, it may be helpful to know that through the centuries, theologians have held tenaciously to the equality of God's sovereignty and man's responsibility. One is not supreme over the other. A quote regarding the decrees of God, taken from the *London Baptist Confession,* with comments by Peter Masters, explains this well:

God has decreed in Himself *(decided by Himself)* from all eternity, by the most wise and holy counsel of His own will, freely and unchangeably, all things which shall ever come to pass. *(Nothing forced Him in the making of any of His plans, and all His intentions will be carried out without the slightest alteration.)*

Yet in such a way that God is neither the author of sin, nor does He have fellowship *(mutual responsibility)* with any in the committing of sins, nor is violence offered to the will of the creature *(no one is made to sin)*, nor yet is the liberty or contingency of second causes taken away, *(i.e.: nor is the free working of the law of cause and effect interfered with)* but rather established.[16]

When I think of God in this way, I am in awe of His wisdom and power. Aren't you? Let's now consider *what* God is, and in the next chapter we'll focus on *who* God is, as we continue laying the foundation upon which to anchor our faith.

What Is God?

The *Westminster Confession of Faith*, written in 1646, has served Christians well for centuries. Although it is not a complete statement of what God is, the Westminster divines agreed on some of His fundamental characteristics. First, they said God is "spirit." They described Him as "infinite, eternal, and unchangeable in His Being, wisdom, power, holiness, justice, goodness, and truth." I can't adequately explain all of these things about God, but a brief overview of the scriptures supporting this lofty description of Him will help us. Let's look at each aspect of God's nature independently. Then we'll apply those to specific characteristics of His Being.

God Is Spirit

As recorded in John 4:24, Jesus revealed to the woman at the well *what* God is: a spirit. William Hendriksen, a popular contemporary Bible commentator, remarked about Jesus' statement in his commentary on the gospel of John:

> Completely spiritual in His essence is God! He is not a stone-deity or tree-deity, neither is He a mountain-deity so that He has to be worshiped on this or that specific mountain. He is an independent, incorporeal, personal Being.[17]

Simply put, God is an omnipresent, omniscient, and relational Being. Understanding this helps us in our worship of God. We're not to think we can only relate to God in a church building or during a worship service. Worship is an everyday, every-minute experience. Knowing this also anchors our faith in Him because we know nothing takes place outside of His presence and thus outside of His plan and power.

God Is Infinite

How on earth do we finite beings comprehend infinity? "Can you discover the depths of God? Can you discover the limits of the Almighty?" one of Job's counselors asked him. The obvious answer is "No!" In the *London Baptist Confession*, the writers described God's

Being, wisdom, power, holiness, justice, goodness, and truth as *infinite*. "How unsearchable are His judgments and unfathomable His ways!" wrote the Apostle Paul in Romans 11:33. We may put out of our minds the idea that God is limited in ways such as we are.

God Is Eternal

Although any effort to illustrate the concept of eternity will surely be incomplete, perhaps an attempt would still be worthwhile. Imagine a line appearing from one end of the universe and disappearing out of the other end. To us as humans living within the boundaries of time, the line represents all of history. Each event is a *point* on the line, and the chain of events—the causes and effects, the actions and reactions— proceed along the line as time progresses. Each of our lives—a collection of events—occupies a tiny segment of the extensive line of time.

But God sees it differently. *Because He stands outside of time, He sees the entire line—all of history—at once, as a single point.* This is why He says He is "declaring the end from the beginning" (Isaiah 46:10).

The Psalmist expressed His praise to God by declaring,

> *Before the mountains were born, or Thou didst give birth to the earth and the world, even from everlasting to everlasting, Thou art God (Psalm 90:2).*

I'm not sure our minds can fathom such timelessness. But understanding this aspect of God's nature is significant because it helps us realize that God is always the actor, never the *reactor*—the First Cause and the initiator of all things. He is never surprised by events.

Because He lives outside of time, He is the only One who can preside over it. Understanding His eternal nature helps us comprehend how He could see and know *all* the sins of *all* His people throughout *all* of history. On that day when Jesus satisfied God's infinite justice by dying on the cross, He bore all the sins of His people at one time. And because God is eternal—viewing this world from a position outside of time—He DID know *all* of us on the day Jesus died. He DID forgive the sins of *all* of His people. He DID reconcile us to Himself through Jesus' shed blood on the cross. Knowing this gives us confidence that not one sin escaped His notice and that *all* is paid for. It is DONE.

If we can imagine God looking at the entire timeline of the history of mankind, we may be able to bring together these two concepts:

God's eternal nature and its relationship to Jesus' atoning death for us. He *foreknew* us before we were created; He *knew* us on the day Christ died; He *knows* us today; and He *sees us in Christ,* forgiven and seated at His right hand in heaven. His perspective is eternal because He is eternal.

Without this eternal perspective of the atonement, we have no basis for understanding how God could justify *us* along with every other believer at *one point in time* in history. The completed work of our salvation, justification, and sanctification *was determined outside of time.* It was *accomplished at one point in time*—at the Cross. Why is this important for Christians to understand? Because otherwise we may think that God forgave our sins individually, person by person, throughout history, at the moment each one of us prayed and asked Him to. What the Bible tells us, though, is that God decided and made a plan to forgive us all together, before He ever made the world (Ephesians 1:4). If our thinking about the way God determined to save us is not correct, we will wrongly reason that *we are the initiators of events,* and that God *reacts to our prayers*—or lack thereof. Such backward reasoning is like the proverbial tail wagging the dog. This makes our faith very shakable.

But having this eternal perspective of the atonement provides a solid rock for a stable faith. Knowing our salvation was planned and administrated *from eternity* and is being worked out *in history* contributes to our assurance because it isn't based on our own actions, or on the hope that we did the right thing, prayed the right prayer, or made the right decisions. It is anchored in God's work through Jesus Christ in eternity rather than in a shakable man-centered perspective of life. This truth inspires me to declare with the Apostle Paul in Romans 11:33,

> *O, the depth of the riches both of the wisdom and knowledge of God!*

In summary, we see the glory of God's eternal nature in this: His people are not justified one at a time as they choose to believe in Christ. Instead, because *they already have been justified* in Christ from eternity, God grants them repentance and faith in Jesus Christ when *He* chooses, as He applies the saving work of Jesus to them through the ministry of the Holy Spirit. When we see Jesus Christ living His life *in us,* we know *we were* in Him at the Cross and *are now* in Him in the heavenlies. That's why we say we *have* eternal life in Jesus Christ. Hallelujah!

God Is Unchangeable

In a world that is constantly changing and where people often change their minds every few minutes, God's immutability draws me to Him. Does it draw you? Our faith finds a resting place in One whose Being never changes. The Apostle James described our heavenly Father in this way:

> *Every good thing bestowed and every perfect gift is from above, coming down from the Father of lights, with whom there is no variation, or shifting shadow (James 1:17).*

This important quality allows us to hold onto His promises with a sense of confidence, all through our lives until the moment we enter eternity. We can know that when we get there, God will still honor His promise:

> *Whoever believes in Him will not be disappointed (Romans 10:11).*

The Son of God, Jesus Christ, is portrayed in Scripture as being as unchangeable as His Father. The writer of Hebrews wrote, "Jesus Christ is the same yesterday and today, yes and forever" (Hebrews 13:8). What security this gives us! The eternal, infinite Word of God remains true—and this is our basis for an unshakable faith.

Consider how things have changed over the centuries—creeds and doctrines, papal bulls and church edicts, attitudes and values of cultures, governments and world leaders. But God NEVER changes! He Himself is our most dependable anchor.

He Is Infinite, Eternal, and Unchangeable in His *Being*

Now let's apply these attributes of God's nature to specific characteristics of His Being. Since God exists outside of time, there is no past or future for Him. Therefore when Moses asked God what he should tell the Egyptians if they asked, "What is the name of the God of your fathers?" God answered with a description of His *Being*. He said, "I AM WHO I AM. Thus you shall say to the sons of Israel, 'I AM has sent me to you'" (Exodus 3:14). Perhaps the ever-present God addressed Moses with such a name because he needed to know that God would be with him at every moment. Like Moses, we also need the assurance that God always IS. He isn't a "WAS" or a "WILL BE." Our faith rests in the infinite, eternal, unchangeable nature of His Being.

He Is Infinite, Eternal, and Unchangeable in His *Wisdom*

As the affairs of our lives unroll in history, what confidence do we have that things are not out of control and simply left to fate? The Scriptures tell us that all things are being done according to God's great wisdom. I hope the following verses encourage your faith like they do mine as you consider that "His understanding is infinite" (Psalm 147:5b).

> *O Lord, how many are Thy works! In wisdom Thou hast made them all; the earth is full of Thy possessions (Psalm 104:24).*

> *The Lord by wisdom founded the earth; by understanding He established the heavens (Proverbs 3:19).*

> *The Lord is exalted, for He dwells on high; He has filled Zion with justice and righteousness. And He shall be the stability of your times, a wealth of salvation, wisdom, and knowledge; the fear of the Lord is his treasure (Isaiah 33:5-6).*

He Is Infinite, Eternal, and Unchangeable in His *Power*

"Great is our Lord, and abundant in strength!" wrote the psalmist in Psalm 147:5. God's power has no limits. When I think of God's power, immediately His most awesome display of strength comes to mind: the removal of the sins, the guilt, and the power of the flesh from His elect. How can we fathom the infinite power that can remove our sins as far from us as the east is from the west? Can we grasp with our minds the power of One Who only needs to speak and a universe is created, with all its order and design? Indeed, who can understand the power of God, Who forms light and creates darkness, Who causes well-being and creates calamity for all His creatures? He said, "I am the Lord who does all these" (Isaiah 45:7).

Believers need to understand the power of God. The Apostle Paul prayed for the Ephesians that they would know the "surpassing greatness of His power toward us who believe" (Ephesians 1:19). Peter wrote that it is the power of God that protects us through faith for a salvation ready to be revealed (1 Peter 1:5). Although we can't wrap our minds around such power, our faith is sustained by it, and we can rely on it!

He Is Infinite, Eternal, and Unchangeable in His *Holiness*

God often spoke of Himself to men in the Scriptures, but no picture of Himself is recorded more often than, "I am holy." About Himself God said,

> For I am the LORD your God. Consecrate yourselves therefore, and be **holy**, for I am **holy** (Leviticus 11:44).

Understanding God's holiness is important because of its place in our own lives as we relate to God. His holiness is important to our faith's foundation because our worship of Him is linked to His holiness. For instance, when Isaiah saw the Lord, he was impressed with His holiness (Isaiah 6). John, at the revelation of Christ, also saw Him surrounded by creatures crying, "Holy is the Lord God, the Almighty" (Revelation 4). In the Psalms, God is said to speak and swear "in His holiness" (Psalm 60:6; 89:35; 108:7). When God swears, our faith has an eternal foundation in which to be anchored. God swears for *us*! He certainly doesn't need to do it to make His word surer for Himself. Perhaps now would be a good time to pause and meditate on this glorious truth that God is infinite, eternal, and unchangeable in His holiness. Shall we join the everlasting throng of worshipers at the feet of Jesus in humble adoration and praise?

He Is Infinite, Eternal, and Unchangeable in His *Justice*

Perhaps it may surprise you to learn that God cannot forgive like we forgive. When we say we forgive a person for his offense, we usually mean that we will try not to bring it up anymore and we'll not hold anything against the offender. In a way, because we don't have the power to bring about justice, the sin is allowed to slip by unpunished. But God cannot allow sin to go unpunished because He is infinite, eternal, and unchangeable in His *justice*. His throne in heaven rests partially on His justice. Notice how the writers of the Psalms understood that God is just:

> *Righteousness and justice are the foundation of Thy throne; lovingkindness and truth go before Thee (Psalm 89:14).*

> *He loves righteousness and justice; the earth is full of the lovingkindness of the Lord (Psalm 33:5).*

> *For the Lord loves justice, and does not forsake His godly ones; they are preserved forever; but the descendants of the wicked will be cut off (Psalm 37:28).*

The mouth of the righteous utters wisdom, and his tongue speaks justice (Psalm 37:30).

Clouds and thick darkness surround Him; righteousness and justice are the foundation of His throne (Psalm 97:2).

And the strength of the King loves justice; Thou hast established equity; Thou hast executed justice and righteousness in Jacob (Psalm 99:4).

The works of His hands are truth and justice; all His precepts are sure (Psalm 111:7).

When our faith relies on the finished work of Jesus Christ on the cross, we are believing that something actually took place there— eternal justice was accomplished! God was doing so much more than giving mankind an emotional reason to love Jesus and choose to accept Him as their Savior. If God has not put our sins upon His precious, spotless Lamb and executed justice, then we are still in our sins. On the other hand, if the Lamb of God did bear our sins, then justice has been served.

I love the way the Apostle Paul wrote about God's justifying sinners. Look at how our justification relates to God's own character:

But now apart from the Law the righteousness of God has been manifested, being witnessed by the Law and the Prophets, even the righteousness of God through faith in Jesus Christ for all those who believe; for there is no distinction; for all have sinned and fall short of the glory of God, being justified as a gift by His grace through the redemption which is in Christ Jesus; **whom God displayed publicly** *as a propitiation in His blood through faith.* **This was to demonstrate His righteousness**, *because in the forbearance of God He passed over the sins previously committed; for the demonstration, I say, of His righteousness at the present time,* **that He might be just and the justifier of the one who has faith in Jesus** *(Romans 3:21-26).*

God did not permit His Son to be put to death in a corner, so to speak, hidden from the world. Instead, Jesus was "lifted up" for the entire world to see. God advertised the sacrificial atoning work of His Son—making it the central point in history. In so doing, He highlighted the justness of His own character. His justice demanded that He not pass over sins like we do when we forgive. Rather, payment was made in full, and God's requirement for justice was satisfied. Authentic faith in Jesus Christ is faith that stands on the solid rock of what God is: infinite, eternal, unchangeable justice!

He Is Infinite, Eternal, and Unchangeable in His *Goodness*

Perhaps no other aspect of God's character is more viciously attacked because of the presence of sin and evil than the goodness of God. How can God be considered good if He is in control of *all things*, and some of those things are hurtful, tragic, and intensely repulsive? What kind of a God is it that allows evil to exist and prosper? These are difficult questions to answer. However, one of the first things we must do is relinquish a man-centered definition of "good."

If we define "good" by our own standards, we find ourselves trapped by evil like a victim cornered by a gang in a dark alley. There's no way out! There are no answers that satisfy us. Our tendency is to view the events of life from our finite, temporal, selfish perspective rather than from God's infinite, eternal perspective.

For instance, is an earthquake that kills a hundred people a "good" thing? If we consider it from the perspective of human loss, we surely answer, "No!" However, we who believe in God have another perspective upon which to stand. God is sovereign over all events, so we know that somehow the earthquake fits into God's purposes. It would be evil if you or I caused the earthquake because we are not God. But if God permits it, then it is ultimately good—because God is good—even if we, as finite humans, cannot see this from our limited perspective. Only in heaven will we understand such things.

One of my favorite Old Testament stories portrays God's *goodness* as God's *glory*. Moses asked God to show him His glory. In answer to Moses' request, God caused His goodness to pass before him. God hid Moses in the cleft of a rock and placed His hand (figuratively speaking) over Moses as He passed by. Then God removed His hand and allowed Moses to "see His back." The scriptures in Exodus 33:19 and 34:6-7 record that, while passing Moses,

> *... He said, "I Myself will make all My goodness pass before you, and will proclaim the name of the Lord before you; and I will be gracious to whom I will be gracious, and will show compassion on whom I will show compassion."*

*Then the Lord passed by in front of him and proclaimed, "The Lord, the Lord God, compassionate and gracious, slow to anger, and **abounding in lovingkindness** [KJV: goodness] and truth; who keeps lovingkindness for thousands, who forgives iniquity, transgression and sin; yet He will by no means leave the guilty unpunished, visiting the iniquity of fathers on the children and on the grandchildren to the third and fourth generations."*

God demonstrated His goodness when He chose to show compassion and kindness to sinners. It is amazing that, in order to show His goodness without compromising His justice, He had to sacrifice His Son! He shows compassion on whom He wills, and that is His infinite, eternal, and unchangeable goodness.

We might think God is *uncompassionate* since He doesn't show compassion to everyone. However, God can do with His mercy what He wishes. Not one of His creatures deserves God's good favor. Nothing in us disposes Him to be merciful; rather, our sinful rebelliousness warrants His wrath and indignation. We should all be amazed at God's willingness to show mercy to anyone—and even more so if we are the recipients of such goodness!

How great is Thy goodness, which Thou hast stored up for those who fear Thee, which Thou hast wrought for those who take refuge in Thee, before the sons of men (Psalm 31:19)!

He Is Infinite, Eternal, and Unchangeable in His *Truth*

In the passage in Exodus 34, you'll notice the phrase that God "abounds in truth." Many of the Psalms also declare the glorious dimensions of God's truth:

Into Thy hand I commit my spirit; Thou hast ransomed me, O Lord, God of truth (Psalm 31:5).

For Thy lovingkindness is great to the heavens, and Thy truth to the clouds (Psalm 57:10).

Lovingkindness and truth have met together; righteousness and peace have kissed each other (Psalm 85:10).

The works of His hands are truth and justice; all His precepts are sure (Psalm 111:7).

For His lovingkindness is great toward us, and the truth of the Lord is everlasting. Praise the Lord! (Psalm 117:2).

God's trustworthiness toward us is sure because the truth of the Lord is everlasting. Currently, the antichrist culture imagines that there is no such thing as absolute truth. The contradiction seems obvious: *"It is an absolute truth that there is no such thing as absolute truth."* That's ridiculous! We've seen the fruit of this lie: a society with no moral bearings destroys what is most valuable to its well-being—that is, truth. We can be thankful that God has given us an anchor! When we read His Word and bank on it, we are resting our souls on Truth that is everlasting. "Thy Word is truth," confessed the Lord Jesus to His Father (John 17:17). How else can we have a faith that endures all things unless it stands firmly on infinite, eternal, unchangeable truth?

As we review these qualities about God, we probably ask why a number of words we can think of are omitted from the *Westminster Confession's* list of God's fundamental characteristics. The reason is that not every quality of God's character can be applied universally, as God's wisdom, power, holiness, justice, goodness, and truth can be. For instance, we would expect God's love to be infinite, and it is! But there are different kinds of love, and God has one kind of love for His enemies and another kind for His elect. God's love cannot be described as infinite, eternal, and unchangeable *to everyone.* The same may be said for other qualities that usually fall under a discussion of God's character, such as jealousy and patience.

What Is God?

God is spirit. He is *infinite, eternal, and unchangeable* in His *Being, Wisdom, Power, Holiness, Justice, Goodness, and Truth.* If we begin with this understanding of what it means to be God, our theology and doctrine have a firm foundation upon which to build. In the next chapter, we will consider *Who* God is. Is it possible that we can know this great, awesome, eternal Being? The good news is that we can!

Seventeen

Who Is God?

Who is God? Is He the pantheistic deity of the New Age? The gods of the Hindus? Allah of Islam? The god of the Mormons or Jehovah's Witnesses? Is He the God of Baptists, Catholics, Methodists, Presbyterians, Lutherans, or Pentecostals? There are hundreds of religions in the world, and they either speak of the true God or of false gods. They can't *all* be right! How does one know for sure who God is? What is His identity? These are the questions we will explore in this chapter.

Beware of False Conceptions of God

First of all, when we ask, "Who is God?" we are asking about His *identity*. We have solid evidence that throughout history, God revealed His identity to many men. These men wrote down what they heard and saw, and God ensured the accurate recording and preservation of their writings. But also throughout history, other philosophers and so-called theologians—hostile to the true and living God—ignored or denied the revelations of God. Instead, they looked to their own corrupt logic and fallen natures to answer the questions about God's identity. So today, we need to know the true God and at the same time beware of the false conceptions of God, which all deny His true nature.

For example, *pantheism* is an ancient but persistent belief that the world and nature are divine, and that God is in everything. Pantheists reject God's revelation of Himself as a divine, personal Being who is distinct from and infinitely exalted above His creation. Instead, they identify God more as an impersonal force, existing entirely *within* creation.

Another popular yet erroneous view of God casts Him as a personal but *finite* being. This is not a new idea. In an effort to make God more like us and thus more appealing, some religious philosophers asserted that God is limited in His power and is still "growing" in His own knowledge and being—an "evolving" deity. These men believed that this "higher power"—friendly, and communing with man more as an equal than an authority—met their practical, experiential, and emotional needs through religion.[18]

Still other philosophers portrayed God as a personification of an abstract idea. Such thinking considers the title "God" as symbolic, standing for some cosmic process, a universal force or power, or perhaps just a lofty ideal.

All of these philosophies have one thing in common: They allow man to be his own god and to create a "god" of his own liking, one who serves man's needs and fits his social ideals or cultural norms. The false religions always glorify man, his nature, or his free will, always find ways for men to justify themselves, and always worship man-made gods that are inferior to the true and living God.

So what can we know about the *real* God? Where do we go for a reliable answer to our question about who God is?

God Has Made Himself Known Through Nature

The first place we should go is to the universe itself. When we look at the order, complexity, and design throughout nature, we must reasonably infer that all this is surely the work of an intelligent Designer. The theory of evolution, which denies the existence of God and claims that life came from a long series of lucky accidents, is a vastly inferior explanation of origins when compared to the idea of a Creator. Why? Because whatever chance may create, chance may also destroy. There is no logical reason to think that the wonders of nature are mere accidents.

In every area of life, the existence of something presupposes a creator of that thing. Only in the scientific arena have men been so foolish as to claim existence without a creator! The following fascinating story clearly makes the point:

That a maker is required for anything that is made is a lesson Sir Isaac Newton was able to teach forcefully to an atheist-scientist friend of his. Sir Isaac had an accomplished artisan fashion for him a small-scale model of our solar system which, when completed, was to be put in a room in Newton's home. The assignment was finished and installed on a large table. The workman had done a very commendable job, simulating not only the various sizes of the planets and their relative proximities, but also so constructing the model that everything rotated and orbited when a crank was turned. It was an interesting, even fascinating work, as you can imagine, particularly to anyone schooled in the sciences.

Newton's atheist-scientist friend came by for a visit. Seeing the model, he was naturally intrigued, and proceeded to examine it with undisguised admiration for the high quality of the workmanship. "My! What an exquisite thing this is!" he exclaimed. "Who made it?" Paying little attention to him, Sir Isaac answered, "Nobody."

Stopping his inspection, the visitor turned and said: "Evidently you did not understand my question. I asked who made this." Newton, enjoying himself immensely, no doubt, replied in a still more serious tone, "Nobody. What you see just happened to assume the form it now has." "You must think I am a fool!" the visitor retorted hotly. "Of course somebody made it, and he is a genius! And I would like to know who he is."

Newton then spoke to his friend in a polite yet firm way: "This thing is but a puny imitation of a much grander system whose laws you know, and I am not able to convince you that this mere toy is without a designer and maker. Yet you profess to believe that the great original from which the design is taken has come into being without either designer or maker! Now tell me by what sort of reasoning you reach such an incongruous conclusion?"[19]

May God help us not to be blind to the truth conveyed through this story! The entire universe with all its wonders cannot possibly be the result of simple chance. The monkey tapping away on a computer keyboard does not produce a dictionary. Neither can the mere *presence* of energy nor the *power* of force create order or design. For instance, a pile of lumber hit with a flamethrower does not produce a house. And the tornado going through the forest does not create a log cabin.

To create something with order and design, someone needs to put information into it, and that requires a Creator. It is far more reasonable to look at the universe—at *creation*—and infer the existence of a *Creator*. The question that nature should cause us to ask is this: "Has the One who created the universe revealed Himself in more specific ways and in words that we can understand?" And the answer is, yes, He has.

God Has Revealed Himself So We Can Know Him

I mentioned earlier that most religions of the world seek to justify and glorify man, but that through history God has revealed Himself to many men, overseeing and preserving the records of their encounters with Him. Why has He done these things?

Close examination of the universe leads us to answer with a second reasonable inference: Not only does the Creator *exist,* but He also *wishes to be known.* This is a simple deduction. Such order, complexity, and design as we see would be wasted without an intelligent audience to appreciate it. Contrary to pantheistic, finite, or abstract gods that glorify man, the Creator of this intricate and symbiotic universe obviously wants us to know and delight in *His* glory. If by the *intricacy* of the things He has designed we can deduce that He *wishes* to be known, then by the *intelligence* and *power* demonstrated by His design, we can conclude that He *will* make Himself known. Nothing could thwart the wishes of such a Being.

So He did not stop at creating the universe in order to reveal His nature and character. He went on to demonstrate His power and unveil His love among men in history, so that we can know Him and honor Him for who He is. Of course, to people who have never considered this or who have disbelieved it, I could say much more. But since it is probable that most readers of this book will be Christians who accept these ideas, I'll keep the line of reason simple so that only the most important basic concepts are laid out plainly.

God Has Made Himself Known Through the Bible

Not only has God revealed Himself through nature, but He has also done so through the testimonies of men throughout history. For several hundred years, men recorded God's revelation of Himself to them, and it is vital to note that of all the religions with notions of a god or gods in history, only the God of the Bible has historically verified eyewitness testimonies of His communication with man. What would you think if you heard a voice from the sky, received a message through a messenger who told you details of an event to come next year, or watched a man command the wind and waves of a lake to be still—and they did so? Do you think you might value those words or that experience? Incidents such as these are exactly what we should expect from someone claiming that the God of history spoke to him, and the Bible is filled with testimonies of such incidents.

But why should we believe these testimonies? Since we live in a day when God's Word is commonly denigrated or dismissed, let's digress for a minute to simply state why we can believe what God has said about Himself.

The Bible Is Inspired

The Bible claims to be "inspired"—that is, "breathed by God." Why should we accept this claim? Remember that God *wishes* to be known, so He did things *in order* to be known. It is rational to expect the God of creation not only to be able to communicate to His creatures, but to do so in such ways that His creatures would know without question they had heard from Him, that is, by doing unnatural or supernatural things. We might also expect the true God of history to make Himself known by foretelling historical events and then confirming His word by perfectly bringing those prophecies to pass. God has fulfilled these reasonable expectations. Further still, it is reasonable to expect that God—because He is God—is certainly capable of delivering His words first-hand to some men through experience, and second-hand to others through the written testimonies of those who experienced His power. It is irrational to think that God—as God—is incapable of keeping His own testimony about Himself from being messed up by mere men. Therefore, we trust in the process of men writing down their experiences with God, and we call that process *divine inspiration*. The Apostle Peter made this assertion most clearly:

> *But know this first of all, that no prophecy of Scripture is **a matter of one's own interpretation**, for no prophecy was ever made by **an act of human will**, but men **moved by the Holy Spirit** spoke from God (2 Peter 1:20-21).*

Also, according to 2 Timothy 3:16-17, the Holy Spirit of God superintended the recording and compilation of God's acts and words through men for four purposes:

> *All Scripture is inspired by God and profitable for teaching, for reproof, for correction, for training in righteousness; that the man of God may be adequate, equipped for every good work.*

So we believe that the Bible is the divinely inspired record of God's revelation of Himself to man. This book is our most trustworthy means of coming to know God. Other religious books telling of other gods cannot meet the standards of authenticity that the Bible meets. All other religious books pale by comparison and prove to be nothing more than the contrivances of men.

The Bible Is Trustworthy

In addition to God's fulfilling our expectations that he would make Himself known and keep the testimony about Himself reliable, we also have the "big picture" aspect of how the Bible is comprised, giving us great confidence that it is not a contrivance of men.

Contrary to popular understanding, Christians who believe the Bible are not placing their trust in a single book but rather in a virtual library about God. Over a 1500-year period, 66 distinct accounts authored by over 40 men have been collected and compiled to constitute what is now commonly called *The Bible*. Many of the accounts were historical records of what God said and did. Others are teaching letters of men who knew Jesus Christ personally and were eyewitnesses to His life and teachings. Every book within the Bible tells of men's interactions with the sovereign God who has revealed Himself in historical events, in the lives of individual men, and in His only begotten Son. The variety, both of the authors He inspired and the cultures they lived in, along with the vast range of time over which the books were written, make the unified testimony of the Bible all the more amazing. These combined features argue powerfully for the trustworthiness of the Bible as a true witness for God.

The Bible Is a Progressive Revelation of the True God

Consider also that over those 1500 years, God didn't reveal all of Himself to mankind at once, yet the later revelations of Him are consistent with the earlier ones. In the same way that we might develop a relationship with someone, where we divulge information about ourselves progressively, so God shared more about Himself to His creatures as history advanced. God prophesied to men His intentions specifically for the purpose of making Himself known. (In the book of Ezekiel, for example, God prophesied at least seventy times what He would do and then added a statement like, "Then they will know that I am the Lord.")

And God told Isaiah,

> "For I am God, and there is no other; I am God, and there is no one like Me, declaring the end from the beginning and from ancient times things which have not been done, saying, 'My purpose will be established, and I will accomplish all My good pleasure'" (Isaiah 46:9-10).

When He subsequently performed the acts that He had previously declared He would do, those men knew for sure that God had spoken to them. His perfect record of prediction and fulfillment distinguishes the God of the Bible from all other so-called revelations and gods.

For example, the Book of Mormon claims to be a further, newer revelation from God. But unlike the Bible, the prophecies and historical record in the Book of Mormon are not supported by historical and archeological evidence. No other religions boast of a god who controls history and calls the end from the beginning with one hundred percent accuracy! Because of this true historical revelation, we confidently accept the Bible as our rule for faith and practice.

The Bible Is a Standard by Which to Think and Live

Those words which the men of old knew to be God's Word have become the standard by which all subsequent revelations of God are judged. They have also become a standard in life for the wise and a judgment against the foolish. Believing that God has revealed Himself in the Bible, our faith has a resting place, and we have a faithful guide for our doctrine and our lifestyle.

Rock-solid faith can only stand on ideas that are anchored in historical revelation by a personal God who relates intimately with men. This is the God revealed in the Bible. It is the inspired compilation of accounts about the true God who has revealed Himself to men, creating for us a standard by which to judge our own lives and other claims about God. These are the reasons that we turn to the Bible to answer our question, "Who is God?"

So let's return to the first focus of this chapter. Who does God declare Himself to be in the Bible?

God Is One

God in the Old Testament revealed Himself this way:

> *Hear, O Israel!* **The Lord is our God, the Lord is one!** *(Deuteronomy 6:4).*

In the New Testament, the Apostle Paul spoke for believers when he wrote to the Corinthians,

> *Yet **for us there is but one God**, from whom are all things, and we exist for Him (1 Corinthians 8:6).*

So who is God? He's the *One* from whom all things flow, according to Romans 11:36. There is only *one* God—*one* source, or origin, of supply for the entire universe. I want to be clear about this because we live in a day when many people have a philosophy of tolerance about religion, saying we should not exclude from the arena of truth people who believe in other gods or have a faith different from our own.

You've probably heard the idea that all the world's faiths and religions are simply different roads up the same mountain, and they all lead to God. But of course this can't be true because the claims about God from all these faiths contradict each other. Remember in the beginning of this chapter I mentioned just a few of the many differing conceptions of God.

The God of the Bible and many of the other so-called gods claim exclusivity—that is, they demand worship of themselves alone. In fact, the very term "God" is exclusive. Consider what it means to be God: the *source* of all, the *cause* of all, the *ruler* of all. Yet the biblical God's claims about Himself are very different from those of the other gods. Neither are their requirements of men the same. Such dissimilar "roads" cannot lead to the same god in eternity. Because God by definition must be a single source, cause, and ruler, the idea of *many true gods* is oxymoronic, and the belief in a *single god that reveals himself by different names in contradictory ways* is illogical. So the proposal that all roads lead to God can only come from men who don't want to argue about religion, but not men who want to discover if there is a true God. There can only be *one* true God.

God Claims Supreme Authority, With Jurisdiction Over His Creation

God also declares Himself the Supreme Authority over all He has created. Earlier in this chapter we considered how nature calls us to believe in an intelligent Designer who created everything. God's creating *power* and His *word* are related to each other. According to the Bible, when God created everything, He did so by *speaking it into existence*. This gives us a basis for understanding the important concept of *jurisdiction*. A crucial aspect of our faith being firmly anchored in Christ is the idea that God has jurisdiction over every area of our lives. The term comes from two words meaning "law" or "authority" and "to speak." Together they communicate the concept of "the one who has the right to speak" in a particular sphere.

One of the jurisdictional principles by which we live on a daily basis is this: the one who creates a domain has the right to speak over it. For instance, an employee listens to the CEO because either he created the business or was given jurisdiction by the one(s) who created it. No one questions his right to speak or give directions as to how the business operates. Why does he have that right? Because the right to speak into any sphere is inherent with being the owner or creator. The same is true for God and His creation. He has the right to speak into every part of His creation, and He has always done so.

Think about what God has done in history as He revealed Himself to men: He ordained a worldwide flood, parted the waters, used a large fish and a talking donkey, entered history in the form of a man, calmed the sea and wind with a word, healed the sick, and resurrected the dead. These stories would be unbelievable if God did not prepare the hearts of men to receive them as truth! Now think about the *implications* of believing in a God who so controls creation. Those who believe that God did *these things* must also acknowledge God's jurisdiction over *them*! For this reason, unbelievers often dismiss the Biblical stories as myths rather than face the alternative, that God has the right to speak over their lives and destinies.

Natural man—in his sin—is the only creation in the entire universe that refuses to submit to its Creator. The fall of man and the entrance of sin into the world brought tragic consequences to us—blindness and hardness toward God, self-deception about our spiritual condition, and eternal death.

Conversely, Christians—mercifully enlightened by the grace of God—believe that the true God is the One revealed in the Bible. Our lives become anchored in Him. If God had not revealed Himself or had not spoken to mankind throughout history, there would be no such thing as faith at all, much less an unshakable faith. But we have a basis for happiness and direction in life because the invisible Creator God has revealed His being, purposes, and will to us.

You may have noticed that people who reject the God of the Bible or who have never heard of Him have no basis for a steadfast faith, no understanding of themselves and life, and no hope for the future. **Those who do know the God of the Bible and have believed His Word are privy to the mysteries of life.** As they study and grow in wisdom and understanding, **they** learn God's **answers to life's most troublesome questions.** Most of these questions pertain to the most catastrophic event of human history—the entrance of sin into the world—and its accompanying consequences. Let's press on to discover more about God, His purposes, and our relationship to Him as we look at God's purpose for the fall of man.

Eighteen

God's Great Purpose

Praise God from Whom all things flow! Did you notice that I said "all *things*," not "all *blessings*," as the Doxology proclaims? Certainly all blessings do flow from God. But what I'd like to address in this chapter is of much broader scope. The Bible teaches us that "all things" flow from God, and once we grasp this magnificent truth, we will be much more firmly anchored in Jesus Christ. As we look carefully at what the Scriptures teach about God's work and purposes in *all things*, we can really get to know God, our Creator!

His Word assures us that nothing is outside His purposes and control, especially sin and its consequences. This idea is a real mind-twister if you've never heard it before. But it is ultimately a source of great peace for our souls once we see that our God is really big enough to glorify His name in even the most trying and tragic events of life. The Scriptures have much to say on this subject, and we will cover many of them in the rest of this book.

In these next few chapters, I want to build a case for the truth that God *designed* the Fall of man and the entrance of sin into the world. We can be sure that everything God created, He created with intent. We will see how *purpose* predetermines *all* actions of the Creator. We will learn that God decreed man to be created with a desire in his heart to be like God. We will understand why He gave a law with the threat of death for disobedience, and why He authorized Satan to tempt Adam. *In all these things*, He was working with a goal in mind: to glorify Jesus Christ in history.

The Great Mystery of God Is Revealed in the Bible

The Apostle Paul called this truth a *mystery* in his letter to the Ephesian church. A mystery is something outside the range of unassisted comprehension. Man would never understand God's purposes unless God revealed them through His Word and by His Spirit. The amazing thing, according to Paul, was that this mystery of God's purposes has been revealed!

> *In Him we have redemption through His blood, the forgiveness of our trespasses, according to the riches of His grace, which He lavished upon us. In all wisdom and insight* **He made known to us the mystery of His will,** *according to His kind intention which He purposed in Him* **with a view to** *an administration suitable to the fulness of the times, that is,* **the summing up of all things in Christ,** *things in the heavens and things upon the earth (Ephesians 1:7-10).*

Paul's insight recorded here is that all of history will be summed up in Christ. If you take every event from the creation of the earth until the last event in history and stack them on top of each other, much as you would an addition problem, the sum of them will be "the glory of God in Jesus Christ." *God's glory is God's purpose for everything!*

Does this surprise you? If it does, could the reason be that you've been trained to focus on God's love for His creatures and to believe that our comfort and happiness are His primary purpose in all He does? I don't want to diminish the truth of His love for us and His delight and joy in providing for us, but the Bible clearly teaches that in all God does, He is purposely revealing Himself to us so that we may see His glory. And as we know Him in truth, we praise Him, bow before Him, and tell others about Him. In short, we glorify Him. We just can't help it! This fellowship that happens as we walk with Him in the truth of who He is really delights us both.

(or doesn't do) passive power

Remember that unbelievers cannot understand "the mystery" as Christians do: *that all the events of time will glorify His Son, Jesus Christ.* This foundational fact abounds within the covers of the Bible. We just looked at Ephesians 1:9-10. Where else do we see this idea? The Apostle Paul restated it in Romans and Colossians:

> *Oh, the depth of the riches both of the wisdom and knowledge of God! How unsearchable are His judgments and unfathomable His ways!... **For from Him and through***

Thats where faith comes in.

"praise God from whom ALL THINGS flow"

Him and to Him are all things. To Him be the glory forever. *Amen (Romans 11:33, 36).*

*For by Him all things were created, both in the heavens and on earth, visible and invisible, whether thrones or dominions or rulers or authorities—**all things have been created by Him and for Him.** And He is before all things, and in Him all things hold together. He is also head of the body, the church; and He is the beginning, the first-born from the dead; **so that He Himself might come to have first place in everything.** For it was the Father's good pleasure for all the fulness to dwell in Him, and through Him to reconcile all things to Himself, having made peace through the blood of His cross; through Him, I say, whether things on earth or things in heaven (Colossians 1:16-20).*

In the book of Revelation, the Apostle John recorded the scene in heaven, as God's purpose is fulfilled and Jesus Christ sits enthroned before all creation as Lord of the history of mankind:

... "Worthy is the Lamb that was slain to receive power and riches and wisdom and might and honor and glory and blessing."

*And **every created thing** which is in heaven and on the earth and under the earth and on the sea, and all things in them, I heard saying, **"To Him who sits on the throne, and to the Lamb, be blessing and honor and glory and dominion forever and ever"** (Revelation 5:12-13).*

The world and all that is in it exists for the glory of God in His Son, the Lord Jesus Christ. Our faith is firmly anchored in this truth. When tragedies occur in our lives, we may turn with eyes of faith unto Christ, the author and perfecter of our faith. Through all such trials, we may draw near to Him and hold firmly to God's promise in Romans 8:28 and 29 that He will conform us into the image of His Son. In this assurance, we have peace. And through this peace, we glorify Him.

So God's purposes are being fulfilled in every event through all of time. Yet there are some foundational facts regarding the fall of man and sin that I think are vital for us to grasp in order for our faith to stand. In the next chapter, let's examine the impact sin has had on mankind. How has the Fall affected you and me? Understanding what God's Word records about the fall of man into sin gives us great insight into God's purpose for the Fall and the condition of our hearts. Knowing the truth about these two things helps us relate to God and worship Him in spirit and truth when we find ourselves windblown by life's challenges.

Nineteen

Did God Blow It?

Have you ever thought that God "messed up" by allowing Adam and Eve to sin, by giving a law to make sin possible, or by "letting" Satan tempt Adam and Eve? Why didn't God banish Satan from the domain of Earth into everlasting darkness after Satan tempted Adam and Eve? Almighty God could have sent Adam and Eve into eternal damnation immediately and started over. Why didn't He? Perhaps you've wondered why God "let" the Fall occur if He could have prevented it.

Many people harbor thoughts like these that suggest God has blown it—big time! From the beginning of the history of man right through to the present, in large and small details of life, men have held God's motives and plans suspect. Consequently, they don't have very good *feelings* about God. But you don't have to feel that way!

As we think through the fall of man and the entrance of sin into the world as recorded in Genesis, we will see that God is much bigger than our minds conceive Him to be. I believe that when you finish this study, you will understand God better, and you will love and praise Him all the more. In this chapter we'll talk about *what* happened when Adam, the first man, fell into sin. I will introduce some concepts that may be new to you and contrary to your current understanding of God, man, and God's purposes in creating the universe. These concepts are not new, but if you have never heard them before, they may surprise you. In the next chapter, we'll discuss *why* the Fall happened, and *how* God's purpose to glorify Christ was fulfilled by the fall of man. Please consider and ponder with me as I develop what may be a new line of thinking for you on this subject.

Questions Should Lead Us to Truth

The most obvious consequence of Adam's fall into sin was that man's relationship with God was broken beyond man's ability to restore it. The subsequent millennia have been one long demonstration of the heart of man as a result of this separation. Yet instead of blaming ourselves for the evil in the world, men tend to blame God. They know that whoever God is, He *must* be all-powerful and all-knowing. So if He knew that such evil would come upon the earth with Adam and Eve's fall into sin, why didn't He keep it from happening? How do we reconcile His purported *power and goodness* with His *non-intervention* to keep this world from becoming such a mess? *Did God blow it?*

Questions like these are honest, understandable, and natural. Yet we must be careful. Some people will use such questions to blame God and so excuse themselves from responsibility before Him. A wrong attitude prompting questions like these essentially "puts God on trial." I think calling on God to defend Himself before us reveals the ultimate pride of man and hostility against God. But God's intention for us when these kinds of questions provoke us is that we search out the truth. In the process, we will find Him. There's nothing wrong with asking questions if we are searching for the truth. God has supplied answers for us. He understands us and provides us with the knowledge of His purposes.

God Does Everything With Purpose

In Chapter 18 we looked at how God's purpose predetermines *all* His actions. This must include, therefore, creating, sustaining, and ruling over the universe. Paul gave us insight about this when he wrote to the Ephesians that God "works all things after the counsel of His will" (Ephesians 1:11).

In thinking about God's predetermining purpose, it has helped me to consider that we human beings, who are the highest expression of God's creation, made in His image and likeness, never act without purpose predetermining *our* actions. No act of our wills is free and uninfluenced from a previous act or thought. For instance, the artist selects the purpose of his drawing, and from that moment every stroke of his pencil follows as an effect of that purpose. A potter sees the finished product in his mind as he works with the clay. An inventor purposes first to solve a problem or provide a service before beginning one step of research and development. Is it therefore even remotely possible that God works randomly in His creation as though He had no mind or purpose in it, when His creatures clearly act in their creations according to *their* mind and purpose? I don't think that is reasonable.

This line of thinking about purpose and its relationship to actions raises some other questions. If God does *everything* with a purpose, then did He *design* the fall of man? Did God know the Fall was going to take place? Or did the fall of man surprise God, or frustrate His plans? Did God *allow* sin, or did He *decree* sin? Does God have a *good* purpose for sin in man? In this chapter, we will begin to answer these questions as we look at the first two of four foundational facts about the fall of man and the presence and purpose of sin in man.

The first fact is very important to our faith. If we don't believe that God has a purpose and is in complete control of all things—especially sin and suffering—then our faith is shakable. When we have a wrong understanding of God's ways and purposes, we have nothing solid to hold onto when the storm winds blow. The questions above need to be answered, and we need to have a clear understanding about the fall of man and the entrance of sin into history if we are to grapple with the problem of sin in this world and in our lives.

The Fall of Man Was a Part of God's Plan

God absolutely did not "blow it" when He failed to keep Adam from sinning in the Garden of Eden. In fact—and this is the first foundational fact—*He intended the fall of man and the entrance of sin into the world*. He *decreed* it. (If this idea is shaking you up, please stay with me. Remember, we are looking for truth, and God has provided it in His Word.) What do I mean by saying God *decreed* it?

When theologians talk about the events of history and God, they sometimes speak of God's decrees. A decree may be thought of as an *irrevocable* command or judgment of God. Larry Richards, in his book, *Expository Dictionary of Bible Words*, wrote,

> The Hebrew words translated "decree" carry the image of cutting or engraving on rock. Therefore we get the idea that we're talking about "divine judgments, irrevocably inscribed in the bedrock of God's moral character or his eternal purpose."[20]

Anytime you read a scripture where God states that something is going to occur or He is going to do something, you are reading a *decree of God*.

Here are some decrees of God from both the Old and New Testaments:

> And He said, *"I Myself will make all My goodness pass before you, and will proclaim the name of the Lord before you; and **I will be gracious to whom I will be gracious, and will show compassion on whom I will show compassion."** But He said, **"You cannot see My face, for no man can see Me and live"** (Exodus 22:19-20).*

> At that time Jesus answered and said, *"I praise Thee, O Father, Lord of heaven and earth, that **Thou didst hide these things from the wise and intelligent and didst reveal them to babes.** Yes, Father, for thus it was well-pleasing in Thy sight"* (Matthew 11:25-26).

Dr. Wayne Grudem, author of *Systematic Theology*, describes God's decrees as "powerful, creative words from God... that cause something to happen. These decrees of God include not only the events of the original creation but also the continuing existence of all things."[21] Therefore, we know God *decreed* that Adam and all his offspring would be dead in sin through Adam's fall. He set up the players and the events, so to speak. Yet in so doing, God cannot be considered as either the *author* of sin or as *mutually responsible* with Adam for the fall of man. But why is this true?

A Nagging Question

Though it is hard for us to envision from our mortal frame of reference, we must accept the fact that God is not responsible in the way we are responsible. Being God, it is perfectly right for Him to do things that we as humans have no right to do and for which we will be held accountable to God if we do them. Whatever God does is right *because He is God*, the purpose and source of all things. All of creation belongs to God. It's His to do with as He wishes. He's not operating in the same frame of reference as we are. We are under *His* jurisdiction. But God, as the ultimate sovereign Being over the whole universe, is not subject to anyone's judgment.

In His work as Creator, God has the authority or jurisdiction to do with His creation whatever He pleases (Psalm 115:3). We don't like that, do we? We want God to do what seems right to us, and it just doesn't seem right that He can with impunity set up an environment in which sin is sure to occur. Like rebellious little children who want their parents to live by the same rules they must live by, we scowl and fume at the perceived *unfairness* of it all. Yet God addresses this attitude plainly, saying in Psalm 50:21, "You thought that I was just like you; I will reprove you, and state the case in order before your eyes." And Paul picks up the rebuke in Romans 9:20, putting us in our proper place with this retort: "On the contrary, who are you, O man, who answers back to God?"

So God is free to do with His creation as He wills and cannot be rightly accused of any wrongdoing or injustice, while we humans are rightfully held accountable by God when we do not follow His Law. We cannot presume that God should be held to the same standards as we are; to do so would be grasping equality with God.

All Things Exist for Jesus Christ

Remember that God's purpose is to glorify Himself through His Son. In previous chapters we have noted that nothing exists unless Jesus speaks it into existence by and for Himself (Colossians 1:16-18, 1 Corinthians 8:6, and Romans 11; 33, 36). We learned that "all things"— which by definition must include the fall of man, sin, and suffering— have come by and through Jesus Christ. Even these things fulfill His purpose. Sometimes this idea is hard to accept, for we hesitate to assign blame to Jesus Christ or to God for things we would call evil or bad. But as we get a clearer understanding from God's Word about His purposes, we will see that God has a good reason—even today—for sin's existence and for the fall of man.

God's creation of the universe and all that is in it, the fall of man into sin, and His redemption through Jesus Christ to the glory of God the Father are all aspects of His great plan. The biblical record shows that history is a *demonstration,* not an *experiment.* It demonstrates the full nature and character of God, primarily as a contrast to the full nature and character of man. This demonstration includes God's grace and mercy by His plan of redemption through Jesus Christ. In other words, God did not set up the Garden of Eden as an experiment "to see what would happen."

Rather, we read in Ephesians 1:11 that *all things* were determined "by the counsel of God's will." Isaiah recorded God's "declaring the end from the beginning and from ancient times things which have not been done, saying, 'My purpose will be established, and I will accomplish all My good pleasure'" (Isaiah 46:10). So God's purposes are being fulfilled, and He is working according to His decrees. All that happens is somehow "from Him and through Him," for His glory (Romans 11:36). Therefore, nothing surprises Him—not even Adam and Eve's fall into sin.

These declarations from God's Word about Himself leave us with only one possible conclusion: God created all the elements of the Fall *for a reason*, and that is *to glorify Himself throughout history and eternity by demonstrating His infinite, eternal, and unchangeable nature and character through His Son on behalf of His people.* Therefore, reconsidering the familiar scriptures above, we may rightly conclude that God *predetermined* for sin to enter into the entire human race. This is God's plan, which He has been carrying out through His decrees. So we've looked at the first foundational fact: *God decreed for sin to enter the world.*

God Intended for Sin to Enter *Through Adam*

The second fact is that *God intended for sin to enter the world through one man: Adam.* Remember as you read the following verses that they are not just statements of fact about events that occurred, as though God had "Plan A" but then had to switch to "Plan B" because someone made a mistake. These scriptures are *expressions of God's decrees that fulfilled His foreordained purpose.* As the Author of Life who is writing the Story of Redemption, "Plan A" is the only one God has or needs. The only possible alternative to this is that God was surprised by Adam's sin because He was not fully in control—which we know is not true. Do you see how the purposes of God have been perfectly carried out?

*Therefore, **just as through one man sin entered** into the world, and death through sin, and so death spread to all men, because all sinned (Romans 5:12).*

*For since by a man came death, by a man also came the resurrection of the dead. **For as in Adam all die**, so also in Christ all shall be made alive (1 Corinthians 15:21-22).*

Of course, this entrance of sin into the world had a grave effect on the hearts of Adam and all his offspring. But God's goal was for His people to *need a Savior*, by Whom the magnitude of His glory would

be revealed. We'll look in detail at these ideas in Chapters 21 through
23. But first I would like to continue enlarging our understanding about
God's predetermination for sin to enter the world *through Adam*. It was
an important aspect of God's plan that what happened in the Garden of
Eden did not happen only to Adam and Eve. Their sin did not create some
kind of random "glitch in the software" of *some* of Adam's offspring,
whereby occasionally—or even frequently—another human would fall
from the glory of his first state and remove himself from the grace of
God. Rather, when Adam sinned and sin entered into mankind...

Man Became Useless *All Together*

In Romans 3:12, Paul quoted an Old Testament passage (Ps. 14:3)
that, through hindsight, revealed more of God's plan: the whole human
race would go astray *at one particular time.*

> *All have turned aside, **together** they have become useless;
> there is none who does good. There is not even one.*

I would like to point out that mankind became useless *together*—
not one by one—as we transgressed God's law. *All at one time, all* of
mankind became useless. This is contrary to the popular notions that
each person is born good and with a free will either to choose Christ
for the glory of God, or else to not choose Christ at all. There are some
who believe that sin enters into our lives individually as we reach an
"age of accountability." With this idea in their foundation, they conclude
that each of us became disqualified from salvation one at a time as we
consciously sinned against what we knew was right. The scriptural record,
however, is that mankind became useless all at one time—*together*.

Why is this idea important? First, it is important because God's Word
teaches it. Second, as we discussed in Chapter 16, in the section entitled
"God Is Eternal," the belief that people become disqualified individually
as they sin, and then saved individually as they repent, leads us to the
wrong conclusion that *we are the initiators* of whatever we do and that
God *responds or reacts* to our sins, repentance, and prayers.

Third, sometimes people feel compelled to establish an age when
children become accountable for their sin—an age which cannot be
found in the Bible. Fourth, they may also believe that all children who
die before they reach an age of accountability are saved and will go to
heaven—again, an attractive idea that cannot be explicitly supported by
Scripture. Fifth, once they believe a child cannot be held accountable for

sin unless he is old enough and conscious of his sin, they open the door for excusing *any* sin in *any* person if he is ignorant of God's requirements or if he didn't intend to commit that sin. Without consciously thinking about what God's Word says, people seem to naturally conclude that it simply can't be right to hold children and others who have never heard of God accountable to Jesus Christ.

I think you can see where this road leads us: to irresponsibility regarding our own sin, repentance, and putting to death the deeds of the flesh, and to a lack of concern for the spiritual destiny of the millions of children who are killed by abortion, and also to a lack of urgency to share the gospel with children and others who we think are not in eternal danger since they have never heard it. Haven't you heard the question, *How can God condemn the man in Africa who has never heard the gospel of Jesus Christ?* Though the question is often posed by unbelievers, many Christians seem to share its sentiment. Consequently, their missionary zeal may be stifled. One who asks such a question, or who is unconcerned about his own sins or the sins of others, or about the spiritual state of children, reveals a faulty foundation on this point: He doesn't believe in the Fall's effect on *all* mankind.

However, Paul wrote in 1 Corinthians 15:21-22 that death entered the human race "in Adam" *and everyone died.* Acting as the federal head of the human race, Adam brought condemnation and death upon all his offspring:

> For since by a man came *death, by a man* also came the resurrection of the dead. For **as in Adam all die,** so also in Christ all shall be made alive.

We see the heads of two races in those verses. Through Adam, the head of the *human* race, sin and death entered the history of mankind, and man was "disqualified" for righteousness through his own works. However, through Jesus Christ, the head of the *redeemed* race, sin and death were conquered, and the redeemed are now qualified for eternal life.

Usually Christians have no problem agreeing that God has decreed, *all who are in Christ are made alive.* But if we are going to be consistent, we must also recognize that God has likewise decreed, *all who are in Adam died when he sinned.*

Isn't God *Still* Responsible for the Fall?

All right, up to this point we've seen that God planned for sin to enter the entire human race through Adam. He didn't "blow it" but rather designed the Fall "by the counsel of His will." Everyone "became useless" at the same time—when Adam sinned—so every person is equally responsible before God, regardless of his age or ignorance. But doesn't that *still* mean that *God* is responsible for the presence of evil in the world? How can I be held accountable for sin when God is the One who decreed it? I hope to answer these questions in the next chapters as we continue to consider the Fall from God's point of view.

Whoahhh yeah how does that work?

Twenty

Created in God's Image

In the last chapter we asked: *If God planned for sin to enter the human race, then why isn't He responsible for all the evil in the world? Why is mankind held accountable for sin?* I answered briefly that *God has the right to do what He wills with His creation, but man is under His Law and must not try to grasp equal standing or rights with Him.* God had a purpose to display His glory, especially through the demonstration of His goodness, mercy, grace, power, and love. Therefore, He designed and brought into being all the elements of the Fall, *but He did so without committing any unrighteousness or injustice.* There are three considerations leading us to this understanding, which we will look at more closely in these next three chapters. What were the elements of the Fall that God designed?

Man Was Created in God's Image

We see God's design in His creating man in His own image. Although there are many aspects to what this means, I want us to focus on one: *the prevailing motive of the heart, which predetermines the choices of every individual.* Let's explore this idea.

What do I mean by the "prevailing motive of the heart"? Our heart consists of our conscience (1 John 3:19), mind (Proverbs 23:7), and spirit (Ezekiel 11:19). Most theologians consider the heart to be the inner control center of our lives. According to Jesus, all of our actions flow out of our hearts (Mark 7:21). The same is true with God. The values of His

(the values of Gods)

heart motivate all His actions toward us. There is in the heart of God, as well as in our hearts, a *prevailing motive*—the predominant value—that governs the choices we make. What is that motive? For God, it is to glorify Himself as God. We have already looked at many scriptures that tell us these things.

Truth be Gods word is Truth

To be Gods for is the source of all

I believe that part of what God means when He says we were created "in His image" is that He has given us a motive of heart to be like Him. What does this mean? Before we can understand what it means to be like God, we need to know what it means to be God. It means to be the source of all things, the first cause of all things, and the end of all things. This is what motivates God to do all that He does, so that He might glorify Himself as God. So what did it mean that Adam and Eve, being created in His image, wanted to be like God? Ultimately it meant that they had the desire to control their lives and their environments and that they sought glory for themselves as they did so. These were the attractions to them in Satan's temptation of "having their eyes opened" and "knowing good and evil" (Genesis 3:5).

if adam was created in Gods image God is not created him total

When we consider these ideas in relation to God Himself, we find no problem. He is the self-existent Creator and Judge, the independent sovereign ruler who sees all and knows all. He is God. He is holy—absolutely unlike created men. It is right for Him to glorify Himself in these ways in our sight.

It is also right for God to have created Adam "in God's image" so that he would want to rule over those areas where God had given him the right to do so, as in naming the animals and caring for the Garden of Eden. It is right for God to have designed His creatures to function as He functions, so that their wills would act according to what their hearts would want.

We might think of the analogy of a father and son. Young sons wish to be like their fathers. I believe God has placed it in their hearts. In the same way—by design—Adam wished to be like His Father. Is there anything morally wrong with God's designing Adam and Eve to have the same inclination of heart as He had? No! There was no evil and no failure of any kind in His design. He Himself proclaimed His finished creation "very good" (Genesis 1:31), and David tells us that in wisdom God has made all of His many works (Psalm 104:24). So we know that because of His goodness and wisdom God had a positive purpose for creating Adam and Eve with the motivation to be like God as the highest value in their hearts. However, this desire plays a vital role in the fall of man into sin.

From God's vantage point, the way He designed Adam's heart to function was not a problem, but rather a necessity in order for Jesus Christ to be glorified in history. So if everything God does is with the ultimate goal of glorifying Himself, how does Adam's heart inclination fulfill that purpose? It puts in place the first element necessary for the Fall to occur. The fall of man makes redemption through Jesus Christ necessary. And our redemption through Christ exalts Him beyond measure as worthy of all praise!

> And they sang a new song, saying, "Worthy art Thou to take the book, and to break its seals; for Thou wast slain, and didst purchase for God with Thy blood men from every tribe and tongue and people and nation.... Worthy is the Lamb that was slain to receive power and riches and wisdom and might and honor and glory and blessing." ... And every created thing which is in heaven and on the earth and under the earth and on the sea, and all things in them, I heard saying, "To Him who sits on the throne, and to the Lamb, be blessing and honor and glory and dominion forever and ever" (Revelation 5:9-13).

So should we excuse mankind for sin and blame God because He designed His creatures with a prevailing motive of heart to be like Him? No. We must find God's purpose in the events of life, beginning with the fall of man, if we're to have peace rather than blame God and excuse ourselves from responsibility. Knowing God's purposes is where peace comes from in the midst of trials, temptations, and losses. We have been given a progressive revelation of God in the Scriptures. It is our responsibility to search through His Word for truth. If all God had done were to make Adam and Eve desire to be like Him, everything would have continued in perfect bliss. More elements needed to be created. So God did something else, without which the Fall could not have occurred. Let's continue our search for the next element of His design.

Twenty-one

God Gave a Law

Thus far we've said that God doesn't do anything without purpose, and we've concluded that God was righteous to make Adam in His image. Now we want to consider another element of the Fall: God gave Adam a law for a purpose.

> But from the tree of the knowledge of good and evil you shall not eat, for in the day that you eat from it you shall surely die (Genesis 2:17).

Why did God give Adam a law, knowing that it would bring about sin? Why did He forbid eating the fruit of the tree? Why did He not give some other law? These are good questions to keep us on the right track. As long as we're asking these questions in a search for the truth, we should not be afraid. Let us pray for understanding as James encouraged his readers to do and as the father of Proverbs admonished his son:

> But if any of you lacks wisdom, let him ask of God, who gives to all men generously and without reproach, and it will be given to him (James 1:5).

> The beginning of wisdom is: Acquire wisdom; and with all your acquiring, get understanding (Proverbs 4:7).

God did not have to give Adam a law, but He did so to serve His predetermined purpose: to reveal the hearts of Adam and Eve and to glorify His Son, Jesus Christ. We can be sure that God wasn't acting spontaneously or whimsically when He created that tree and told Adam not to eat from it. He knew exactly what He was doing. In fact, since He declares "the end from the beginning" and says, "My purpose will be established, and I will accomplish all My good pleasure" (Isaiah 46:10), we can be sure that He gave the law to Adam because it was absolutely necessary in order for all things to occur according to His plan.

From the Scriptures, we can know God's purpose for law: It makes sin possible. Without the law, there can be no sin. Do you see this principle in the following passages?

> For the Law brings about wrath, but **where there is no law, neither is there violation** (Romans 4:15).

> For while we were in the flesh, the sinful passions, **which were aroused by the Law**, were at work in the members of our body to bear fruit for death.... What shall we say then? Is the Law sin? May it never be! On the contrary, **I would not have come to know sin except through the Law**; for I would not have known about coveting if the Law had not said, "You shall not covet." But sin, taking opportunity through the commandment, produced in me coveting of every kind; **for apart from the Law sin is dead** [that is, indefinable, unrecognizable] (Romans 7:5, 7-8).

> The sting of death is sin, and **the power of sin is the law** (1 Corinthians 15:56).

This means that without a law, sin has no power to exist. How can there be a transgression or a falling short of a standard if no law or standard has been established? God surely understood that He was giving power to sin when He gave that prohibition to Adam. Had He not wanted Adam to sin, He would not have forbidden Adam to eat from the tree of the knowledge of good and evil. *There can be no violation without law.*

This principle of law has a way of bringing to life innate passion and desires. Maybe you can relate to an experience I had in the Minneapolis airport. While deplaning, I noticed a sign, "WET PAINT. DO NOT TOUCH." The walls to the walkway were being repainted, and a decorative stripe added. Signs had been placed along the walkway as well as yellow tape to keep passengers from rubbing up against the freshly painted walls. Being the last one off the plane, I realized no one would see me if I were to touch the wall. I'm embarrassed to say the thought even crossed my mind to reach out and verify if the new stripe on the wall was still wet. The warning actually drew my attention to the wet paint! Did I do it? No, but I doubt if the thought would have crossed my mind if there had been no signs or yellow tape.

So why did God make a law, knowing it would provoke Adam to sin? Four reasons come to mind: *(faith w/o works is dead)*

• The law instituted a covenant of works.

• The law incorporated God's people into Adam's race and fall.

• The law gave sin and death a way to enter history so God could glorify Jesus Christ.

• The law defined righteousness.

Let's look at each reason individually.

Reason One: The Law Instituted a Covenant of Works

When God gave the law, He instituted a covenant of works with Adam and his posterity. What is a covenant of works? First, a covenant is an agreement between two parties involving a promise on the part of one party and the performance of some act or acts on the part of the other party. (Deuteronomy 30 shows an example of a covenant.) According to God's purposes, He determined that mankind would initially relate to Him on the basis of law: man would receive blessing for obedience, and a curse for disobedience. Such a relationship is sometimes called a "covenant of works," based on keeping God's law, and is contrasted in the New Testament with the "covenant of grace," administered by faith.

We should ask, "*Why* did God institute a covenant of works?" The answer to that question (and in fact, all questions along this line) is found in Jesus Christ. *The covenant of works prepares the way for the covenant of grace in Jesus Christ.*

Remember that God's purpose for having created everything is to glorify Himself, and He chose to do this through His Son, Jesus Christ. We discovered in a previous chapter the meaning of Ephesians 1:10, that all of history will be summed up in Jesus Christ. God needed a way to highlight His Son's glory. He gave the law so sin could enter the human realm, man's righteousness would be eliminated, and God's righteousness would be clearly seen. Man's fall was *necessary* in order for salvation to be *by grace through faith.* By creating an environment where sin could occur, God was also creating an environment where our need for a Savior became abundantly evident. God's intention was *always* for our need to be met *only* in the person and work of the Lord Jesus Christ.

God purposed before the beginning of time to bring redemption through His Son. Furthermore, He purposed to give His Son the only name by which men could come to God. Therefore, He had to create a *need* for men to come to Him through His Son. We've seen so far that He created men with a heart motivation to glorify themselves, and He created an environment in which sin could occur. Therefore, in order for His Son to be glorified, it was necessary also to institute a covenant of works on the basis of law.

We see God's redemptive plan in the words of the prophet, Isaiah. The covenant of grace was established between God, the Father, and His Son, Jesus Christ, before the foundation of the earth was laid. Can you see the agreement between the Father and the Son in the following passage?

> *But the Lord was pleased to crush Him, putting Him to grief;* ***if He would render Himself as a guilt offering,*** *He will see His offspring, He will prolong His days, and* **the good pleasure** *of the Lord will prosper in His hand. As a result of the anguish of His soul, He will see it and be satisfied; By His knowledge the Righteous One, My Servant, will justify the many, as He will bear their iniquities.*
>
> ***Therefore, I will allot Him a portion with the great,*** *and He will divide the booty with the strong;* **because He poured out Himself to death,** *and was numbered with the transgressors; yet He Himself bore the sin of many, and interceded for the transgressors (Isaiah 53:10-12).*

If this was God's redemptive plan, then the covenant of works and the fall of man were necessary from the beginning. The covenant was not an "afterthought"—just some idea God threw out to Adam to show him who was "Boss"—and the Fall was neither an accident nor a surprise. If you do not believe this, then you must believe the alternative, that God's world was out of His control from the very beginning.

Furthermore, the covenant and the Fall were also necessary in order for salvation to be by grace through faith and *not* by works of the law. These elements set the stage for Jesus to fulfill the covenant we broke. His righteousness becomes ours through the means of faith.

Consider Paul's words in Romans 4:16:

> *For this reason it is by faith, that it might be in accordance with grace, in order that the promise may be certain to all the descendants, not only to those who are of the Law, but also to those who are of the faith of Abraham, who is the father of us all...*

Paul told us why God gave the law. It was given so faith in God's promises might come to us who believe. If there were no law, there would be no sin. If there were no sin, we could not define God's grace, forgiveness, mercy, compassion, justice, wrath, or holiness. This is very important! How is God defined as good except as He relates to us in contrast to our sin? These are the things into which angels long to look—the mystery of the gospel (1 Peter 1:12). Without the law and sin, man would not know that he has a need for God's righteousness, to walk in humility, or to seek God.

Reason Two: The Law Incorporated God's People Into Adam's Race and Fall

God's plan always flows

The second reason God gave the law issues out of the first one. As part of His plan to glorify His Son, God gave Him all things, which included two major responsibilities. The first was to atone for and redeem His people, who were created in Him before the foundation of the earth. The second was to subdue and exercise judgment against all God's enemies. These truths are also seen on the previous page in the verses from Isaiah 53. In order for all these things to occur, all those whose salvation was purposed from eternity had to be *lost* in Adam so they could be *found* by Christ.

Most evangelicals consider everyone who is not a believer to be "lost." But something can't be lost unless it was previously owned and misplaced. For instance, if I lose my car keys, I go looking for them until I find them. In the same way, technically, the lost are those who have belonged to God from all eternity. They have been incorporated into the entire fallen human race so that Jesus might "come to seek and to save that which was lost" (Luke 19:10). In each of the parables about the lost sheep, the lost coin, and the lost son that Jesus told in Luke 15, what was lost *belonged* to one who was responsible for it—the shepherd, the woman, and the father. Similarly, those who have been lost in Adam have *belonged* to God, even since before He made the

based misconception

he understood it because the spirit dwelt within him and was writing thru him so... its like a verse I've read but but don't remember the name.

168   *Anchored in Christ*

world. The Apostle Paul understood this, for He wrote to Timothy and the Ephesians,

> *... who has saved us, and called us* with a holy calling, not according to our works, but *according to His own purpose and grace* which was granted us in Christ Jesus *from all eternity* (2 Timothy 1:9).
>
> Blessed be the God and Father of our Lord Jesus Christ, who has blessed us with every spiritual blessing in the heavenly places in Christ, just as **He chose us in Him before the foundation of the world,** that we should be holy and blameless before Him (Ephesians 1:3-4).

Wow

Reason Three: The Law Gave Sin and Death a Way to Enter History So God Could Glorify Jesus Christ

The third reason God gave a law to Adam is this: The entrance of sin and death into the world was necessary for God to glorify Jesus Christ. Having established the relationship with His people on the basis of law and not grace, God knew He was giving sin an avenue by which death could enter the human race. Remember that without law, sin has no power to disqualify mankind from a righteousness of his own.

Furthermore, without the entrance of sin and "the wicked," there is no canvas upon which the history of grace, forgiveness, mercy, compassion, righteousness, and justice can be painted. Perhaps you have seen a white cross emblazoned on a black background. The contrast between black and white is what makes the cross so outstanding. So it is with the fall of man. Jesus' righteousness stands alone in glorious contrast to the desperate condition of man in his sin and separation from God.

None of these redemptive qualities or acts of God can be displayed, or even known, without the contrasting agents of wickedness and sin. Life seems valuable only when it is contrasted with death. The writer of Proverbs stated, "The Lord has made everything for its own purpose, even the wicked for the day of evil" (Proverbs 16:4). The NASB side notes for that verse tell us the word "its" may be translated "His." So we could also read this verse, "The Lord has made everything for His own purposes, even the wicked for the day of evil."

The "day of evil" is not the Day of Judgment. It is any day in which a wicked deed is done against someone. For believers who are victims of evil, the sin committed against them may draw out a gracious response as they trust in Jesus Christ. The "day of evil" is a *necessity* in order for grace and goodness to be made evident to others who are watching. Through these daily events, when the wicked act and the righteous respond with grace, God is glorified. Knowing that this is God's purpose should motivate us to return grace to the wicked who come aginst us, shouldn't it?

Granted, there are times when believers don't respond graciously. However, when a believer responds wrongly and then repents, relies on Jesus' sacrifice, and makes restitution where needed, Jesus Christ is glorified. Whether a believer responds graciously or selfishly, God uses it to glorify His Son. Therefore, the entrance and empowering of sin and death were necessary. The law that God gave to Adam made a way for that entrance—and *Jesus Christ is glorified as a result!*

Reason Four: The Law Defined Righteousness

I have a friend who is an engineer for a firm that makes doors for aircraft. He told me that these doors must be tested to see what pressures and stresses they can endure. They don't want to sell a product to an aircraft manufacturer and then have them call one day to say they lost a door in flight! So they test their doors in order to *establish a definition and set a standard* for a secure aircraft door. Without the test, there can be no definition or standard with which to assure the manufacturer.

In the same way, God defines what righteousness is by giving man laws, which are the standard set by His own character and nature. He then tests men to illustrate that their character and nature do not measure up to His. However, one might raise another question at this point: *Is it right for God to test His creatures?* When I say "test," I don't mean "experiment with." An experiment is performed to discover something previously unknown. But God already knew everything that was in Adam's heart because He designed it. What I mean by "test" is "demonstrate." God used the tree of the knowledge of good and evil to *demonstrate* the prevailing motive of Adam's heart.

We've already seen that we can't fault God for providing the prevailing heart motive of being like God and making an opportunity for Adam to demonstrate righteousness. God is also just and righteous to *test* Adam. Remember our discussion about jurisdiction? The creator has the right or authority to speak over that which he has created and to do with it what he wishes. God's test of Adam in the Garden of Eden offered Adam the opportunity to *demonstrate his own righteousness*. Like the aircraft door that endures without failure the pressures and stresses of the test it undergoes, so a person's actions can only be *accounted* as righteous when he *actually obeys* the law. We call this a *positive righteousness* in contrast to a *potential righteousness*. That's why Jesus' fulfilling the law of God is so important and vital to our salvation. Jesus Christ *actually performed* righteousness in history on our behalf. Therefore, we are dressed before God in the *positive righteousness* of Jesus Christ who passed without failure all the tests of God's law. Hallelujah! There may be more reasons why God gave the law to Adam, but these four are enough to confirm that God gave the law with good purposes. Let's review them:

- The law instituted a covenant of works.

- The law incorporated God's people into Adam's race and fall.

- The law gave sin and death a way to enter history so God could glorify Jesus Christ.

- The law defined righteousness.

Why the Tree of the Knowledge of Good and Evil?

Although we know there were many trees in the Garden of Eden from which Adam and Eve could eat, there were two trees that were unique:

> And out of the ground the Lord God caused to grow every tree that is pleasing to the sight and good for food; the tree of life also in the midst of the garden, and the tree of the knowledge of good and evil (Genesis 2:9).

The two trees obviously are a contrast to one another. One brings life and the other brings death.

Why did God create a tree that Adam and Eve couldn't use? *God designed the tree of the knowledge of good and evil as a test for man, not as a source of nourishment.* Remember my story about the freshly painted walls at the airport? The forbidden object has a direct appeal to the inclination of the heart of man. God already knew good and evil, but Adam did not.

Adam's heart's desire was to be like God. When God created the tree of the knowledge of good and evil, He purposely was making an object of temptation that appealed to Adam's nature. He certainly knew that Adam would act on the basis of his own nature, and He knew Adam's choice would open the door for sin and death to enter the world, God "set the stage" for Adam to do just what was necessary for all of His purposes in history to unfold—sin, redemption, and glory. He had created a heart, a tree, and a law. *Then God allowed Adam to act according to his own nature.*

The great eighteenth-century theologian and preacher Jonathan Edwards called God's actions in the Garden of Eden His "passive power"— that is, setting up the environment where sin could enter, then releasing Adam and giving him freedom to act.[22] God gave the law and the tree so that Adam would have to choose between doing things his way or doing things God's way. We know which he chose!

I've said this before, but it is worthy of repeating: When God forbade Adam and Eve to eat of the tree of the knowledge of good and evil, He wasn't merely performing an experiment. It was a demonstration. God set it up, and He had the right to do so. Adam's heart was inclined to grasp equality with God; thus God knew exactly what was going to happen when He gave Adam free agency. We might be tempted to think this was not "fair," but God has a right to do what He wants with His creatures and His creation. We have to acknowledge and accept this fact. Once we do, we can thank God that He designed the fall of man to glorify Himself and to provide salvation for us through His Son Jesus Christ. Because of sin, we know our God in so many ways that we could not otherwise!

Let's look at what we've seen so far and consider the height, breadth, and depth of God's purposes:

- God created the plan for our salvation through the covenant between the Heavenly Father and the Son.

- God created Adam with an inclination of heart to be like God.

- God created the tree of the knowledge of good and evil in order to test Adam and thereby demonstrate the inclination of his heart.

- God gave Adam a law not to eat of that tree, thus creating an environment in which sin and death could occur.

The Angels Are Impressed!

Considering these things leads us to ask further questions like, "Why didn't God just make everyone perfect? Why deal with sin at all?" Perhaps we can answer those questions from 1 Peter 1:12. Why is it that the ministering angels "long to look into the things of the gospel

Wow Never thought of that

and our salvation"? I think it is because they can't experience what we experience. Not having fallen out of favor with God, they cannot experience the knowledge of Him in all that He is. We have a relationship with God they don't have and cannot experience.

Thinking about angels leads to another question. What about Satan? Did God have a purpose for Satan? Does God have a purpose for Satan's interaction with people on earth? The answer to these questions leads us to consider the third element of God's design of the fall of man.

→ Because the angels haven't fallen away from God and don't know evil, or more like experianced it so they can't experince Gods Grace like we can... Because we humans fell away from God in the Garden and are seperated from him (face to face) while on earth.

→ This raises a few questions, where did the angels come from? where they created or w/God (trinity) from the beginning?

are the Angels perfect like christ is perfect (perfectly good and holy)

are some angels ranked higher than others?

Twenty-two

Satan, the Tempter

Not only did God design man in His image and give him a law through which sin could be introduced, but He also *created* and *authorized* the jurisdiction of spiritual darkness to be under one who was created for destruction—that is, Satan. God *authorized* Satan to come into the realm of this world at a designated time to tempt Adam. He was *sent* with a purpose to act according to his nature. God has postponed Satan's destruction until he accomplishes all the purpose for which God created him.

Does this language trouble you? This is an entirely new way to think about Satan, isn't it? I remember how hard it was for me when I first started to discover the truth about Satan in the Scriptures. Nevertheless, let's keep asking questions and searching the Scriptures for answers. Our quest is for truth in our foundation so that our faith can endure every test in life. Satan's presence and work often are a source of great testing of our faith. If we're to find peace in this life, we must set our anchor firmly in the Scriptures in order to come to the truth about Satan's purpose.

Satan Was Created for Jesus Christ

We learn of the lordship of Jesus Christ over Satan and the entire realm of dark spiritual forces from Colossians 1:15-16:

*And He is the image of the invisible God, the first-born of all creation. For **by Him all things were created**, both in the*

*heavens and on earth, visible and invisible, whether **thrones
or dominions or rulers or authorities**—all things have
been created by Him and for Him.*

We see here that through Jesus Christ, God created even Satan. And
we have learned that He must have done so with the purpose of glorifying
Himself through His Son. Satan is the *archenemy* of God, but he is not
an *equal* enemy to God. He is actually merely an errand boy for God to
accomplish His purposes. This may seem like an audacious claim, but I
believe the Scriptures support it, and in this chapter we will look at some
that do so. I hope you will begin to think of Satan in proper perspective
as you encounter his works throughout God's Word. Notice that Satan is
never out of God's control, regardless of what *he* thinks. Satan is in the
heavens, and God allows him to manifest his presence on earth.

As we read through the gospels, we can't help but notice that the
demons were in subjection to Jesus Christ. He cast them out of people
who came to Him because of the suffering the demons caused them
(Mark 5:13). He silenced them when they sought to subvert the work
of the Holy Spirit (Mark 1:25). He told Peter that Satan had demanded
permission to sift him like wheat, and God had granted it (Luke 22:31).
We usually consider Pilate to be Satan's puppet, but Jesus said he would
have had no authority unless it had been given to him *from above* (John
19:11). Finally, Jesus *was led by the Holy Spirit into* the wilderness *for
the purpose of being tempted by the devil* (Matthew 4:1).

It may surprise you to know, the Scriptures reveal that since the
fall of man, Satan has never disobeyed the directions of Jesus Christ.
In fact, anytime there is a reference involving both Satan and God,
Satan is portrayed as a servant—a creature sent on a divine mission.
However, that doesn't mean that God *makes* Satan do what he does.
God exercises *passive power* with Satan just as He did with Adam
(allowing the creature to act according to his nature), and so Satan acts
according to his nature within God's purposes.

God's Purposes for Satan With Regard to the Wicked Are to Torment, Tempt, Deceive, and Destroy

Consider what the following verses say about Satan's purpose as he
relates to the wicked:

> Now the Spirit of the Lord departed from Saul, and **an evil
> spirit from the Lord** terrorized him (1 Samuel 16:14).

And the Lord said, "Who will entice Ahab to go up and fall at Ramoth-gilead?" And one said this while another said that.

Then **a spirit came forward** and stood before the Lord and said, "I will entice him."

And the Lord said to him, "How?"

And he said, "I will go out and be a deceiving spirit in the mouth of all his prophets."

Then He said, "**You are to entice him and also prevail. Go and do so**."

"Now therefore, behold, **the Lord has put a deceiving spirit** in the mouth of all these your prophets; and the Lord has proclaimed disaster against you" (1 Kings 22:20-23).

With regard to King Saul, we know the writer was not saying that God is evil. The evil spirit was *sent by* God to accomplish His purpose of tormenting Saul. The deceiving spirit who influenced the false prophets of Ahab's day apparently came up with his own plan and was granted success by God. Why? Because it accomplished the purpose of God: to destroy Ahab.

There are many other verses in the Old Testament that reveal Satan's fulfilling the purposes of God with regard to *the wicked*. However, God's use of Satan with regard to *His people* is different—not in method, but in purpose.

God's Purposes for Satan With Regard to the Righteous Are to Tempt, Destroy, Discipline, and Teach

It is comforting to know that God's purposes for Satan's work with the righteous are quite different from His purposes with the wicked. Satan and the powers of darkness play an important role in God's plan for redemption and sanctification. They exercise a disciplinary, testing, instructing purpose—much like a second-string football team playing a scrimmage game against a first-string team.

Regarding the events in the Garden of Eden, God certainly could have prevented the Fall by keeping Satan out of Adam's domain. Why didn't He take this step? We can be certain that according to His wisdom and purpose, God authorized Satan to enter this realm and tempt Adam. We know from the book of James that God Himself does not tempt anyone.

Yet we are told in Deuteronomy that He *does test* His people. He has a good purpose for temptation and testing: they either expose weakness and sin or reveal strength and righteousness in the heart.

> *And you shall remember all the way which the LORD your God has led you in the wilderness these forty years, **that He might humble you, testing you, to know what was in your heart,** whether you would keep His commandments or not.... Thus you are to know in your heart that **the LORD your God was disciplining you just as a man disciplines his son** (Deuteronomy 8:2, 5).*

> *Let no one say when he is tempted, "I am being tempted by God"; for God cannot be tempted by evil, and **He Himself does not tempt** anyone. But **each one is tempted when he is carried away** and enticed **by his own lust** (James 1:13-14).*

Why then was Satan sent and authorized to tempt Adam and Eve? We might further ask, "Why is he sent to tempt us?" I see at least three things that are revealed through the work of Satan: the weakness of flesh without the Holy Spirit, the futility of the natural life without the indwelling life of Jesus Christ, and the glory of God as Christ overcomes and destroys the work of the devil.

Satan's nature makes him the perfect adversary for God's glory. The Scriptures tell us that Satan is the father of all lies, all murder, and all wickedness. If you recall, such things characterized Satan's work with Adam and Eve. Look at how Jesus referred to Satan in John 8:44:

> *You are of your father the devil, and you want to do the desires of your father. He was a murderer from the beginning, and does not stand in the truth, because there is no truth in him. Whenever he speaks a lie, he speaks from his own nature; for he is a liar, and the father of lies.*

In the Genesis account, notice how Satan used lies to appeal to the prevailing motive of Eve's heart:

> *Now the serpent was more crafty than any beast of the field which the Lord God had made. And he said to the woman, "Indeed, has God said, 'You shall not eat from any tree of the garden?'" And the woman said to the serpent, "From the fruit of the trees of the garden we may eat; but from the fruit of the tree which is in the middle of the garden, God has said, 'You shall not eat from it or touch it, lest you die.'"*

*And the serpent said to the woman, **"You surely shall not die!** For God knows that in the day you eat from it your eyes will be opened, and **you will be like God,** knowing good and evil" (Genesis 3:1-5).*

God apparently authorized Satan to tempt Adam and Eve according to the prevailing motives of their hearts—their desire to grasp equality with God. Without the law, Satan could not have brought about death. But Satan, having the law, could pervert it and use it to spiritually murder our first forefather—and so he did!

The New Testament is replete with examples of God's using Satan as His agent to accomplish His redemptive purposes in the lives of the righteous. Twice the Apostle Paul exercised his jurisdiction as an apostle to the church and employed Satan to accomplish God's work. In both cases, the individuals were assumed to be members of the body of Christ, yet were unwilling to listen to God's Word or their fellow brothers in Christ. When they did not listen to those who were there in God's name to bless and instruct them, then the jurisdiction of darkness and destruction in the physical realm was employed to get their attention. Notice the ends for which Satan was used by the apostle:

> *I have decided to deliver such a one to Satan **for the destruction of his flesh, that his spirit may be saved** in the day of the Lord Jesus (1 Corinthians 5:5).*

> *Among these are Hymenaeus and Alexander, whom I have delivered over to Satan, **so that they may be taught** not to blaspheme (1 Timothy 1:20).*

It is important to note that, with one who is born again, the *flesh* may be destroyed, but the *spirit* cannot be.

Satan Must Ask Permission From God to Work

Remember also Satan's work in Job's life and how he was authorized by God to bring destruction to Job (Job 1:12, 2:6). Job's heart was tested, and the result of the test was that Job's heart and testimony toward God were purified (Job 42:1-6). The story of Job reveals that Satan knew of Job's weakness and had to ask God's permission before unleashing destruction and temptation upon him. If Satan needed permission to tempt Job, he must also have needed permission to tempt the father of the human race.

God's purpose in allowing Satan to attack Job was the same as His purpose in permitting Satan to tempt Adam and Eve—to glorify His Son, Jesus Christ, and to make His power known. Did Satan know that was God's purpose for him? I doubt if he did, nor do I think he does today. He's in the dark!

Jesus Came to Destroy All the Works of the Devil in the Lives of the Righteous

What wonderful news the gospel brings to mankind! Jesus' work destroys Satan's works in the lives of those who are justified by faith in Jesus Christ. That's why I said that God's purpose in permitting Satan to tempt Adam, Eve, and Job was for the glory of His Son. In Romans 3:25-26, Paul wrote that the work of Christ was *to demonstrate God's righteousness in passing over sins previously committed*—including the sins of Adam, Eve, and Job. Later, in Romans 9, Paul explained God's purposes for Pharaoh. He wrote,

> *For the Scripture says to Pharaoh, "For this very purpose I raised you up, to demonstrate My power in you, and that My name might be proclaimed throughout the whole earth"* *(Romans 9:17).*

The same thing may be said regarding Satan. He was raised up (created and sent to this earthly domain) so that God might demonstrate His power and make His name great in destroying the devil's work.

Jesus came to destroy all the works of the devil in the lives of the righteous—hallelujah!

> *The one who practices sin is of the devil; for the devil has sinned from the beginning. The Son of God appeared for this purpose, **that He might destroy the works of the devil** (1 John 3:8).*

What works did He destroy? Let's look at just a few. First, sin was made powerless.

> *Knowing this, that our old self was crucified with Him, that our body of **sin might be done away with** [NASB: **"made powerless"**], that we should no longer be slaves to sin (Romans 6:6).*

The flesh with all of its deeds has been removed.

And in Him you were also circumcised with a circumcision made without hands, **in the removal of the body of the flesh by the circumcision of Christ** *(Colossians 2:11).*

Death was conquered.

And God raised Him up again, **putting an end to the agony of death,** *since it was impossible for Him to be held in its power (Acts 2:24).*

The devil himself was rendered powerless.

Since then the children share in flesh and blood, He Himself likewise also partook of the same, that through death **He might render powerless him who had the power of death,** *that is, the devil...*

Fear and the slavery it produces were conquered.

... and might deliver those who through fear *of death* **were subject to slavery** *all their lives (Hebrews 2:14-15).*

God's plan and purposes for sin, Satan, and the Fall *magnify* His glory, *enable* us to see Him and experience His love in ways the angels never could, and *cause* us to love Him in return to a far greater degree than we otherwise could. Praise the Lord!

God Created the Elements for the Fall, Yet He Is Without Sin

Before continuing our discussion in the next chapter about the effects of the fall of man, let's review who is responsible for what. God created man in His own image, gave him a law, and authorized a trial to test his creatures' hearts. Was it righteous for God to do these things or not? In all of this, we cannot assign any sinful act to God. He did not transgress His own character; in fact, He acted well within His rights as the Creator.

Additionally, Adam and Eve's decision was entirely their responsibility as they acted contrary to God's law when Satan tempted them. On whom shall the blame for the transgression be laid? There is none other but Adam to blame. He sinned by his own decision and fell from his former position of blessing. No one coerced him to sin—not even his deceived wife, Eve (Genesis 3:6, 12-13).

So far, we've seen that the fall of man was not only *decreed* by God, but was actually *designed* by Him—for good. In this design, He did not commit any acts of unrighteousness. When God made Adam in His image with a desire to be like God, He knew Adam would be tempted at that very point. He also knew when He gave Adam a law that sin would be given an opportunity to come into being. Furthermore, God knew when He sent Satan into the garden to tempt Adam that Adam would choose to disobey God's command.

God Could Have Done Otherwise If He Had Wished

Knowing that God's purpose predetermines all of God's actions, we conclude that God never has acted capriciously. He doesn't do things on a whim. He does everything with perfect knowledge and according to the counsel of His own will.

God easily could have created Adam with a different prevailing motive of heart, but He didn't. He could have withheld from man the power to choose contrary to His will, like the angels in heaven who serve as ministers to God's people. But He didn't.

God also could have related to Adam *without* law. His creation of the tree of the knowledge of good and evil was purposeful. If He had not wanted sin to exist, God easily could have *not* created the elements of heart motive, the tree, and the law. No one made Him do these things.

Furthermore, God could have refused Satan permission to enter into the realm of His creation to tempt Adam. In fact, we could entertain the notion that God didn't have to make Satan at all! Since Jesus is the Creator even of dominions (Colossians 1:16), we know that Satan didn't somehow evolve and surprise God. And the timing of Satan's entrance into the Garden is too supernatural for us to think he just happened upon our first parents while he was crawling around the universe. Considering all these things, we can only conclude that God *purposed* for the Fall to occur and that He designed each element of the Fall.

If our faith is to stand in the midst of a sinful world, it must stand on the knowledge of God's purposes. So let's review what we've learned in the last few chapters about His purposes for sin and the Fall, and in the next chapter we'll consider from the Scriptures another foundational fact about the fall of man.

1. God's decrees were pre-determined "by the counsel of His will."

2. God has a purpose for every element of His creation.

3. God decreed the fall of man and the entrance of sin into the world.

4. God intended for sin to enter the world through one man, Adam.

5. God purposed that Adam and all mankind in him would be dead in sin through Adam's fall.

6. God decreed that life would come through one man, Jesus Christ.

7. God created man in His image with a prevailing motive of heart to be like God.

8. God gave man a law in order to make sin possible.

9. God designed the jurisdiction of darkness to test men's hearts.

10. God could have designed the world with different elements if He had wanted to.

11. The only conclusion we can draw from these scriptural revelations of God is that He had a purpose for the fall of man.

As I think about God and what He has done in creation and history, I am reminded of what the Apostle Paul wrote to the Romans after explaining the fall of man and the gospel:

> Oh, the **depth of the riches both of the wisdom and knowledge of God**! *How unsearchable are His judgments and unfathomable His ways! For who has known the mind of the Lord, or who became His counselor? Or who has first given to Him that it might be paid back to Him again? For from Him and through Him and to Him are all things. To Him be the glory forever. Amen (Romans 11:33-36).*

Twenty-three

Ruined by the Fall

Of all the calamities to befall man throughout the entire course of history, nothing could have been more tragic than man's plunge into sin. Since that day in the Garden of Eden, sin has permeated mankind, and its effects have pervaded the whole earth. Professor Louis Berkof, author of *Systematic Theology*, wrote,

> Sin is one of the saddest but also one of the most common phenomena of human life. It is part of the common experience of mankind...[23]

This truth leads us to the third foundational fact about the fall of man: *The condition of the heart of every man since Adam is one of self-service, darkness, and death.* In this chapter we will look at what the Scriptures say about *how* sin has affected our hearts and made us incapable of doing anything to save ourselves.

What is the nature of sin? What are its effects? Since sin separates us from God, it is important to know the answer to these questions. Throughout history, the essential character of sin has been debated. Prominent theologians have proposed various theories regarding sin. Some have suggested that sin is an illusion, an unavoidable defect, or a lack of God-consciousness that disappears when a sense of God awakens. Others have thought sin to be simple selfishness, or a lack of trust in God due to ignorance, or the opposition of the lower tendencies in human nature to a developing moral consciousness.

Is Sin a Result of Environmental Conditioning?

Some people believe the notion that everyone comes into this world good, innocent, and with a clean slate before God. Having this view, they tend to view sin as a sickness or something learned or conditioned by one's environment. What's the matter with that? *If they believe sin arises from conditioning, then they will believe man can be reconditioned not to sin. Their answer to the problems of society is not a need for atonement, forgiveness, or a relationship with God in Jesus Christ, but a change of environment or outward conditions.* Humanism and much of psychology are based on this shaky foundation with regard to the entrance of sin at the Fall.

In contrast to the view described above, the Bible teaches that everyone comes into the world a slave of sin and guilty before God. We believe that any man is capable of any sin because the seeds of every sin are inborn from the Fall. Believing this, when we deal with "broken" people, we realize the solution to their problems doesn't lie in convincing them to improve themselves. We also understand that while we may help them improve themselves in outward behavior, if the Spirit of God doesn't transform them on the inside, they will remain condemned for eternity.

You will never understand why people do evil things to others if you don't understand where sin comes from. You'll find yourself shaken to the core when someone you trust surprises you by committing a terrible sin. When you are surprised, you're a very small step from blaming God or someone other than the sinner who is responsible. Though you may not realize it, your shocked response to the sin of another person arises from an expectation that he or she would not do anything contrary to either your will or God's.

However, if you do understand that every man became a sinner in Adam's fall, you'll not be shocked when they sin. I often joke with first-time counselees, "There's nothing you can tell me that will make me think less of you. I already think as little of you as I possibly can." What I mean is that I know that because of the Fall, there is no sin of which they are not capable. I am not likely to be surprised or shaken by whatever they may tell me.

A Popular View of Sin

Let's get a little historical perspective on the most popular current view of sin. The British theologian Pelagius (ca. 350-430 A.D.) moved to Rome in the early 400's. Although he was highly educated, the Pope and his contemporaries considered him a "layman." During his stay in Rome, Pelagius composed several works, the most popular being a commentary about the Apostle Paul. As church leaders closely examined this work, certain teachings came to light that they ultimately condemned as the "Pelagian heresy." *Great books, Mrs. Oden*

Pelagius viewed sin as consisting only of *separate acts of the will.* His presupposition was that there is no such thing as a sinful nature or sinful dispositions, and he therefore rejected the idea that these could exist in man. Consequently, he taught that the fall of Adam into sin did not affect the hearts of all men who came after him. In his opinion, sin is always—with each individual—a *deliberate choice of evil by a perfectly free will that can just as well choose to follow what is good.* The church condemned this teaching. *False belief*

The idea that man's will is free and able to choose good is built on another false presupposition: *If God has commanded man to do what is good, then man must have the ability to do it.* Is this what you believe? This conclusion is based on a popular but unbiblical notion regarding the first moral state of Adam: that he was created *morally neutral* rather than with *positive righteousness.*[24]

What do I mean by these terms? We looked briefly at the idea of positive righteousness in Chapter 21 when I said that we are dressed in the positive righteousness of Jesus Christ (that is, in His perfect righteousness demonstrated through tested endurance without failure). The belief that Adam was morally neutral means that he had neither righteousness nor unrighteousness in his being. It's the idea that Adam was morally a "blank slate."

We have no biblical basis for thinking Adam's original moral state was one of neutrality. God considered His creative state "good" (Genesis 1:31). However, God apparently also considered it necessary for Adam's righteousness to be tested and proven in order for him to stand before God in *positive* righteousness. Remember that in order for *positive* righteousness to be demonstrated, *potential* righteousness must be tested. Thus God gave Adam a law forbidding him to eat of the tree of the knowledge of good and evil. With this command, God provided not only a basis for displaying positive righteousness, but also a basis for defining sin.

The point for us in this study is that there is no biblical evidence that God created Adam as a *moral blank slate*. However, there is abundant scriptural evidence that He created Adam with the ability to understand God and to make a choice either in keeping with or contrary to His revealed will.

What Is the Scriptural Idea of Sin?

So if Pelagius was in error, then what is an accurate biblical idea of sin? First, we can say sin is *a specific kind of evil*. Usually we are right to think of sin as *not doing what God commands*. Sometimes we use the term *transgression*, which refers to *doing what God forbids*. We call various sicknesses, injuries, and tragedies *evil*; but *sin* is specifically a reference to that which is *unethical* or *immoral*. It is not a *lesser degree* of goodness, but it is a *positively exhibited* evil. There is no neutral ground when it comes to sin.

When we talk of sin, we usually are referring to a relationship with God and His will. That is why we often talk of sin as *missing the mark* or as *falling short* of God's standard or law.

We associate guilt and corruption with sin. We think of *guilt* as the state of deserving condemnation and punishment due to a transgression. *Corruption* signifies being brought into an inferior or worse condition, usually with a destructive effect. In Romans 8:21, the Apostle Paul refers to the condition of creation as being under bondage to corruption—an effect of Adam's sin.

When sin is referred to in the Bible, it is often associated with the heart. The heart of man is like the root of a tree, and the acts of a man are like the fruit of a tree. As the fruit of a tree develops from the sustenance supplied by the tree roots, so the acts of a man develop from his heart. The tendencies of the heart give rise to the sinful acts of the will.

Finally, when we think of sin, we don't limit it to outward actions. One can have sinful habits that rise out of a sinful state of soul, which numerous scriptures refer to as "the flesh."[25] Some of these sins may rarely be revealed because they are secretly harbored in the mind, will, and emotions.

I'd like to take you with me on one of the most eye-opening journeys through the Scriptures I've ever undertaken. Let's survey the Scriptures regarding sin's effect on mankind. Do you know what the

Bible teaches about the effects of the Fall? In short, we're told that through sin mankind was totally disqualified for relationship with God and for glory. Mankind was ruined by the Fall.

The Extent of Sin's Corruption

What is the extent of the corruption of man because of Adam's transgression? When Adam transgressed God's law in the Garden of Eden, the entire human race was totally polluted and condemned before God. Every function of man was infected. We read in Romans 8:7 that the flesh (our human nature under the dominion of sin) is hostile to God and cannot subject itself to God's law. Jeremiah described the human heart as deceitful and desperately sick (Jeremiah 17:9). The spirit of man, his thinking, and his conscience are all functions of the heart (Ezekiel 11:19; Proverbs 23:7; 1 John 3:19-21). We've already discussed how the will reflects the condition of the heart. The Bible explicitly says that the extent of the corruption because of Adam's sin reaches the entire being of every person born from Adam's race. "Evil inclinations" have zeroed in on our hearts.

One of the first indications of sin's devastating effects is found in Genesis 6:5:

> Then the Lord saw that the wickedness of man was great on the earth, and that every intent of the thoughts of his heart was only evil continually.

Look at this verse carefully. *Every* intention, not some of them, is evil. Notice also the seat of the evil is the heart because the heart is what controls the will. Sin's effect is so extensive that *every* motive and intent of the heart is evil. Still further, notice how sin so polluted the hearts of men that their intents and thoughts were *only* evil. There was absolutely no good to be found within the heart of men as a result of the fall of Adam. Lest we think this was a description of man on a bad day, the Spirit also added that the intents and thoughts were only evil *continually!* The Holy Spirit left no room for us to conclude there is any good in man.

What is the significance of this truth? If every intention of the thoughts of the heart is only evil continually, will any human being ever choose what is good (by God's standard)? Is the will of man actually free to choose God's will? The answer is a resounding "No!" It is not possible for man to choose good according to God's standard of good as long as every intent of the thoughts of man's heart is only evil continually.

Comparing man and God

Hearing to God

What is God's standard of good? It is Himself! God is passionately committed to one thing: *His own glory.* Consider the difference between God and man. He has a passion for *His* glory, and we have a passion for *our* glory. He is motivated for *our* good, and we are also motivated for *our* good—but apart from Him. His love delights in *giving*, but our actions are motivated by *self-lust*.

Someone might raise the question about all the *good* that people do even though they are not believers. Isn't the professional athlete who contributes millions of dollars to a charity doing a *good* thing? What about the unbelieving statesman who serves his constituents well? Isn't he doing *good*? The answer to these questions depends upon the perspective. From man's perspective, determined by how man is benefited, the answer to these questions is "Yes." But from God's perspective, determined by how God is glorified, the answer is "No." The natural man does good deeds and gives to others for his own glory, not God's glory. How is God glorified? God is glorified most when His creatures delight in Him because His love has been poured out on and through them. They give glory to God because they once were dead in sin and separated from God, but now they are alive in Christ and reconciled through Him to God.

Man in Sin Is Dead, Helpless, and Incapable

we were dead before Christ

Although the testimonies of the Old Testament should suffice to convince us of man's spiritual condition after the Fall, specific New Testament scriptures leave us no doubt as to what desperate straits man is in, in our "pre-faith" state. There is no way we can relate to God or do His will. The Apostle Paul described the state of all men before faith comes in Chapter 2 of Ephesians. He said we were *dead in our sins.* When used in this context, *dead* expresses the idea of separation and alienation.

> And you were **dead in your trespasses and sins**, in which you formerly walked according to the course of this world, according to the prince of the power of the air, of the spirit that is now working in the sons of disobedience. Among them we too all formerly lived in the lusts of our flesh, indulging the desires of the flesh and of the mind, and were by nature children of wrath, even as the rest (Ephesians 2:1-3).

When writing to the Romans, the apostle described us as *helpless.* If we could *choose* to get ourselves out of the mess we are in, we wouldn't be helpless. The glory of the gospel is that it tells us God justified us through His grace, even while we *couldn't do anything* to right ourselves!

> For while we were still **helpless**, at the right time Christ died for the ungodly (Romans 5:6).

Paul further expounded the point of man's helplessness in Chapter 8, verses 3, 7, and 8, when he explained to the Romans the liberating work of the Holy Spirit in our salvation. He wanted the Romans to understand that man's problem doesn't lie with the law of God; it lies with flesh that is too weak and incapable to do what God requires. He wrote,

> For what the Law could not do, **weak as it was through the flesh,** God did: sending His own Son in the likeness of sinful flesh and as an offering for sin, He condemned sin in the flesh.... because the mind set on the flesh is hostile toward God; for it does not subject itself to the law of God, for **it is not even able to do so;** and those who are in the flesh cannot please God.

Is Man Free to Choose?

If by this question we are asking whether God *makes* a man *choose to accept or reject Jesus Christ,* the answer is "No." However, if we are asking whether God *allows* man to *act naturally on the inclinations of his heart*—that is, whether God exercises *passive power* over him—the answer is "Yes." This is just what He did with both Adam and Satan. The natural man is "free" in only two ways: he can either reject Jesus Christ completely, or else he can "choose" Jesus Christ in an attempt to *use* God for his own purposes. Either way, he continues in his alienation and hostility of mind against God. Yet God is not compelling him to do so. He is freely choosing to act in concert with the sinful nature to which he is enslaved. The Apostle Paul made some strong statements about this bondage of the will to the sinful disposition of man's heart:

> But thanks be to God that though **you were slaves of sin**... (Romans 6:17).

> For we know that the Law is spiritual; but **I am of flesh, sold into bondage to sin** (Romans 7:14).

If God chooses to intervene and grant a man a new disposition of heart—that is, a new nature resulting from new birth by the Holy Spirit—then the man will trust in Christ and do so for the glory of God.

When he turns from faith in himself and from his sinful practices to faith in Jesus Christ to follow Him, he freely chooses to do so without any feeling of being made to do so against his will. But as he knows how he once hated God and loved himself, and as he now perceives the glorious grace of God in Jesus Christ, he doesn't see how he can continue to sin against such love and grace! He feels he *must* trust in Christ and follow Him if he is to enjoy the promises of God in Christ. This man will be very cognizant of and grateful for the new heart that God gives him.

Man Needs a Change of Heart

Now we can begin to understand how no offspring of Adam can choose to change his own heart. He is not free, as Pelagius proposed, to simply choose to do right. As Abraham believed, so do we believe: *God gives life* and *calls into being that which does not exist* (*Romans 4:17*). Primarily what He calls into being is new hearts! Unless the Holy Spirit is at work, an evangelistic appeal to such a natural heart to accept Christ in order to avoid spending eternity in hell only encourages him to "do evil"—that is, to act solely for his own benefit. He may pray a prayer, walk down an aisle, raise a hand, or do anything within the limits of his selfish nature that will put himself in a state of blessing rather than peril. But his deceived last state is worse than his previous one; for now he thinks he has won God's favor! The natural man may do things we consider good, *but he will do them with the wrong motive,* and thus be further deceived about his true state of enmity with God.

This is a very serious consideration when we think about popular methods of evangelism. Knowing that man is dead, helpless, and incapable of glorifying God in his choices—because of the Fall—helps us realize that salvation must be more than an emotional appeal to the will of man. A man in the flesh, trapped in bondage to sin in the heart, cannot glorify or please God. Our gospel must reach beyond the mind and the will and into the *heart*, relying entirely on the power of the Spirit of God to convert the soul and create a new heart through the gospel message. Let's look now at several descriptions of the natural heart of man.

Man in Sin Has Evil Intentions

What does the Bible teach us about the heart of man as a result of the Fall? Genesis 8:21 gives us insight from God's perspective regarding the heart of man from the beginning:

> *And the Lord smelled the soothing aroma; and the Lord said to Himself, "I will never again curse the ground on account of man, for the **intent** of man's heart **is evil from his youth**; and I will never again destroy every living thing, as I have done."*

When the scripture says the intent of man's heart is evil from his youth, it isn't referring to men when they are young. Mankind is being viewed from the beginning, *from his youth.* The intention of the human heart—your heart, my heart—is toward evil, unless we experience the new birth. When we consider a person's intent, we are thinking about his purpose, design, or plan. *Purpose* usually suggests determination, but not necessarily success in carrying it out. *Design* implies careful preliminary planning or preparation.

Romans 3:10-18 illustrates this evil intent in the heart of man quite vividly. The Apostle Paul was making his case that no man can justify himself before God. Paul's description of God's appraisal of mankind was almost like a bullet list:

- *There is none righteous, not even one;*

- *There is none who understands, there is none who seeks for God;*

- *All have turned aside, together they have become useless; there is none who does good, there is not even one.*

- *Their throat is an open grave, with their tongues they keep deceiving, the poison of asps is under their lips;*

- *Whose mouth is full of cursing and bitterness;*

- *Their feet are swift to shed blood,*

- *Destruction and misery are in their paths,*

- *And the path of peace have they not known.*

- *There is no fear of God before their eyes.*

Therefore, it is easy to see how an appeal to accept Christ and be saved made to the fallen, corrupted emotions and intellect of a man

[handwritten margin note: what kind of faith are we promoting]

may lead him into a deeper deceit than he is in already. In his pride, he may think he can do good for himself and for God by responding to the appeal. If the Holy Spirit isn't converting the soul and giving him a new heart, he will do what he's told for his own glory rather than for God's. Self-protection and self-preservation may be strong motivations convincing him to respond favorably to the appeal. But will he be concerned about God's name and God's glory? Will this faith be the kind of faith God reckons as righteousness (Romans 4:4-13)? It is interesting to note that Peter's second epistle opens with a salutation "to those who have received a faith *of the same kind as ours...*" We should be asking ourselves, in our evangelism, what kind of faith are we promoting?

For parents of small children and children's ministers, this truth is crucial. We'll talk more about this in the chapter on leading your children to Christ.

Man in Sin Has a Heart of Deceitfulness

The Scriptures also portray the condition of the heart of the natural man as being selfish and darkened. And if that were not enough, deceit and spiritual sickness reign within. Jeremiah 17:9 indicates that the heart of man is more deceitful than all else, and is desperately sick. Think about what this means. The condition of men's hearts since the Fall has left such a testimony in history that God can find nothing more deceitful in all of human existence!

Verse 10 of Jeremiah 17 reveals God's testing and judgment of the heart of man. He says, "I test the mind, even to give to man according to his ways, according to the results of his deeds." I think the deceit in the human heart is beyond our comprehension. We can think we're loving God and doing good and not be aware that our motives are sinful.

Consider whom the deceitful heart deceives: its owner! A deceitful heart may trick the people around it, but not usually. Others can usually observe the selfishness of someone's lifestyle, but the person himself may not be able to do so.

How does the deceitful heart deceive? Psalm 36:1-4 provides insight:

> *Transgression speaks to the ungodly within his heart; there is no fear of God before his eyes. For **it flatters him in his own eyes, concerning the discovery of his***

iniquity and the hatred of it. The words of his mouth are wickedness and deceit; he has ceased to be wise and to do good. He plans wickedness upon his bed; he sets himself on a path that is not good; he does not despise evil.

Sin in the heart speaks to the heart of the natural man regarding sin, "It's okay. Don't be so concerned. It's not so bad. You know it's not as bad as So-and-so's sin. Besides, God's not watching. No one will ever know."

[handwritten: Be awear of this in your own heart]

Man in Sin Has a Heart That Is a Treasury of Evil

In addition to these things, there is further explanation for why men sin. We find in Mark 7:14-23 Jesus' explanation for the sinfulness of men.

> *And after He called the multitude to Him again, He began saying to them, "Listen to Me, all of you, and understand: there is nothing outside the man which going into him can defile him; but **the things which proceed out of the man are what defile the man.** If any man has ears to hear, let him hear."*

> *And when, leaving the multitude, He had entered the house, His disciples questioned Him about the parable. And He said to them, "Are you so lacking in understanding also? Do you not understand that whatever goes into the man from outside cannot defile him; because it does not go into his heart, but into his stomach, and is eliminated?" (Thus He declared all foods clean.)*

> *And He was saying, "That which proceeds out of the man, that is what defiles the man. **For from within, out of the heart of men,** proceed the evil thoughts, fornications, thefts, murders, adulteries, deeds of coveting and wickedness, as well as deceit, sensuality, envy, slander, pride and foolishness. **All these evil things proceed from within and defile the man.**"*

Why do men sin? It is because their hearts are treasuries of evil. That's how much the Fall affected the human race. Consider what Jesus said. What hurts us is not what people do to us, but what comes out of us in response. What we are filled with is what is going to come out of us when we are shaken.

[handwritten: like a shaken up soda can]

Imagine my standing in front of you with a glass of apple juice in my hand. A fleeting moment of evil erupts in you and you grab my wrist and shake it violently, slinging apple juice all over the room and us. Look at this mess! How did this happen? The obvious answer is that you lost your composure and shook my hand, thus making the mess. But another answer is also true. The room and we are spotted with apple juice because there was apple juice in the cup. Had the cup been empty, there would be no mess to clean up.

In life, we're faced repeatedly with people and situations God sends our way to shake our spiritual cups. Whatever we are filled with when we get shaken is what comes out! That's what hurts us—and others. If we are filled with the love and righteousness of Jesus Christ, then *He* comes out when we are shaken.

But the Bible teaches us that since Adam's fall, sin has completely, one hundred percent, darkened the human heart, making it a treasury of evil. Anytime it is disturbed, out of that treasury of evil come wickedness, darkness, destruction, and death. Until one is born from above, nothing else *can* come out! (Again, see Romans 8:7-8.)

Man in Sin Has a Heart That Doesn't Fear God

Perhaps this seems extreme, but we must remember that God's view is the one that counts, not ours. Mankind naturally entertains a higher view of himself than God does. Paul quoted the Psalms when he told the Romans about God's view of mankind. I quoted these verses above, but notice again how Paul concluded the descriptive list of our condition without Christ:

There is no fear of God before their eyes (Romans 3:18).

Man in Sin Has a Hard, Calloused Heart

Ephesians 4:17-19 illustrates the hardness of heart in the human soul:

This I say therefore, and affirm together with the Lord, that you walk no longer just as the Gentiles also walk, in the futility of their mind, excluded from the life of God, because of the ignorance that is in them, because of the hardness of their heart; and they, having become callous, have given themselves over to sensuality, for the practice of every kind of impurity with greediness.

Because of a hardness of heart, a man living in the flesh can neither walk after God nor choose to believe in a way that brings glory to God in Christ. Because his spirit is not alive in Christ, his heart is characterized by hardness and sensuality. *" but you have made us alive togette w/ christ "*

Therefore when we tell an offspring of Adam, whose heart lacks the work of the Spirit of God, to choose to believe or to live in such a way as to glorify God, the condition of his heart will be exposed. The spiritual deadness and darkness will surface. The undiscerning person may try to believe. He may respond to a gospel invitation and attempt to live a "Christian" life, but if the Spirit of God has not converted his heart, he can only do what his heart leads him to do. His own darkness will be his light. His natural "light" will lead him to put on a form of godliness, but it will lack power. Jesus taught this in the Sermon on the Mount when He said,

> *"The lamp of the body is the eye; if therefore your eye is clear, your whole body will be full of light. But if your eye is bad, your whole body will be full of darkness. If therefore the light that is in you is darkness, how great is the darkness!" (Matthew 6:22-23)*

The typical unbeliever who attends church usually isn't attending to glorify God or to seek the true God, according to Romans 3. This poses a significant problem when it comes to our philosophy of ministry. If a church appeals to the selfish nature of man, offers self-serving programs, and accentuates the sensual, unbelievers *will be attracted.* But the problem is that they are attracted for the wrong reasons. Looking to appease their guilty consciences and wishing to feel good about themselves, they're looking for "Jesus Lite." If ministers don't understand the spiritual condition of the hearts of unbelievers, they won't address the issues of their hearts. Instead, they will encourage them to appease their consciences by doing religious things, and this practice will inoculate them to true faith and knowledge of Jesus!

John MacArthur hit the nail on the head in his book, *Ashamed of the Gospel: When the Church Becomes Like the World.* He wrote,

> Pragmatism ignores doctrine and focuses more on achieving "success" than on communicating God's Word unashamedly. Tragically, this theology emphasizes church growth over church doctrine, makes entertaining congregations more important than feeding them spiritually, and views truth as being secondary to "what works."[26]

I'm not suggesting that every minister interested in growing a church is wrongly motivated, but if ministers do not understand what God's Word says about the nature of man, they won't apply the truth to how they minister or evangelize.

Understanding the nature of man enables one to see the danger of a philosophy of ministry that emphasizes appealing to what people like to hear and do. We should consider this: whatever we use to *get* them, we must continue to use to *keep* them! In the following verses, Paul wrote,

> **But you did not learn Christ in this way, if indeed you have heard Him and have been taught in Him,** *just as truth is in Jesus, that, in reference to your former manner of life, you lay aside the old self, which is being corrupted in accordance with the lusts of deceit (Ephesians 4:20-22).*

Tragic conditions develop in the visible church when we resort to worldly philosophies and methods based on ignorance regarding the hearts of men. Churches using such tactics may have not only a large front door, but also a gaping hole in the back where people may slip or wander away. They may fall away after a time because their faith was of a natural generation rather than by the Holy Spirit. They may hear of a better "show" happening at another church in town. They may become discouraged due to their emptiness and lack of spiritual power. Or, on the other side of this tragic coin, others will keep trying harder to please God and prove their sincerity, remaining under a spirit of law and never knowing true grace.

These tragic conditions describe many today who have become discouraged with Jesus and Christianity. What they thought was the Christian experience was not! Perhaps they were not told the truth about the hardness of their hearts and were led to believe they were genuine believers by others who also didn't understand the natural condition of the heart of men or God's purpose for sin and the Fall.

Man in Sin Has a Foolish, Darkened Heart

In the chapter regarding God's purpose for the Fall, we discussed how the choices of men flow out of the spiritual condition of their hearts. Ever since the fall of Adam, men's hearts have been focused on serving themselves, the creature, rather than their Creator. Adam and Eve made their choice to break God's law simply because they were focused on what they wanted for themselves.

Romans 1 describes the attitude and the condition of the person who has not been born again by God's Spirit. From this description, we can know what choices the natural man will make because of the prevailing motives in his heart. Paul wrote,

> For the wrath of God is revealed from heaven against all ungodliness and unrighteousness of men, who suppress the truth in unrighteousness...
>
> For even though they knew God, they did not honor Him as God, or give thanks; but they became futile in their speculations, and **their foolish heart was darkened**. Professing to be wise, they became fools, and exchanged the glory of the incorruptible God for an image in the form of corruptible man and of birds and four-footed animals and crawling creatures.
>
> Therefore God gave them over in the lusts of their hearts to impurity, that their bodies might be dishonored among them. For they exchanged the truth of God for a lie, and **worshiped and served the creature** rather than the Creator, who is blessed forever. Amen (Romans 1:18, 21-25).

What will every offspring of Adam choose? They will choose to serve the creature because their hearts are foolish and darkened. Men under God's wrath are given over to the lust of their hearts—to serve themselves. That's how to discern those who are under God's wrath: they live to serve themselves. They'll never see things differently until God reveals Himself to their hearts. Everything in their lives will be viewed from their own perspective.

In the rest of Romans 1, Paul further described the choices of those who are foolish and darkened in their understanding. Since they don't acknowledge God, they are given over to their depravity, to act out the wickedness of their hearts.

> And just as they did not see fit to acknowledge God any longer, **God gave them over** to a depraved mind, to do those things which are not proper, being filled with all unrighteousness, wickedness, greed, evil; full of envy, murder, strife, deceit, malice; they are gossips, slanderers, haters of God, insolent, arrogant, boastful, inventors of evil, disobedient to parents, without understanding, untrustworthy, unloving, unmerciful; and, although they know the ordinance of God, that those who practice such things are worthy of death, they not only do the

same, but also give hearty approval to those who practice them (Romans 1:28-32).

In the hearts of those God created in Christ Jesus before the foundation of the world, this "giving over" serves a valuable purpose. This is God's way of teaching them about the power of sin, their helplessness, and their need of righteousness and grace through Jesus Christ. In Chapter 6 of John's gospel, Jesus commented that everyone who comes to Him must be taught of God (verse 45). They must first be convinced of the bad news that they are under God's wrath and cannot deliver themselves before the good news in Christ has power. As the wrath of God is revealed from heaven, the Holy Spirit begins the work of redemption in the heart.

Someone who *sees* his own self-service shows evidence of the work of the Spirit of God. Perhaps you noticed that the scripture above states, *"God gave them over."* Therefore, a person who is *convicted* of his selfish nature shows signs of God's mighty hand at work in his heart, granting him repentance. God has given him over to himself and then opened his eyes to see his sinfulness in order that he might repent and trust in Christ. Perhaps God is "shaking his cup" so he can see what fills him and repent, in order to save him.

We've seen from the Scriptures that the extent of the corruption of the Fall in the heart of the natural man pervades every intent of the heart, leaving the heart...

• Dead in sin

• Helpless to change itself

• Incapable of choosing good for God's glory

• Full of evil intentions

• Deceitful

• A treasury of evil

• With no fear of God

• Hard

• Calloused

• Foolish

• Darkened

The terrible things men have done against one another throughout history may be explained by the impact of the Fall. Mankind has lacked self-control ever since Adam rebelled against God, and therefore we have appeared to be out of control. Do you think God's world is out of *His* control? How can God be glorified in a world that has fallen from the state in which He originally created it? Let's see!

God shows His glory by being good to us, sinners, who do not deserve goodness or love. This is how we know true love.

Twenty-four

The Fall of Man and the Glory of God

The fourth foundational fact about God's purpose for sin and the fall of man has to do with the glory of God in His Son, Jesus Christ. *God's purpose for the fall of man and the presence of evil and death is to display His goodness, which is His glory.* It is the glory of God for Him to be good to sinners who are undeserving, alienated, and hostile toward Him. Wouldn't you agree? God's goodness is seen in His redemptive purpose in the history of mankind. He has not chosen to *destroy all men*, although He would be righteous in doing so, but has chosen to *save some*.

The connection between God's goodness and God's glory are seen in Exodus 33:18-19. God spoke to Moses about His glory.

Then Moses said, "I pray Thee, show me Thy glory!"

*And He said, "I Myself will make **all My goodness** pass before you, and will proclaim the name of the Lord before you; and **I will be gracious** to whom I will be gracious, **and will show compassion** on whom I will show compassion."*

The goodness of God is displayed in His compassion for His enemies. He has purposed to be compassionate to some who should otherwise spend eternity separated from His goodness. When Adam transgressed God's law, sin and death entered into the world. If God had not had a purpose for sin and death, He would have displayed His ultimate wrath immediately.

Mankind Is on Probation

If you recall, after Adam sinned, God passed judgment upon Adam, Eve, and Satan. He didn't immediately send them into eternal punishment, though He could have, since justice demands retribution. He didn't bring *final* judgment upon them, but instead put them *on probation*. This interesting concept is found in the works of Jonathan Edwards and other great preachers of previous centuries. Noah Webster defined *probation* as a "moral trial; the state of man in the present life, in which he has the opportunity of proving his character and being qualified for a happier state."[27]

Today when we say someone is on probation, we mean that they have transgressed the law and their punishment has been suspended. During the time of probation, the offender is being *tested* scrutinized and observed to see if he has reformed. A probation officer holds the transgressor accountable throughout this period of time. If the person commits another offense, the sentence is then enacted. The judge's finding him guilty and suspending his sentence *should* produce in him a fear of perpetrating another crime. The fear of the wrath to come *should* motivate him to do what is right. But this often is not what happens. Offenders fail their probation and suffer the consequences.

Adam was the first of mankind to be "put on probation," after disobeying God's law. God suspended the sentence of death and put Adam and Eve and all their offspring on probation so there could be no question about God's judgment when He says, "There is none righteous, not even one" (Romans 3:10). As each offspring of Adam is born and lives his life, his wicked heart displays the truth of God's declaration.

When God put Adam and Eve on probation, the *means* of this "moral trial" were not the same as the means He used in the original test of their hearts in the Garden. But the *question* to be answered by this trial was essentially the same: *Will you trust Me in what I tell you, or will you trust yourself?*　Jesus

All of mankind goes through life on earth under a similar "moral trial." Each person is "under probation" until he sins the first sin. The testing of every human being has yielded a completely consistent judgment: Man is reprobate. Noah Webster defines this word this way: "Not enduring proof or trial; rejected; abandoned in sin; lost to virtue or grace; abandoned to wickedness and eternal destruction."[28] Romans 3 tells us that without exception, every single person has violated his God-given conscience, breaking God's laws and expecting to be delivered *[handwritten annotation at top: we take for granted the "kind, sweet, merciful" side of God and forget that there is baking soda in the cake too (Judgment)]*

from the consequences. Disbelieving or ignoring the sentence hanging over them for eternal damnation, men take for granted the kindness of God, which should lead sinners to repentance (Romans 2:5) but so often doesn't. That's how wicked our hearts are. Neither time nor kindness will bring about reformation. Man is totally ruined unless God is merciful. The sentence of death still hangs over mankind and will rightly fall on all who die in Adam—in their sins.

God's Riches of Glory Are Known Through Vessels of Mercy

The questions before us are these: Why has God chosen to endure wicked people, "vessels of wrath prepared for destruction"? Why has He put up with millennia of evil and wickedness? Why hasn't He sent Satan into the outer darkness? Why has He demonstrated such patience? The Apostle Paul gave a direct answer to these questions: God purposed to show forth the riches of His glory through believers in Christ, "vessels of mercy" created in His Son before the foundation of the earth.

> *What if God, although willing to demonstrate His wrath and* *[handwritten: That's us]* *to make His power known, endured with much patience vessels of wrath prepared for destruction? And **He did so in order that He might make known the riches of His glory upon vessels of mercy, which He prepared beforehand for glory, even us,** whom He also called, not from among Jews only, but also from among Gentiles (Romans 9:22-24).*

Paul taught that the mystery concealed through the ages was that all of history exists for one purpose: to bring forth the sons of God into the glory of Jesus Christ! All history is to be summed up in Him. He alone is the author of life, the Redeemer and Savior of men.

Through the fall of man, God ordained that mankind would be "put down" (abased) so Jesus Christ might be exalted. I'm not saying God "put us down." As we've already discussed, our abased spiritual state passed to us through Adam's sin. Without a work of God's Spirit, man won't choose righteousness or good (by God's standard), won't choose to obey for God's glory, and won't choose life (Romans 3:10-12). When compared to our spiritual state of poverty, the glory of God appears like unfathomable wealth! God is glorified as He supplies everything we need through the glory of Jesus Christ. Jesus' glory rises and abounds through His ministry to us in our spiritual poverty. We can see why Paul prayed for the Ephesians and Philippians as he did:

I pray that the eyes of your heart may be enlightened, so that you may know what is the hope of His calling, what are the riches of the glory of His inheritance in the saints (Ephesians 1:18).

And my God shall supply all your needs according to His riches in glory in Christ Jesus (Philippians 4:19).

The contrast between man's helpless and hopeless condition and God's goodness and mercy ought to generate in us worship and glory to God through Jesus Christ. It did in the mind and heart of the Apostle Paul:

*It is a trustworthy statement, deserving full acceptance, that **Christ Jesus came into the world to save sinners, among whom I am foremost of all.** And yet for this reason I found mercy, in order that in me as the foremost, **Jesus Christ might demonstrate His perfect patience,** as an example for those who would believe in Him for eternal life.*

Now to the King eternal, immortal, invisible, the only God, be honor and glory forever and ever. Amen (1 Timothy 1:15-17).

Notice how the great apostle saw the patience of God when he considered his own sinfulness and God's mercy demonstrated through Jesus Christ. God used Paul's sinful life to manifest His glory in Christ. In writing to Titus, Paul included himself with other sinners so he could talk about the riches of God's grace in Christ.

*For we also once were **foolish** ourselves, disobedient, deceived, enslaved to various lusts and pleasures, spending our life in malice and envy, hateful, hating one another.*

*But when the **kindness of God our Savior and His love for mankind appeared, He saved us,** not on the basis of deeds which we have done in righteousness, but according to His mercy, by the washing of regeneration and renewing **by the Holy Spirit, whom He poured out upon us richly** through Jesus Christ our Savior (Titus 3:3-6).*

What do these words speak to your own heart? Were you once foolish, disobedient, deceived, and enslaved to the lusts and pleasures of this life? Has God chosen to reveal to you His goodness and grace in Jesus Christ? If your answer to both of these questions is "Yes," then you cannot help but be in awe of God's goodness to you. And if you have seen God's goodness to you, then you cannot help but speak of it and thank Him for it. Indeed, you glorify Him when you do so, and that was God's plan! *declare his goodness + glory!*

Summary of Four Foundational Facts About the Fall of Man

1. God decreed the fall of man and the entrance of sin and death.

2. God designed the fall of man and the entrance of sin and death with a purpose.

3. The condition of the heart of every man since Adam is one of self-service, darkness, and death.

4. God's purpose for the fall of man and the presence of sin and death is to display His goodness and glory in His Son, Jesus Christ.

God has determined that Jesus Christ shall get all the glory in the salvation of men. He wisely devised a way for man to disqualify himself for glory by transgressing God's law. God's plan did not violate Adam's will nor remove his responsibility before God. He did not *cause* Adam to sin, but once Adam did so, God *imputed* his sin to all his offspring (that is, attributed it to us, or charged it to our accounts). Our powerlessness and inability to do anything about our condition makes Jesus' sacrifice and God's mercy in Him toward us wonderful and glorious.

We all stand guilty and condemned before God. How can God justify the guilty and still remain righteous? How does one know if he is right with God? In the next chapter, we'll enjoy the wonderful truths about God's glorious grace through His Son, Jesus Christ!

Twenty-five

Reconciled by God

A re you ready for some good news? I hope so. Having seen what
God's Word reveals about the condition of the heart of the natural
man, we are ready to answer questions naturally arising about our
relationship with God. How can we human beings, whose intentions
of heart are "only evil continually," ever gain favor with Him? Can we
ever do right in God's eyes and obtain peace with Him? How can we be
reconciled to a just and righteous God?

The situation seems even more hopeless when we consider what
we've learned about God. A righteous God cannot allow even one sin to
go unpunished. We would consider a judge unjust if he were to allow a
guilty person to go free without retribution. Have you ever considered
that God's character demands perfect obedience and conformity to His
own standard of righteousness? If you have, then you know we're faced
with some important questions. How can God be just in saving even one
person? Furthermore, is it really possible that God justifies a person as
a result of his simply choosing or accepting Christ? Or can a person's
so-called good choices to go to church, sing in the choir, tithe from his
income, or teach a Sunday school class earn him a righteous standing
with God while he continues practicing sin?

Before we answer these questions, we want to remember an important
fact. Choosing to accept Christ can be nothing more than a work of the
flesh *unless* the Spirit has done His work in the heart first. This was what
Nicodemus didn't understand, and it is widely misunderstood by the
evangelical church today.

The Only Answer

There is really only one answer to the questions above. Salvation must be accomplished entirely by God because man is helpless to do anything to secure God's favor. We certainly have nothing *in ourselves* to cause God's heart to turn toward us, do we? Additionally, man by himself cannot *merit* right standing in God's sight. The Apostle Paul told the Romans that no man can justify himself by any works of righteousness (Romans 3:19-20). This leaves man with only one hope: That God has devised a way to justify Himself as well as sinners, without either compromising His character or ignoring His declaration that the "wages of sin is death."

What Does Justification Mean?

Justification is applied two ways—first, to God and, second, to His people. Let's begin by asking what it means for God to justify Himself. How has God justified Himself in forgiving those He calls to Himself? What must God do to justify Himself and provide righteousness for His people? Larry Richards wrote in *The Expository Dictionary of Bible Words* that justification "has important judicial meanings. A person whose actions are in question will be justified if those actions are examined and found to have been right."[39] It carries the idea of acquittal, vindication, or a pronouncement of righteousness. When we talk of justification, we mean that God is pronouncing His people righteous in His sight.

The problem we face is God's examination of us. He declares that none of us are righteous:

> ... for **all** have sinned and fall short of the glory of God... (Romans 3:23).

> For **all of us** have become like one who is unclean, *and **all** our righteous deeds are like a filthy garment*; and **all of us** wither like a leaf, and our iniquities, like the wind, take us away (Isaiah 64:6).

A just God cannot pass over sin. Every sin must be accounted for; the debt must be paid. So how can God proclaim us righteous and yet remain just Himself?

God Vindicated Himself at the Cross

The great news is this: *God satisfied His own justice through His Son Jesus Christ. Jesus' righteous life and sacrificial death fully satisfied His Father's just and righteous demands on all of us.* Jesus secured redemption for His people. His sacrifice was the only possible means to fully pay the penalty for our sins without merely excusing them.

In the following passages written by Paul, notice how *God demonstrated His own righteousness* while reconciling sinners to Himself through His Son, Jesus Christ:

> ... *even the righteousness of God through faith in Jesus Christ for all those who believe; for there is no distinction; for all have sinned and fall short of the glory of God, being justified as a gift by His grace through the redemption which is in Christ Jesus; whom God displayed publicly as a propitiation in His blood through faith.* **This was to demonstrate His righteousness**, *because in the forbearance of God He passed over the sins previously committed;* **for the demonstration, I say, of His righteousness at the present time, that He might be just and the justifier of** *the one who has faith in Jesus. Where then is boasting? It is excluded* (Romans 3:22-27).

How could God pass over the sins previously committed? How could He declare everyone past, present, and future to be righteous in His sight when the Law demanded death? Jesus' death on the cross satisfied *both* God's own righteous character *and* the demands of the Law. He is *just* as well as *justifier.* Hallelujah! In Paul's letter to the Romans, he again emphasized God's work in His Son at the cross to fulfill what the Law required:

> *For what the Law could not do, weak as it was through the flesh, God did:* **sending His own Son** *in the likeness of sinful flesh and* **as an offering for sin**, *He condemned sin in the flesh, in order that* **the requirement of the Law might be fulfilled in us**, *who do not walk according to the flesh, but according to the Spirit (Romans 8:3-4).*

Can you see why God can forgive all of our sins and be just in doing so? Through the sacrifice of His perfect Son on our behalf, God has given our consciences a basis for peace with God. Not only has God demonstrated His justice at the cross, but He has also justified sinners in Christ.

God's Basis for Our Justification

We've seen that God must have a just way to save men from their sins and yet vindicate Himself. He must also have a just way to declare sinners righteous in His sight. *The foundation for our right standing with God is our union with Jesus in His death and resurrection.* Because God has made our union with Christ the basis of our justification, He may now justly apply to us *every aspect* of salvation.

What does it mean that you, personally, are united with Christ in His death and resurrection? It means that before you were even born, God knew you in Christ! He justified you in Christ! He forgave you in Christ! He made you righteous in Christ! These truths give us great reason to rejoice. Before He made the world, God placed *all* who are His into Jesus Christ and declared us righteous before Him. He did so in order to justify us and thus reconcile us to Himself. Because He did this *in eternity*, our standing before Him is not subject to change. Since He *predetermined* to make us righteous in Christ, our sins do not affect our eternal security in Him. (When I say this, I do not mean at all that we are excused from right living and good works. We'll consider this idea at length in Part 3 of this book. But understanding our union with Christ sets us free from the anxiety caused by our failures in our performance-driven culture.) Notice this wonderful truth in the following verses. Consider the number of your sins and the shame, hostility, and massive breach they have caused between you and your Creator, and let these scriptures wash your conscience clean!

> *Blessed be the God and Father of our Lord Jesus Christ, who has blessed us with every spiritual blessing in the heavenly places in Christ, just as* **He chose us in Him before the foundation of the world,** *that we should be holy and blameless before Him. In love* **He predestined us to adoption as sons through Jesus Christ to Himself,** *according to the kind intention of His will, to the praise of the glory of His grace, which He freely bestowed on us in the Beloved (Ephesians 1:3-7).*

> *Therefore if any man is in Christ, he is a new creature; the old things passed away; behold, new things have come.* **Now all these things are from God, who reconciled us to Himself through Christ,** *and gave us the ministry of reconciliation, namely, that* **God was in Christ reconciling the world to Himself, not counting their trespasses against them,** *and He has committed to us the word of*

reconciliation. Therefore, we are ambassadors for Christ, as though God were entreating through us; we beg you on behalf of Christ, be reconciled to God. **He made Him who knew no sin to be sin on our behalf, that we might become the righteousness of God in Him** (2 Corinthians 5:17-21).

Doesn't your heart rejoice that God has done it all! But then, how did you get into Christ? By accepting Him? By believing? By doing something good for Him? Absolutely not! _God put you in Christ_ in order to demonstrate His grace in justifying you:

But **by His doing you are in Christ Jesus**, who became to us wisdom from God, and righteousness and sanctification, and redemption, that, just as it is written, "Let him who boasts, boast in the Lord" (1 Corinthians 1:30-31).

When God put His people in Christ, He did so for the purpose of presenting us before Him as if we had never sinned. Isn't it amazing? With the hymn writer, we exult, "Amazing love! How can it be that Christ, my God, should die for me?" The good news is that we have peace with God, with ourselves, and with others because of what God has done, not because of what we have done. _Therefore, the basis for our justification is what God did for us in and through Jesus._ Look! What a wonderful thing God has done for us who believe in His Son:

And **through Him to reconcile all things to Himself**, having made peace through the blood of His cross; through Him, I say, whether things on earth or things in heaven. And although you were formerly alienated and hostile in mind, engaged in evil deeds, yet He has now reconciled you in His fleshly body through death, **in order to present you before Him holy and blameless and beyond reproach** (Colossians 1:20-22).

Before we move on, this is probably a good place to make an important point: when God justified us in Christ, He didn't _do_ anything _to_ us. As we learned previously in this chapter, justification is a declaration, a pronouncement of right standing.

Why is this important? Because if we do not understand the doctrine of justification, we may think our right standing before God depends on something _we do_. Most people probably think this way. A popular evangelistic presentation recommends asking people where they think they will go when they die. A common response is, "I hope

I'll go to heaven." When asked a follow-up question, "Why should God let you into His heaven when you die?" those same people usually say they believe He should allow them into heaven because they aren't bad people. They expect that God will accept them because of the good things they have done. They may cite their church membership, the day they invited Christ into their hearts, their baptism, or the fact that they give annually to the United Way.

Even those who hear frequently that salvation is not the result of their own works may still think their right standing before God came about by something *they did*—particularly, "choosing Jesus." They think God's peace came to them in the first place because they made the right choice, and that His peace remains because they continue to do good. So they tend to relate to others on the same basis. (Again, I am not saying that our right living and good works don't matter; they do. But I am talking about *how* we obtain peace with God—by *His* work and declaration, not by *ours*.) These believers do not understand that the faith they have is both a gift from God and a condition of their hearts. They believe they have responded to God in faith and obedience *out of their wills*, so they expect others to do the same. When others don't, they often feel intolerant toward them.

For instance, when someone does not respond favorably to a presentation of the gospel, they may think, "What's the matter with him? *I* chose to follow Christ when *I* heard the good news. Why doesn't *he*?" Worse yet, when someone sins against them, they have no basis for forgiveness and can be quite unmerciful toward that person. This opens the door for anger, bitterness, and unforgiveness to take root in their lives. Only when the unbeliever becomes a believer or the offending party quits hurting them and behaves as they desire are they finally at peace—and it is a very fragile peace.

Therefore, when the Holy Spirit convicts them of sin, or they are accused by the devil, or condemned by others, they usually try to assuage their guilt with some kind of "righteous" performance—for example, a streak of church attendance, Bible reading and prayer, giving, or kind deeds for others. In reality, they live in fear of not performing well enough to remain in God's favor. *What if they should die before they are able to offset their guilt?* Do you know anyone who thinks or feels this way? What a miserable way to live—or die! I hope you will share with them the true basis for a Christian's peace: God put us in Christ and made us one with Jesus in His death and resurrection, justifying us through His death and reconciling us to Himself. And He did this before He ever made the world. Our peace with God is not based on our performance! *Praise the Lord*

Then what *are* the results when we "behave badly"? The consequences of our behavior will shake us, but they will not jeopardize our salvation or annul our justification. God will continue His work of conforming us to the image of His Son (Romans 8:29).

I'll speak for myself, and perhaps you can relate to my experience. My soul needs an anchor when I am shaken by the Holy Spirit's conviction of sin. When faced with the tremendous number of my sins, and the depth of my shame because of them, and the consequences others and I suffer because of them, my heart needs a basis for hope that is unshakable. Because I know that God is righteous and just, my conscience must have an anchored response against the storms of conviction, accusations, and condemnation if I am to remain secure and peaceful. Furthermore, my soul also needs a basis for forgiving the sins of my brothers and sisters in Christ. Understanding *how* God has justified me, as well as knowing that *I am justified* before God, gives my soul the solid anchor I need for peace with God, as well as peace with my fellow man.

A Change of Heart Indicates Justification

Rejoicing in the way God has righteously dealt with our sin and reconciled us to Himself, we are ready to enjoy another aspect of salvation—the new birth by the Holy Spirit. How does God change the heart? And how do His people know that He has called them to be His children, and also has justified them? *How do we know?*

The way God has chosen to manifest His favor upon His people is seen in the work He does in their hearts. God does something no man could ever do on his own. He gives him the grace to believe in his heart in Jesus Christ alone as the only means by which he is reconciled to God. *By the power of His Word and through the Holy Spirit, God grants repentance and faith in the heart.* That is how one knows he has been called and justified by God to be His child. *This is how we know*

This work of God in the heart of man is called *regeneration, the new birth, being born again,* and *conversion.* The Scriptures speak plainly about this wonderful gracious work of God in the hearts of His people.

The work of God in our hearts. It is nothing we can do, have done, or will do. It is 100% Christ

*For **you have been born again** not of seed which is perishable but imperishable, that is, **through the living and abiding word of God** (1 Peter 1:23).*

*Jesus answered, "Truly, truly, I say to you, unless one is born of water and the Spirit, he cannot enter into the kingdom of God. That which is born of the flesh is flesh, and **that which is born of the Spirit is spirit** (John 3:5).*

God Gives Repentance

When God applies justification to the hearts of His people, He gives them repentant hearts. Repentance means "to think again" and "to have a change of mind" about God, self, life, sin, and the world around us. It comes from a combination of two Greek words: *meta* which means "to have a change," and *noia* which means "mind." Having a change of mind about God, self, and life is necessary in order to listen from the heart and seek a relationship with God based on Jesus Christ and what He has done instead of on something we have done.

When God is working repentance in one's heart, leading him to eternal life, that person comes to see that his reliance on his own good works is idolatrous and sinful. He begins to see unbiblical ideas about God or Jesus as expressions of enmity against God and the truth. Whereas previously he was content and adamant that he had earned a place of acceptance with God, he now comes to fear God's judgment and condemnation. In short, he sees his sinful condition and no longer defends or justifies it.

How does a person become a Christian? What I've described above shows that he doesn't just wake up one morning and *decide* to view life through a new paradigm. He doesn't suddenly say, "Today I shall see God in truth and turn from my wicked ways." No, this kind of transformation takes time, and it is the work of God, not originating from anything "good" in the man. *We* may see only the very end of the process, when a person makes a public declaration of faith. Or sometimes we may see much of the process, where changes are evident through a season of time before he proclaims his trust in Christ. But when we see genuine repentance, we can be sure we are witnessing a work of God in the heart of someone for whom Christ died!

You'll notice in the scriptures below that *God grants repentance* to His people:

He is the one whom God exalted to His right hand as a Prince and a Savior, **to grant repentance to Israel,** and forgiveness of sins *(Acts 5:31).*

And when they heard this, they quieted down, and glorified God, saying, "Well then, **God has granted** to the Gentiles also **the repentance that leads to life** *(Acts 11:18).*

And the Lord's bond-servant must not be quarrelsome, but be kind to all, able to teach, patient when wronged, with gentleness correcting those who are in opposition, if perhaps **God may grant them repentance leading to the knowledge of the truth** *(2 Timothy 2:24-25).*

Repentance is necessary because it leads to salvation—that is, trust in God. Paul wrote to the Corinthians:

I now rejoice, not that you were made sorrowful, but that you were made sorrowful to the point of repentance, for you were made sorrowful according to the will of God, in order that you might not suffer loss in anything through us. **For the sorrow that is according to the will of God produces a repentance without regret, leading to salvation;** but the sorrow of the world produces death. *(2 Corinthians 7:9-10).*

Another Scripture reveals the importance of the work of repentance in the heart. Paul taught that there is no salvation without it:

Or do you think lightly of the riches of His kindness and forbearance and patience, not knowing that **the kindness of God leads you to repentance?** But **because of your stubbornness and unrepentant heart you are storing up wrath for yourself** in the day of wrath and revelation of the righteous judgment of God, who will render to every man according to his deeds *(Romans 2:4-6).*

As long as the heart of a man remains unrepentant, he is under the wrath of God! But when God grants repentance to a person, that repentant heart remains throughout his life as evidence of new birth. This is what gives us assurance and hope. An important distinction to make is that God does not regenerate a man *after* he believes. The man believes *because* God has regenerated him. Repentance and faith result from the regenerative work God does in the heart.

The Bible gives us an indication of *how* this work of repentance takes place. The Holy Spirit uses the Word of God to produce repentance. That's why the teaching, preaching, and studying of God's Word is important for the unregenerate. In a biblical example of this, Peter described to the apostles and others his experience of preaching to the Gentiles in Caesarea. The Lord's word was brought back to his mind, producing a change in his thinking. As he told the story, the word of God also changed his listeners' minds:

> *And as I began to speak, the Holy Spirit fell upon them, just as He did upon us at the beginning. And* **I remembered the word of the Lord, how He used to say,** *"John baptized with water, but you shall be baptized with the Holy Spirit."* **If God therefore gave to them the same gift as He gave to us** *also after believing in the Lord Jesus Christ,* **who was I that I could stand in God's way?** *And when they heard this, they quieted down, and glorified God, saying, "Well then,* **God has granted to the Gentiles also the repentance that leads to life** *(Acts 11:13-18)."*

[margin handwritten: The word of God brings repentance.]

God Gives Faith

As God gives repentance to a person, He also produces faith in his heart. We shouldn't think, though, that one necessarily precedes the other. Regeneration precedes them both, but repentance and faith are like two sides of one coin. On one side, repentance is believing that we are *sinners* as God has said. On the other side, faith is believing that we are *forgiven* as He has promised.

The Scriptures are clear about the function of faith, as well as its origin. *Faith is the assurance of things hoped for, the conviction of things not seen (Hebrews 11:1).* We can't *hear* God's declaration of righteousness, nor can we *see* that we were baptized into Christ. So how do we know we are forgiven and seated with Christ in the heavenly places? When God works faith in the hearts of His people, He is placing within their hearts evidence that He has reconciled them through His Son. That's why faith is called an "assurance."

[margin handwritten: God gives us assurance in our hearts that we are safe in Him.]

I have mentioned before that faith is not an act of the will, but a condition of the heart. Meditate on the following scriptures and notice what they say about faith and its relation to the heart of man:

[handwritten: Faith is a heart condition.]

*Now the parable is this: the seed is the word of God. And those beside the road are those who have heard; then the devil comes and **takes away the word from their heart**, so that they may not believe and be saved (Luke 8:11-12).*

*And He said to them, "O foolish men and **slow of heart to believe** in all that the prophets have spoken!" (Luke 24:25).*

*"**Let not your heart be troubled; believe** in God, believe also in Me" (John 14:1).*

*That if you confess with your mouth Jesus as Lord, and **believe in your heart** that God raised Him from the dead, you shall be saved; **for with the heart man believes**, resulting in righteousness, and with the mouth he confesses, resulting in salvation (Romans 10:9-10).*

The gift of faith to the heart assures us that God knows us and we are His! Faith isn't something we can produce. Oh, we can try. But flesh can only give birth to flesh. Paul wrote to the Romans that those who are in the flesh cannot please God. So we're not to think of faith as a *choice* to accept Christ or a *choice* to believe certain facts. Faith is an *assurance*, a *conviction*, not a choice of the mind or an acceptance of the will. However, we also are not to think that faith has *no* impact on our wills. The will does become active when the heart believes. In fact, a faith that doesn't bear fruit in our choices is a dead faith, according to the Apostle James.

I've emboldened phrases in the following scriptures that emphasize the important aspects of faith and its origin and function:

*And after there had been much debate, Peter stood up and said to them, "Brethren, you know that in the early days **God made a choice** among you, **that** by my mouth **the Gentiles should hear** the word of the gospel **and believe. And God, who knows the heart, bore witness to them, giving them the Holy Spirit**, just as He also did to us; and He made no distinction between us and them, **cleansing their hearts by faith** (Acts 15:7-9).*

*And a certain woman named Lydia, from the city of Thyatira, a seller of purple fabrics, a worshiper of God, was listening; and **the Lord opened her heart to respond** to the things spoken by Paul (Acts 16:14).*

only God can truly know our hearts don't expect others to know your heart bc they are NOT God.

But **thanks be to God that** *though you were slaves of sin,* **you became obedient from the heart** *to that form of teaching* **to which you were committed** [the verb tense in the Greek shows that God committed them; they didn't commit themselves], *and having been freed from sin, you became slaves of righteousness (Romans 6:17-18).*

For **by grace you have been saved through faith;** *and that not of yourselves,* **it is the gift of God;** *not as a result of works, that no one should boast. For we are His workmanship, created in Christ Jesus for good works, which God prepared beforehand, that we should walk in them (Ephesians 2:8-10).*

Paul wrote to the Galatians, "Before faith came..." Where does faith come from? How does it come to us? The Scriptures reveal that the Holy Spirit uses the Word of God to produce saving faith in the heart. It is the *rhema* of Christ, the Word of God given by the Holy Spirit, that produces faith in the hearts of God's people. *Rhema* is not just the Word of God known in the head. It is the Word of God applied to the heart.

So *faith comes from hearing, and hearing by the word* [that is, "rhema"] *of Christ (Romans 10:17).*

If faith were just a simple choice—an act of the will—we could have no confidence that we were known by God or reconciled to God. We could have no objective assurance from God that He had made peace with us. But our hearts *are* assured because we know that repentance and faith are gifts from a gracious and merciful God.

Faith generated by the Holy Spirit has many functions besides demonstrating justification. The faith God gives also shields His children, protecting and keeping them until the end of their lives. Faith works God's love into the hearts of His children and remains throughout their lives as evidence and assurance of the new birth. Enjoy the hope the following verses about faith bring:

In addition to all, taking up the **shield of faith** *with which you will be able to extinguish all the flaming missiles of the evil one... (Ephesians 6:16).*

To obtain an inheritance which is imperishable and undefiled and will not fade away, reserved in heaven for you, who **are protected by the power of God through faith** *for a salvation ready to be revealed in the last time (1 Peter 1:4-5).*

For in Christ Jesus neither circumcision nor uncircumcision **means anything, but faith working through love** *(Galatians 5:6).*

Justification Is by Faith

Doesn't God require that we repent and believe to be saved? Yes, but the good news is that God works in our hearts, both granting us the repentance and creating the faith that He requires! Isn't that amazing? The very thing God requires of us for salvation, He supplies!

And **without faith it is impossible to please Him,** *for he who comes to God must believe that He is, and that He is a rewarder of those who seek Him (Hebrews 11:6).*

For in it [that is, the gospel] the righteousness of God is revealed from faith to faith; as it is written, **"But the righteous man shall live by faith"** *(Romans 1:17).* [Literally in the Greek, "But the righteous by faith shall live."]

God justifies His people on the basis of the repentance and faith in Christ that He produces in their hearts. He counts that faith that He gives us as our own. He also assigns the righteousness of Christ to us, and then counts that righteousness as our own. So salvation is not based upon anything we do, but entirely upon God's gracious work through His Son and His powerful work of regeneration by His Spirit. This is why we say we are saved by grace.

But to the one who does not work, but believes in Him who justifies the ungodly, his faith is reckoned as righteousness (Romans 4:5).

Therefore having been justified by faith, we have peace with God through our Lord Jesus Christ, through whom also we have obtained our introduction by faith into this grace in which we stand; and we exult in hope of the glory of God (Romans 5:1-2).

Repentance and Faith Constitute the Call of God

A popular promise from God's Word, often quoted among Christians, is part of the chain of works God does to accomplish our salvation, which Paul described in Romans 8. It is verse 28, *"And we know that God causes all things to work together for good to those* who love God, to those who are called according to His purpose." What does it mean to be "called of God?" How can you know that God has called you? I have great news for you! The call of God consists of His gifts of repentance and faith. He gives these gifts to those whom He predestined to glorify His grace through their lives. Drink in the wonder of God's grace in these scriptures:

> For whom He foreknew, He also predestined to become conformed to the image of His Son, that He might be the first-born among many brethren; and whom He predestined, **these He also called**; and whom He called, these He also justified; and whom He justified, these He also glorified. What then shall we say to these things? If God is for us, who is against us? (Romans 8:29-31).

> What if God, although willing to demonstrate His wrath and to make His power known, endured with much patience vessels of wrath prepared for destruction? And He did so in order that He might make known the riches of His glory upon vessels of mercy, which He prepared beforehand for glory, **even us, whom He also called,** not from among Jews only, but also from among Gentiles (Romans 9:22-24).

> I pray that the eyes of your heart may be enlightened, so **that you may know what is the hope of His calling,** what are the riches of the glory of His inheritance in the saints (Ephesians 1:18).

Is God's Call Irresistible?

Often people have asked me if someone can resist the call of God. I think they usually are referring to the call of the preacher instead of the call of God. Although it is possible—in fact, inevitable—that the unregenerate man will resist and even defy the gospel offer made by a minister, it is impossible to resist the call of *God*.

When God calls someone to Him and intends to separate him from this world and give him eternal life, it is a powerful work. The Scriptures reveal that such a call has been decreed from all eternity. That's why Paul prayed that the Ephesians might understand *the hope of their calling*:

> The Lord says to my Lord: "Sit at My right hand, until I make Thine enemies a footstool for Thy feet. The Lord will stretch forth

Thy strong scepter from Zion, saying, Rule in the midst of Thine enemies." **Thy people will volunteer freely in the day of Thy power;** *in holy array, from the womb of the dawn, Thy youth are to Thee as the dew (Psalm 110:1-3).*

Who has saved us, and called us with a holy calling, *not according to our works,* **but according to His own purpose and grace** *which was granted us in Christ Jesus from all eternity (2 Timothy 1:9).*

In fact, Jesus said that no one *can* come to God unless the Father *draws* him to Himself.

"No one can come to Me, unless the Father who sent Me draws him; *and I will raise him up on the last day" (John 6:44-45).*

The word "draws" is from the Greek word *helkuo,* which means "to drag." It is the same word used in John 21:11-12:

Simon Peter went up, **and drew the net to land, full of large fish, a hundred and fifty-three;** *and although there were so many, the net was not torn.*

Dragging a loaded fishnet was no easy task. In the same way, it takes the power of God to "drag" unbelievers from their sin and selfishness into the light of His glorious grace. Remember that we were "dead in our trespasses and sins" (Ephesians 2:1), and dead men cannot simply decide to live for God. It isn't until He shows us "the day of His power" that we "volunteer freely" to come to Him. The drawing action of God—*helkuo* in the Greek—is certainly an overpowering force on the hearts of His elect. After all, God is sovereign, and we are not. Yet God is *not* dragging us into the Kingdom *against our wills*. Rather, the regenerative work of the Holy Spirit on our hearts makes us *willing* to believe, and as a result, we *choose* to believe. Our salvation is all of His grace, and all the glory goes to Him.

That "day of His power" is when we hear the *particular* and *specific* call of God unto salvation. It is not the same as the *general* and *universal* gospel call to all men, which Jesus described in the Parable of the Marriage Feast when He said, "For many are called, but few are chosen" (Matthew 22:14). The Apostle Paul clearly declared the general gospel call in his second letter to the Corinthians:

Or what agreement has the temple of God with idols? For we are the temple of the living God; just as God said, "I will dwell in them and walk among them; and I will be their God, and they shall be My people. **Therefore, come out from their midst and be separate," says the Lord. "And do not touch what is unclean; and I will welcome you.** *And I will be a father to you, and you shall be sons and daughters to Me," says the Lord Almighty (2 Corinthians 6:16-18).*

But the specific call of God that results in salvation is referred to a number of times by the apostles in their letters:

I, therefore, the prisoner of the Lord, entreat you to walk in a manner worthy of **the calling with which you have been called** *(Ephesians 4:1).*

There is one body and one Spirit, just as also **you were called in one hope of your calling** *(Ephesians 4:4).*

Therefore, holy brethren, **partakers of a heavenly calling,** *consider Jesus, the Apostle and High Priest of our confession (Hebrews 3:1).*

Therefore, brethren, be all the more diligent to **make certain about His calling and choosing you;** *for as long as you practice these things, you will never stumble (2 Peter 1:10).*

Frequently the question is asked, "When were you saved?" Usually people respond with the time or day when they prayed a prayer to "accept Christ." Perhaps it *was* the day the Holy Spirit applied salvation to their hearts, but this puts the emphasis on something they did. A more accurate answer to the question is this: *I was saved at the cross when God put my sins on His Son, Jesus Christ. I am now being saved by the intercession of Jesus Christ and through the faith He has given me.*

Where does assurance come from? How does one make certain about God's calling him? The calling is confirmed by the work you know God has done in your heart. It is not confirmed by your praying a prayer to accept Jesus. Anyone can do that if he is persuaded he ought to do it. But I encourage you as Paul encouraged the Corinthians:

"Test yourselves to see if you are in the faith; examine yourselves! Or do you not recognize this about yourselves, **that Jesus Christ is in you**—*unless indeed you fail the test?" (2 Corinthians 13:5).*

examine your heart

You can test yourself by asking yourself some questions. Has God given you a heart of godly sorrow and repentance for your idolatries and sins against Himself and others? Has God washed your guilty conscience with faith in the Lord Jesus Christ? Do you see your faith working through love for God and others? Do you view the commands of God as a joy to obey instead of a burden? These are evidences of God's having called you to Himself for all eternity.

To God Be the Glory

The one who has repented and believed in Jesus Christ has every reason to lift his or her heart in praise and worship to God for the grace received. We rejoice that salvation began in eternity with God, graciously included us in the life, death, and resurrection of Jesus, and powerfully wrought repentance and faith in our hearts through the work of the Holy Spirit and His Word, in order that we might be reconciled and justified in Jesus. Our hearts are assured by the work of God, not by our own works or decisions. All the glory goes to God in our salvation.

But what did God save you *for*? According to most gospel presentations, you might conclude that the goal of salvation is to go to heaven when you die. Many think of eternal life as a future hope. However, when you look at Jesus' ministry and message, you'll discover something quite different. The Kingdom of Heaven isn't a place to go *after* this life; it is a present reality to be entered into *during* this life. Does this surprise you? I hope as you read the next chapter, you'll be astounded by the simple, profound gospel of our Lord when He came to earth. His gospel is a call to rethink the way we live our lives. The remainder of this book addresses this call and how our response to it can anchor our souls in Christ and draw others into His discipleship.

Part 3

Applying Doctrine to Life

discipleship: Jesus is relational

Twenty-six

Rethink the Way You Live Your Life

Can you think of an instance when Jesus presented to anyone an evangelistic call to accept Him and be saved? It might surprise you to discover Jesus never led anyone to invite Him into his or her heart. His earthly ministry seldom focused on how to be saved. Although He did came to "save His people from their sins" (Matthew 1:21), His primary focus and message was about *discipleship*. The Gospel of Matthew reveals the theme of discipleship in the Kingdom of heaven as the way leading to eternal life. I would like for you to consider the importance of Jesus' message, "Repent, for the kingdom of heaven is at hand" (Matthew 4:17) as a basis for having an unshakable faith.

Rethink Who Teaches You About Life

Who is your teacher? That's how Dallas Willard introduces the eighth chapter of his book, *The Divine Conspiracy.* Who teaches you? Whose disciple are you? Please don't answer the questions too quickly. Honestly consider whose disciple you are. One thing is for sure. You are someone's disciple. You learned how to live from somebody else. There are no exceptions to this rule.

In our western culture, it's difficult to grasp this idea because we prefer to think we are our "own persons." We like to think we make up our own minds, but we think that way about ourselves because *we all learned to live from someone.*

we are not truly independent

someone has tutored us to do so. Today, we consider such independent thinking part of being "modern" or "politically correct." Willard writes, "Probably you are disciples of several 'somebodies,' and it is very likely they shaped you in ways far from what is best for you, or even coherent."[30] We all are students of a few crucial people, living and dead, who have been there in crucial times and periods to form our standard responses in thought, feeling, and action. The good thing about this is that the process is ongoing and is to some extent self-correcting.

We Are All Disciples

Originally we were disciples of our parents or family members. When we entered into life, we knew absolutely nothing about existing and surviving in this new realm. From the early days of our lives, we watched our parents, listened to them, and did what they did. When they smiled, we smiled. When they cooed, we cooed. A laugh from them stimulated a parent-thrilling laugh from us. Most of us took our cues about life from them until we were marched off to school.

a story about Mom.

I remember one of the milestones of life in our daughter Abby's childhood—when she began learning from someone other than her parents. After preschool one day we asked Abby what she had learned. She told us Mrs. Johnson taught her that squirrels make trees. I knew Mrs. Johnson, and I knew she wouldn't teach such a thing. Therefore, I confidently corrected Abby by saying something like, "Squirrels don't make trees, Abby. God makes trees, and He uses squirrels in the process." In tears, she responded with certainty that Mrs. Johnson did indeed say squirrels make trees. I could tell it would not be in the best interest of our relationship for me to insist she had heard the wrong thing. So I talked with Mrs. Johnson the next day before school (we both taught at the same Christian school) and asked her if she might clarify the issue for us. That afternoon, I again asked Abby about what she had learned. She exclaimed that I was right! Mrs. Johnson said God makes trees and He uses squirrels to do it. At that point it was painfully clear that I had been displaced as the primary disciple-maker of my preschool daughter. She had become a disciple of Mrs. Johnson! Her experience was like most of ours, as we graduate from learning from our parents to learning from our teachers at school.

Almost simultaneously we become disciples of our playmates or peers until our late teens. Along with a herd of peers we learn from sports figures, movie stars, musicians, and media personalities. Our culture uses these people to set in stone the major thrusts of our self-chosen identities. Then in college we may open our minds to numerous people, but in a different way. These include some very glamorous and powerful people, like instructors and academic professors, but many are artists, musicians, writers, and professionals. These communicate strong impressions of how life is to be lived—what life is all about. *Try to recognize who your teachers have been*

One of the most enlightening events in life is when we recognize who our teachers have been. It can be convicting and sometimes hard to acknowledge, but if the exercise is honest, it can be life changing.

I hope reading this chapter will be a life-changing exercise, because it is my goal to exhort you to rethink the way you live your life. I would like to look at some scriptures that will make us rethink the way we live, just like they made the first hearers rethink their lives and prepare them for an eternal relationship with God.

God Sends a Forerunner

> From that time Jesus began to preach and say, "Repent, for the kingdom of heaven is at hand" (Matthew 4:17).

It is interesting to note that Jesus' message was the same as John the Baptist's message. Matthew wrote,

> "Now in those days John the Baptist came, preaching in the wilderness of Judea, saying, 'Repent, for the kingdom of heaven is at hand'" (Matthew 3:1-2).

John's ministry was one of preparation for the Lord Jesus' coming. John was the forerunner preparing the way of the Lord. Luke records the angel's remarks about John to his father:

> "It is he who will go as a forerunner before Him in the spirit and power of Elijah, 'to turn the hearts of the fathers back to the children, and the disobedient to the attitude of the righteous, so as to make ready a people prepared for the Lord'" (Luke 1:17).

It was the disciples of John who first recognized the Lord Jesus as the Savior of the world and became His first disciples (John 1:37).

In the same way, Jesus' ministry was a forerunner to the ministry of the Holy Spirit. It is not the Son who applies salvation to men's hearts, but the Holy Spirit. This explains many of Jesus' puzzling statements such as Matthew 16:20:

> *Then He warned the disciples that they should tell no one that*
> *He was the Christ.*

Jesus was jealous for the work of the Spirit whom He and the Father were going to send to do the work of converting the elect of God and manifesting His life in them once He went to be with His Father. As a faithful forerunner, Jesus prepared the way for the Holy Spirit by calling people to discipleship in the Kingdom of heaven, and then with the Father, sent the Holy Spirit as He promised.

Rethinking Is a Preparatory Function

We learned in the last chapter that *repent* is the English form of a Greek word meaning, "to have a change of mind, to rethink."[31] I think Jesus' life and teaching made everyone rethink. Some became disciples and others became persecutors. No one could stay the same. Encountering Jesus demanded a change of thinking. It still does today.

C.S. Lewis expressed great insight when he wrote about Jesus,

> We may note in passing that He was never regarded as a mere moral teacher. He did not produce that effect on any of the people who actually met him. He produced mainly three effects—Hatred—Terror—Adoration. There was no trace of people expressing mild approval.[32]

So what is the significance of Jesus' statement and command, "Repent, for the kingdom of heaven is at hand"? Why should a person rethink the way he lives his life? Because *NOW*—in the person of *Jesus Christ*—the power of the *"kingdom of the heavens"* (as the Greek words are translated literally) is being manifested on earth.

What Is "the Kingdom of the Heavens"?

Before we look more deeply at that idea, I'd like to explore this unusual phrase, "the kingdom of the heavens." Jesus preached that this kingdom *is near*. What was He talking about? When Jesus spoke of "the kingdom of (the) heaven(s)," what did this phrase mean to His first listeners? And what should it mean to us? Also, is there a difference between "the kingdom of heaven" and "the kingdom of God"? Most theologians think the two phrases are synonymous. "The kingdom of heaven" is a phrase occurring thirty-two times in Matthew but never in any other book of the New Testament. On the other hand, "the kingdom of God" occurs only five times in Matthew, yet it is the *only* phrase used in the rest of the New Testament.[33]

We can't be sure why Matthew favored "the kingdom of the heavens." However, we can almost be certain that Jesus' first listeners thought of God's *presence* and *power*. Dallas Willard defined the *kingdom of God* as "the range of His effective will, w[here what He wants] done."[34] So perhaps when Matthew chos[e the kingdom of] God, he was referring to *the fact* that God [rules all.] It's another way of communicating that G[od rules over] nature and the events of men.

Clarifying the two phrases further, W[illard said] *kingdom of the heavens* refers to "the air o[r heavens where] God's will reigns. Included are the present heavens (the environment in which we live), the mid-heavens (the realm of the angels), and the third heaven (of which Paul spoke in 2 Corinthians 12:2). We don't know much about these realms except of Jesus' supremacy over them."[35] So when Matthew chose the phrase *the kingdom of the heavens,* he may have been highlighting not *the fact* of God's determining will but God's *very near presence* where His will was being manifested.

Practically, the difference between the two phrases is minimal, but the impact on us of the command, "Repent, for the kingdom of the heavens is at hand," should be significant. Jesus wanted His hearers to think again about God's authority over all of creation, but more importantly, He wanted to alert them to the manifestation of God's *presence* and *power* in their lives.

God Isn't Far Away

One important thing about Jesus' statement is this: God is not located *only* somewhere out beyond the stars in a place called heaven. He is present *in the space surrounding us* and—even more importantly for those who have believed in Jesus Christ—He is *in us!* Many people unwittingly have been taught to believe that God's throne is in one place somewhere outside of the physical universe where He watches everything happening on earth.

Furthermore, most people think of heaven *only* as the place to which they will go when they die. As I mentioned in the last chapter, this notion is encouraged by the questions asked in many evangelistic presentations.

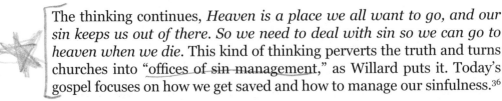

The thinking continues, *Heaven is a place we all want to go, and our sin keeps us out of there. So we need to deal with sin so we can go to heaven when we die.* This kind of thinking perverts the truth and turns churches into "offices of sin management," as Willard puts it. Today's gospel focuses on how we get saved and how to manage our sinfulness.[36]

However, Jesus' message was very different. He didn't come offering a free trip to heaven if we will accept Him and be saved from our sin. He came offering eternal life in the kingdom of the heavens—*right now!* Jesus' statement should cause us to rethink the way we live in light of this truth: God isn't in a throne room way out past the moon waiting for us to arrive after our deaths. The kingdom of heaven is *as near as the space around us, as well as reaching to the furthest conceivable point of the universe.* God is VERY near, and Jesus' gospel declares that the kingdom of heaven is NOW accessible.

One Enters the Kingdom of the Heavens *Now*

So how near is the kingdom of the heavens, and when do we enter it? The scriptures below clearly teach that the kingdom of heaven/God is being manifested in the hearts of men—while we are alive—before we die. The tenses of the verbs and the references to our *present state* in relationship to the kingdom of heaven should cause us to rethink the way we live. Please carefully consider the following verses:

> *Blessed are the poor in spirit, for theirs **is** the kingdom of heaven (Matthew 5:3).*

> *Blessed are those who have been persecuted for the sake of righteousness, for theirs **is** the kingdom of heaven (Matthew 5:10).*

> *Whoever then **annuls** one of the least of these commandments, **and so teaches others** [there will be no need to annul or teach the commandments in the future eternal state], shall be called least in the kingdom of heaven; but **whoever keeps and teaches them**, he shall be called great in the kingdom of heaven (Matthew 5:19).*

> *And He answered and said to them, "To you it **has been granted** [not will be granted] to know the mysteries of the kingdom of heaven, but to them it has not been granted" (Matthew 13:11).*

> And He said to them, "Therefore every scribe who **has become a disciple of the kingdom of heaven** is like a head of a household, who brings forth out of his treasure things new and old" (Matthew 13:52).

> For our citizenship **is** in heaven, *from which* also we eagerly wait for a Savior, the Lord Jesus Christ (Philippians 3:20).

Each of the verses above speaks of the kingdom of the heavens as something one experiences *in this life.* Are you surprised? It is true that when believers die, they will be with Jesus in heaven; however, we should not think of our being in the kingdom of heaven only as a future experience. The kingdom of heaven is *now.* We may know the mysteries of the kingdom of heaven *now.* We are disciples of the kingdom *now.* We are citizens—residents—of heaven *now.*

Not only do we need to think again about *when* we enter the kingdom of heaven, but also it is wise to think again about *where it is located.*

The Kingdom of the Heavens Around Us

We should not be surprised to discover the nearness of God's presence because many verses clearly teach this truth. We also should not fail to recognize the kingdom of heaven as THE main theme of Jesus' Sermon on the Mount, recorded by Matthew. Jesus wanted His disciples to live in light of the reality of the Father's presence.

> But you, when you pray, go into your inner room, and when you have shut your door, pray to your Father who is in secret, and your Father who sees in secret will repay you (Matthew 6:6).

> Pray, then, in this way: "Our Father who art in heaven, hallowed be Thy name" (Matthew 6:9).

> But seek first His kingdom [in this life] and His righteousness [in this life]; and all these things shall be added to you [in this life] (Matthew 6:33).

The Father in heaven is so near to us that He hears our secret prayers. The verses above should cause us to think of God as near, loving, and intimately acquainted with us.

Stephen and Paul obviously testified of the kingdom of heaven being *at hand,* rather than somewhere out beyond space. Just before Stephen was stoned to death, he quoted Isaiah 66, verse 1:

"Heaven is My throne, and earth is the footstool of My feet; what kind of house will you build for Me?" says the Lord; "Or what place is there for My repose?" (Acts 7:49).

I wonder if I am the only one who misread this verse. Without thinking much about it, I somehow assumed God was saying that His throne is *in* heaven. After all, if the earth is God's footstool, then His throne must be farther away, right? Hence, I thought that God is far away from earth. But if we look carefully, we see He was saying *the entire heaven—all the space and sky surrounding us—is His throne!* He rules in the space around us. Furthermore, if the entire earth is His footstool, then there is no place we can go on the earth where His feet— representing His presence and His dominion—are not!

What is the significance of these words to unbelievers? The Judge of all our actions and words is not watching and listening from some far-out place in the universe. His feet are right here with us, and He is taking every word and deed into account so He can judge rightly when the Judgment Day arrives. Paul communicated this same message to the Athenians:

*The God who made the world and all things in it, since He is Lord of heaven and earth, does not dwell in temples made with hands; neither is He served by human hands, as though He needed anything, since He Himself gives to all life and breath and all things; and He made from one, every nation of mankind to live on all the face of the earth, having determined their appointed times, and the boundaries of their habitation, that they should seek God, **if perhaps they might grope for Him and find Him, though He is not far** from each one of us; in Him we live and move and exist, as even some of your own poets have said, "For we also are His offspring" (Acts 17:24-28).*

Why did Paul think it was important to inform his audience that God is as close as the air they breathe, so close that they might even "reach out and touch Him"? He was preparing the way for faith in the Lord Jesus to come to them after they had thought again about the nearness of the kingdom of the heavens and God's presence. Until a person becomes convinced of God's nearness, he cannot come to a saving faith in Christ. It is not the other way around—that we come to saving faith and then become disciples. Being aware that God is watching, listening, and recording every word and action is what brings the fear of the Lord into the heart. The fear of the Lord is the *beginning* of wisdom, leading one to rethink his relationship with God in light of what God has seen and heard. Are you beginning to rethink some things?

The Kingdom of the Heavens Has Been Seen

The kingdom of the heavens is visible when God opens our eyes to see it. God has provided eyewitnesses to its reality and nearness. Jesus promised Nathaniel he would "see the heavens opened, and the angels of God ascending and descending on the Son of Man" (John 1:51). We may safely assume Nathaniel did see what Jesus promised, and it was very near!

Stephen also saw the nearness of the kingdom of the heavens moments before he was driven out of Jerusalem and stoned. Maybe Paul learned about the nearness of the kingdom from Stephen's testimony as those who were stoning Stephen laid their cloaks at Paul's feet. Luke reported,

> *Now when they heard this, they were cut to the quick, and they began gnashing their teeth at him. But being full of the Holy Spirit, **he gazed intently into heaven and saw the glory of God**, and Jesus standing at the right hand of God; and he said, "Behold, **I see the heavens opened up** and the Son of Man standing at the right hand of God" (Acts 7:54-56).*

Do you think Stephen had superhuman eyesight enabling him to peer thousands of miles into space into the room where God is enthroned with Jesus at His right hand? That almost sounds silly, doesn't it? Yet that seems to be how many Christians think about the kingdom of heaven. The scriptural evidence, however, seems to indicate instead that God simply pulled aside the curtain on the heavens in the space surrounding Stephen, and there He was! Jesus stood to receive His faithful martyr. For a moment, Stephen saw both the physical world and the spiritual realm. One would think from Stephen's testimony that the two realms are interrelated.

Another story, found in 2 Kings 6:15-17, illustrates this idea well:

> *Now when the attendant of the man of God had risen early and gone out, behold, an army with horses and chariots was circling the city. And his servant said to him, "Alas, my master! What shall we do?" So he answered, "Do not fear, for those who are with us are more than those who are with them." Then*

*Elisha prayed and said, **"O LORD, I pray, open his eyes that he may see."** And **the LORD opened the servant's eyes and he saw;** and behold, the mountain was full of horses and chariots of fire all around Elisha.*

Elisha prayed for his servant's eyes to be opened to see the forces of God in the heavenlies surrounding them. The veil was removed from his attendant's eyes, and the kingdom of heaven was revealed.

In the book of Acts, Luke's record of Jesus' ascension is enlightening if we can get past our preconceived ideas. Saying that the kingdom of heaven is actually present around us doesn't mean that Jesus didn't *go up* or *ascend* into heaven. He certainly did go up, for we're told in the following passage that He was *lifted up*, indicating elevation from the earth. And we are admonished by the Apostle Paul to think on things *above, where Christ is seated* (Colossians 3:1-2). To the Ephesians, Paul wrote that Jesus "ascended far above all the heavens" (Ephesians 4:10). Furthermore, the writer of Hebrews asserts that Jesus "passed through the heavens" (Hebrews 4:14).

So where did Jesus go when He ascended into heaven or through the heavens? For us three-dimensional thinkers this is difficult for us to comprehend, isn't it? Perhaps it is best for us to conclude that He passed through an invisible veil into the eternal Holy of Holies and is hidden from our sight just beyond the veil. It seems to me that both truths are communicated. He is always present, though hidden from our sight, and He is also exalted above all the heavens at the right hand of the Father.

But I've discovered that many people think His ascension took Him *far away*—and they live like it! We learn through a careful reading of His ascension that He disappeared in a cloud. But for some reason I always pictured that event as Jesus ascending up into the cloud and, like a helium balloon, eventually coming out of the top of the cloud. I imagined the disciples looking on as He became smaller and smaller in their view until He disappeared into heaven, taking His seat on the throne of God somewhere out past the moon. I've discovered from talking with others that I am not the only one who had such a thought. Read carefully the following account. Perhaps the cloud functioned as a cover for His passing through the hidden veil into the presence of His Father. Consider my comments in brackets.

And after He had said these things, He was lifted up while they were looking on, and a cloud received Him out of their sight. [Jesus visually ascended no further than the cloud.]

And as they were gazing intently into the sky while He was departing, behold, two men in white clothing stood beside them; [Where did these two come from? Or were they always there but concealed by the ever-present veil?] *and they also said, "Men of Galilee, why do you stand looking into the sky? This Jesus, who has been taken up from you into heaven, will come in just the same way as you have watched Him go into heaven" (Acts 1:9-11).*

What effect do these things have on you? Do they make you rethink the way you are living your life? They should! The nearness of the kingdom of heaven should make us think again. It teaches us and prepares us for the good news of the gospel, does it not? Rethink the way you live your life, for God reigns in this life over all creation. The manifestation of the presence and power of God (the kingdom of the heavens) is not a figment of someone's imagination, nor is it a religious myth. It is history! Only two or three witnesses are required to verify an event as fact in a court of law. Many more than that testified in the Scriptures to the reality and nearness of the kingdom of the heavens where Jesus reigns. Since we know the kingdom is at hand—it is *here* and *now*, not *far off* and *in the future*—we should also think again about where Jesus is establishing His kingdom.

Jesus Didn't Stay Behind the Veil!

Not only do we need to be aware of God's power and presence manifested in the world around us, but a more amazing truth should capture our hearts: *The kingdom of God is now revealed in the hearts of men as God, the Father, and Jesus, the Son, give the Holy Spirit to them.* Jesus' message declared that God's rule was here—in and through His presence and work. The work of our Lord in performing righteousness on behalf of His people, in atoning for their sin, and in conquering the devil, sin, and death through His resurrection *is the kingdom of heaven at hand*!

Just before Jesus was crucified, He told His disciples clearly what was about to happen: Because He was going to the Father (behind the veil where we can't see Him), they would have the Holy Spirit, the Comforter, sent to them. In fact, when the Holy Spirit came to them, they would then know that He was in the Father and *also in them*. Jesus assured them, He would not leave them alone, but would come to them in the third person of the Trinity, the Holy Spirit.

I will not leave you as orphans. I will come to you. After a little while the world will no longer see Me, but you will see Me; because I live, you will live also. In that day you will know that I am in My Father, and you in Me, and I in you (John 14:18-20).

The Kingdom of Heaven Is Within You!

If you profess to believe in Jesus Christ, do you realize the wonderful, awesome, Jesus-manifesting, kingdom-revealing power of the Holy Spirit within you? Not only is God's presence as near as the air we breathe and His Son enthroned in the heavens, but Jesus is also manifesting the kingdom of God in the hearts of His people through the power of the Holy Spirit. Wherever Jesus goes and works—through you—the kingdom of heaven/God *is at hand.*

Often Jesus taught the multitudes and His disciples the way to enter the kingdom of heaven in this life: *Follow Him, and listen to and act on His words.* This was the message our Lord repeated over and over. The call to follow, listen to, and obey Him is *not* the call to salvation but to discipleship. Jesus was *preparing hearts* to be dwelling places for the Holy Spirit. This call cannot have been to salvation because if it were, then Jesus would have been teaching salvation by works rather than by grace. But the Scriptures are clear and abundant: Salvation is by grace through faith, not of works, lest any man should boast.

Have you ever noticed that Jesus didn't offer what we usually consider to be an evangelistic message about salvation? Why didn't He? And why *did* Jesus call people to follow Him and obey His teaching? Why did He come preaching, "Rethink the way you live your life, for the kingdom of heaven is at hand"? Jesus' ministry was *preparatory* for the ministry of the Holy Spirit. His teaching prepared people for the work of the Holy Spirit, through whom they would know and fellowship with the Father and the Son. Jesus was and is the *way* to the Father in the kingdom of the heavens—here and now—and He is the *truth* in the kingdom of the heavens—here and now—and He is the *life* in the kingdom of the heavens—here and now!

Why do I emphasize the kingdom of the heavens here and now? Because Jesus said some very important things about the here and now, but we have been trained to think that when He said them, He had in mind salvation and going to heaven after we die. Consider with me some examples of these very popular but misunderstood verses.

Jesus Gives Hope for the Present Life

And Jesus said to him, "I am the way and the truth and the life.
No man comes to the Father, but through Me" (John 14:6).

This verse is often used evangelistically to direct unbelievers to think about going to heaven when they die. But the context of this verse is Jesus' going to the Father and sending the Holy Spirit—not only so believers can go to heaven when they die, but also to live in the hearts of believers so that they can know the Father *NOW*, in this life! This chapter is filled with encouragement about how the disciples were to live once Jesus was no longer with them in bodily form. After assuring them of His preparing a place for them with the Father, He instructed them to believe in God and in Himself. He encouraged them that they would do greater works than He had done (perhaps preaching sermons that would result in the genuine salvation of thousands!). He promised them great answers to believing prayer. He reminded them of the importance of obedience for those who love Him. He assured them that His Father would send them His Holy Spirit to teach them and help them remember what He had taught them. He promised He would come to them and disclose Himself to them, and they would behold Him and know Him and live in Him. He comforted them with peace and told them not to be fearful. All of these things portray the earthly lives of believers.

In Jesus' present discourse, recorded in John 14 and 15, Jesus referred 14 times to their abiding in, keeping, remembering, or receiving His words (14:10, 15, 21, 23, 25, 26, 15:3, 7, 10, 12, 14, 15, 17, 20). Furthermore, Jesus repeated the phrase of verse one in verse 27, "Do not let your heart be troubled" after telling them four times to abide in His word. Abiding was an expression of their love for Him and the means by which He and the Father would commune with them. Jesus intended for all these things to give hope to His disciples in this life.

He and the Father would send the Holy Spirit to help them remember what Jesus had taught them. These words would become dwelling places for them in the midst of trial and tribulation—places where they could abide and enter into fellowship with Him and the Father. Through the Spirit's ministry, the disciples would be able to know, remember, understand, and obey what Jesus said. Although these words should be taken as words of encouragement primarily to the disciples, they are also comforting truths for all believers as well. With this idea in mind, John Chapter 14 explodes with hope for the present. Not only do we have the hope of future dwelling with the Father and the Son in heaven, but we also have the present comfort of fellowship with the Father and Son through the ministry of the Holy Spirit in times of trouble here on earth.

Jesus was clearly preparing His disciples for the ministry of the Holy Spirit, through whom they would know the Father and Himself. Obeying Jesus' words enabled them to *experience* eternal life. We usually think of eternal life as beginning after we die. However, in a time of prayer to His Father, Jesus defined eternal life as something we experience *now*. He prayed, *"This **is** eternal life, that they may know You, the only true God, and Jesus Christ whom You have sent"* (John 17:3). Do you see anything future in this statement? Does Jesus have the heaven-when-you-die idea in mind? It surely entails that, but this is clearly a present, in-this-life reality.

In His closing appeal in the Sermon on the Mount, Jesus did not call His disciples to accept Him so they could be saved, nor did He give an evangelistic altar call. Grasp what He said about entrance into the kingdom of heaven and why it is imperative that one enters now, in this life:

> **Enter [the kingdom of heaven] *by the narrow gate;*** *for the gate is wide, and the way is broad that leads to destruction, and many are those who enter by it. For the gate is small, and **the way is narrow that leads to life**, and few are those who find it (Matthew 7:13-14).*

To enter into the kingdom of heaven is to enter into the way leading to salvation and eternal life. What are the "narrow gate" and the "narrow way"?

> *Not everyone who says to Me, "Lord, Lord," will enter the kingdom of heaven* [not "go to heaven when they die" but "enter into the kingdom of heaven"—now, in this life]; *but he who does the will of My Father who is in heaven.* [If Jesus were teaching here about salvation and how to obtain eternal life, then we must conclude that He taught salvation by works. However, nothing in the context leads us to think He's talking about how to be saved.] *Many will say to Me on that day* [the Day of Judgment], *"Lord, Lord, did we not prophesy in Your name, and in Your name cast out demons, and in Your name perform many miracles?"*
>
> *And then I will declare to them, "I never knew you* [you refused to relate to Me on earth as being the way into the kingdom of

heaven]*; depart from Me, you who practice lawlessness."* [You refused to rethink the way you live your lives and let Me teach you how to live.] don't be so proud and stuck for your way of life so that you are not teachable. The most rewarding

Therefore everyone who hears these words of Mine, and acts upon them [this is the narrow gate and narrow way]*, may be compared to a wise man, who built his house upon the rock (Matthew 7:21-24).* way is often the hardest

The entrance into the kingdom of heaven is narrow. Entrance into the kingdom of the heavens for those listening to Jesus amounted to following Jesus' teaching. Jesus was not saying that salvation is by works. Instead, He was pointing His listeners to the way that *leads* to salvation—discipleship *now*. As a person contemplated the way he lived his life in light of Jesus' teaching, he found himself being taught about relationship with God. His heart was prepared for the work of the Holy Spirit as he lived in God's presence—the kingdom of heaven. As you draw Near to Him, faith grows your deeper

For people in our day, Jesus' words written in the New Testament call them to discipleship and to rethink how they live their lives. As they live in the light of God's nearness, their faith in His words grows. They discover that Jesus' words are true and that He is the anchor for their souls, both now and for eternity. As faith comes to them, they experience first-hand the coming of the kingdom of God. Jesus comes to live in them in the God is person and power of the Holy Spirit! They then realize that listening to with us and obeying God's Word and the Holy Spirit is the same to them as it was for those first disciples who listened to and obeyed Jesus Christ.

If we formerly thought that "accepting Jesus" is what leads to salvation, but now we see that salvation comes through being a disciple of Jesus Christ through the indwelling of the Holy Spirit, then what else should we think about again?

We Are to Be Making Disciples of the Kingdom of Heaven

As you rethink the way you are living in light of the truth you have learned, you may be asking, "What are we to be doing for the kingdom?" The popular answer is: *We are to be building the church for the kingdom.* Again, you may be asking, "How is the church to be built today?" And the popular answer is: *By evangelizing the nations and inviting them to accept Jesus into their hearts, we are building His church.* Without realizing it, one who answers the questions this way betrays a fundamental misunderstanding of two facts:

Teach and Train. Build relationships of (long term) discipleship

1. Jesus did not call His disciples to evangelize and ask people to accept Jesus into their hearts through a prayer of invitation. He called them to make disciples and teach them to enter the kingdom of heaven.

2. We cannot build God's church. Only He can (Matthew 16:15-20). He told *us* that we should be making disciples of the kingdom of the heavens.

Before you slam the book down and cry, "Heretic!" please hear me out. I'm not saying that evangelism isn't important. It is. I'm suggesting that most people have the proverbial cart before the horse. I hope you'll read what is often called The Great Commission and see it with a new set of eyes. Remember: The theme of the Gospel of Matthew is *the kingdom of heaven.*

> *And Jesus came up and spoke to them, saying, "All authority has been given to Me in heaven and on earth. Go therefore and* **make disciples** *of all the nations, baptizing them in the name of the Father and the Son and the Holy Spirit,* **teaching them to observe all that I commanded you;** *and lo, I am with you always, even to the end of the age" (Matthew 28:19-20).*

This commandment is the summary of Matthew's whole gospel. Remember, Matthew has used the phrase "the kingdom of the heavens" thirty-two times in this book. Jesus had called forth His own disciples, and now He was telling them to go and make other disciples. Looking at the context of the whole book, it is evident that here at the end, when Jesus told them to go and make disciples, they were to place their confidence in Jesus' presence and power. The person who recognizes Jesus' presence and authority in heaven and earth (the kingdom of heaven) is one who will be saved by the grace of God through faith in Christ. He's also one who will eventually make disciples because He knows of Jesus' presence in him.

Jesus' direction to His disciples was not to go and evangelize and lead people to accept Jesus as Savior; rather, they were to carry on the ministry they had observed for three years. They were to teach about the nearness of the kingdom and call for repentance and faith. Additionally, the ministry of the Holy Spirit was important. I am not saying they were *not* to evangelize, but I think their understanding of evangelism after the coming of the Holy Spirit at Pentecost *was giving the good news about the nearness of the kingdom of heaven in the person of Jesus Christ who manifests Himself in the person and power of the Holy Spirit.*

Jesus taught the disciples that salvation occurs through the process of discipleship. Once a person enters the kingdom of heaven and begins to relate to the Father, the Father teaches him and brings him to Christ through faith.

> *"No one can come to Me unless the Father who sent Me draws him; and I will raise him up on the last day. "It is written in the prophets, '**And they shall all be taught of God**.' Everyone who has heard and learned from the Father comes to Me"* (John 6:44-45).

We should rethink our gospel and our methods of evangelism. We have been thinking this: *Come to Jesus to get your sins managed.* We should be thinking: *The kingdom of heaven is right here and now, and I need to help people understand that. I need to share with them what Jesus said and encourage them to follow Him. As they seek to know what Jesus taught, God will teach them, and then by the power of God they will be born again and receive the promise of the Father and the Son. Once they are born again, disciples of Jesus should walk in the fullness and power of the Holy Spirit who indwells them.*

The modern church has misunderstood the kingdom of heaven, believing it to be *only the place Christians go after they die*. With its extreme emphasis on decision-based evangelism, and its lack of emphasis on living to please the Lord (Ephesians 5:10), the church's message to the world has become distorted. Believers whose lives are little changed now often urge unbelievers to "get saved" so they can "go to heaven when they die." The important question—which usually is *not* asked in modern-day evangelistic presentations—is, "Who teaches these converts *how* to live?"

The answer should be, *the Holy Spirit*. However, when people are led to believe they "get saved" by solely making "decisions for Christ", few of them either know about or are interested in a relationship with the Holy Spirit when they "receive the gospel," and so their lives, for the most part, remain as they always have been. They are less interested in glorifying God through their lives than they are in continuing their pursuit of their personal goals and pleasures. When this happens, (as Paul said in Romans 2:24), "the name of God is blasphemed among the Gentiles" because of them. This is the most tragic result of the church's misunderstanding of the kingdom of heaven as only a place out past the moon where God runs everything and waits for us.

Our gospel should be the same as that of Jesus and His disciples: Rethink the way you live your life in light of the facts that the kingdom

Before you can be a teacher you must first be a student.

of the heavens is *here* and that following Jesus *now* is about walking in the fullness and power of the Holy Spirit.

So how do we make true disciples of Jesus Christ? *We make disciples by first being true disciples of the kingdom ourselves;* that is, by living in an intimate, moment-by-moment, loving relationship with the Holy Spirit. He teaches us how to live as we seek His fullness in our lives, as we are careful not to grieve or quench Him, and as we abandon ourselves to Him. Then we lead others to follow Jesus in the same way, by teaching them what He has taught us: namely, that they may experience the same hope and fullness through a relationship with Jesus Christ, known and revealed in the promised presence of the Holy Spirit.

The Holy Spirit Produces Holy Living

Jesus' gospel message, "Rethink the way you live your life, for the kingdom of the heavens is very near," had a tremendous impact on those who listened to Him during His earthly ministry. Remember, His ministry was one of preparation for the ministry of the Holy Spirit. The purpose of this chapter has been to prepare you to worship the Father in spirit and in truth and to bring you into the presence of God, who is not only as near to you as the air you breathe, but *who indwells you.* He lives in us

If you and your children are to have an unshakable faith, you must be convinced of God's infinite, eternal love and presence as they are revealed in the persons of Jesus Christ and the Holy Spirit. Additionally, you must be convinced of your own love for God. Being a disciple of the kingdom of the heavens (which is the same as living in the presence of God), heeding the words of His Son whom He sent, and walking daily in relationship with the Holy Spirit *are the things that constitute eternal life.* I want to conclude with three probing questions:

1. Who is your teacher in life?

2. Is the kingdom of heaven (life in the Holy Spirit) revealed to others in you?

3. Are you making disciples?

I hope this chapter has caused you to think again about life and made you more Spirit-minded. If you are to have an unshakable faith, anchored in Christ, that faith must be the fruit of His life revealed in you in the fullness and power of the Holy Spirit. He's not waiting for us on the other side of the universe; He's reigning in us now.

Twenty-seven

Evangelism God's Way

The challenge now before us is to take what we have learned about God, man, and God's call and apply it to evangelism so we do it God's way and with His power. It has been important to lay a firm foundation for evangelism so that we may discern what methods and message are going to be anointed with God's power. Wrong ideas about God, man, the Fall, the Atonement, and the way God saves can lead to faulty evangelism, resulting in people who think they are saved when they are not. *don't spread wrong ideas/false Truth*

Applying the foundational truths to evangelism can assist us in our discernment and lead us to know what to share and when to share it with someone who needs to hear the gospel. For instance, when we take into account the holiness of God and the fact that He dwells in unapproachable light, we intuitively know that man can never get to God with good works. Our gospel message should not be about what man can do to be saved. Our gospel must address how mankind can relate to a holy God.

In previous chapters we also have seen that all men have been bound in darkness since Adam's first sin and are at enmity with God. Our gospel must show how this enmity has been overcome if our message is to instill hope.

According to His great mercy, God has chosen and justified a people for His own possession, and He is calling them to Himself. They are being called out of darkness into His marvelous light for the glory of Jesus Christ. What can we do to be instruments of God's redemptive purpose in the world? How does God "call out" through His people?

The Apostle Paul wrote that God has ordained that His calling will come through the foolishness of the gospel message being preached. We want to be sure we preach His message because the gospel is the power of God for salvation. If we don't deliver God's message, God's way, in God's timing, we cannot be confident about the results.

Look at Today's Evangelism

Today's evangelism, for the most part, has been built on a faulty foundation. Great preachers and theologians of the past, such as John Calvin, Martin Luther, John Bunyan, Jonathan Edwards, George Whitefield, J. C. Ryle, C. H. Spurgeon, Thomas Watson, and David Brainerd would be appalled at the evangelistic methods currently endorsed by most evangelical churches. Contemporary theologians and preachers such as Walter Chantry and Drs. D. Martyn-Lloyd Jones, R.C. Sproul, Albert Mohler, Al Martin, and John MacArthur, Jr., have expressed in writing or preaching the errors of contemporary evangelistic methods. Most evangelistic presentations are based on these false notions:

1. Man wasn't totally ruined by the Fall, and his will is free to choose good or evil. Consequently, his good choices have merit before God.

2. Man, having a free will, may choose to accept Christ or reject Him. Therefore, the power to be converted lies within himself.

3. Salvation occurs when a person chooses to confess his sins, accepts Christ, and invites Him into his heart.

So the goal of evangelism today is to persuade people to pray a prayer inviting Christ into the heart. When that occurs, most evangelists believe they've fulfilled the Great Commission. The result of these wrong ideas is evangelism man's way. John MacArthur in his book, *Ashamed of the Gospel*, observed that pastors and theologians today are more interested in what fills their pews and increases their church membership than they are in the truth.[37] Methods often are calculated, canned, coercive, certifiable, and misleading. If you have read any books by the men mentioned above, then I'm preaching to the choir. But if you haven't, then you would do well to become familiar with the writings of these great men. You might be surprised to find how far we have departed from sound doctrine and practice.

You may perhaps argue that we cannot have departed too much, because you and many others were saved as a result of today's evangelistic methods and message. I am not saying that God hasn't saved people through contemporary evangelism. However, such fruit should not be considered a divine endorsement of the doctrine presented or the methods employed. It is instead a demonstration of God's power and grace. God be praised that such methods haven't prevented Him from saving many!

The great tragedy, though, is that there are many more who think they are saved when in fact they are still unregenerate. Since the modern methods appeal to the strength of the flesh, many—perhaps millions— believe they have obtained salvation simply by giving mental assent to certain facts and praying a sinner's prayer. Jesus said the flesh can only give birth to flesh, and this is the tragedy!

Some Thought-Provoking Questions

God's way is quite different. The truths we've discussed so far, if applied to evangelism, will prevent us from adopting a message or methods that can be used by Satan to deceive many. They provide a basis for anchoring us in Christ, the Solid Rock. Before proceeding to the content of the gospel, let's address four frequently asked questions regarding evangelism in light of the truth of God's sovereignty, His election, and Jesus' substitutionary death.

- If God is going to save all of His elect, some may ask, why witness?

- And if you believe Jesus died for His people only, and not for everyone in the whole world, then why offer the gospel to people for whom He didn't die?

- If Christians aren't supposed to lead someone to accept Christ and pray to invite Christ into his heart, what is the aim of evangelism?

- And how does one know when he has effectively "evangelized" someone?

Why Witness?

If God has chosen His people before the beginning of time and He has promised not to lose even one, then why does the church need to witness? God's Word offers the following answers:

Why witness? Because ✓

We've Been Commissioned by the Lord Jesus

First, the church has been commissioned by the Lord Jesus to make disciples (Matthew 28:18-20). This is a command of God:

disciple,
enter into
a deep
relationship
centered
on christ
growing
in Him

> *And Jesus came up and spoke to them, saying, "All authority has been given to Me in heaven and on earth.* **Go therefore and make disciples of all the nations**, *baptizing them in the name of the Father and the Son and the Holy Spirit,* **teaching them to observe all I commanded you**; *and lo, I am with you always, even to the end of the age."*

Although there is reason to believe this commission was primarily given to the apostles, it is obvious from the book of Acts and the letters of the apostles that they believed it applied to everyone. We are to 1) make disciples, 2) baptize, and 3) teach. So first, we witness because we've been commanded to witness.

We've Been Filled With the Holy Spirit

church: The
body, not
the
building

Go.

Second, we witness because the church has been empowered by the Holy Spirit to witness. Jesus Christ is seeking and reaching His lost sheep through His people:

> *And when they had prayed, the place where they had gathered together was shaken, and* **they were all filled with the Holy Spirit, and began to speak the word of God with boldness** *(Acts 4:31).*

Although the empowerment for witnessing that the early church experienced is not shared by every believer today, yet because we are filled with the Spirit, we are lights in the darkness. Often we are led to explain the hope we have within us because of the Holy Spirit's presence and prompting in our lives.

We Have His Life in Us

in Him there is life

Third, we witness because we can't help but share the life of Jesus Christ with those around us. We are a light to the world (Matthew 5:14) because He is the light of the world (John 8:12). Because of our union with Christ, we are part of His continual presence in the world. Whether by our actions or our words, we are constantly testifying of the redeeming life and work of Jesus Christ if we are filled with His Spirit.

Why Offer the Gospel to People for Whom Jesus Didn't Die?

We offer the gospel to all kinds of people because *we* don't know whom God is saving. God certainly knows those who are His; however, the only way *we* can know whom Jesus died for is to share the gospel. As we witness to the truth about God's character, man's alienated condition, and God's work in the world through Jesus Christ, we can see by a person's response if he is being saved by God's Spirit. It is important to remember that a lack of response doesn't necessarily mean God hasn't chosen him; he may turn toward God later. That's why we continue to witness to some people on an ongoing basis.

God's timing for that person's salvation may not be *our* timing. Our first testimony of Christ may be given at a time when the individual isn't "ripe"—he is unprepared by circumstances and truth to receive the truth of the gospel. However, we continue testifying to him while God prepares his heart through the pressure of circumstances, personal failure, and gospel truths revealed in the Scriptures. If God is going to save him, there will come a time when the fruit is *ripe* for picking. We want to build relationships with people so we can be there when their hearts are ready to hear the gospel—when it is relevant to what they are experiencing in life.

God has chosen the gospel as the means by which the elect are revealed. We cannot know the ones for whom Christ did not die. It is both inappropriate and impossible for us to choose whom we think will or will not be saved. We are His servants who both live and speak the *good news* about Christ, expecting that sometimes we will see the harvest of those souls whom God is calling. Just as when the church was first being built by the apostles and their fellow workers, so we also present the gospel to many, as the Spirit gives us opportunities, always hoping to see another of God's elect come to Him as a result of our testimony. We speak because He has commanded and equipped us to do so, and we leave the results to Him.

> *What then is Apollos? And what is Paul? Servants through whom you believed, even as the Lord gave opportunity to each one. I planted, Apollos watered, but God was causing the growth (1 Corinthians 3:5-6).*

What Is the Aim of Evangelism?

Perhaps when you think of evangelism, you picture a person going door to door sharing the Four Spiritual Laws. Or maybe you visualize someone sharing Jesus Christ with his or her work associate. Many think evangelism is what pastors do when they preach a sermon calling for a decision to trust Christ. Although all of these may be evangelistic, I would urge you to consider evangelism in a broader sense. *The aim of evangelism is to be used by God to place the life, message, and work of God in Jesus Christ before others.*

God Uses "Lifestyle Evangelism"

One aspect of evangelism is being God's instrument of light (grace and truth) in the world. Jesus said,

> *You are the light of the world. A city set on a hill cannot be hidden. Nor do men light a lamp, and put it under the peck-measure, but on the lamp stand; and it gives light to all who are in the house.* **Let your light shine before men in such a way that they may see your good works, and glorify your Father who is in heaven** *(Matthew 5:14-16).*

Although proclaiming or sharing the gospel with someone is an important aspect of evangelism, it entails more than merely presenting a message. Powerful evangelism involves three elements: God's Spirit, the believer, and the listener. Through these elements, I have recognized two kinds of witnessing.

The first entails our being Christ-like in our lifestyles. (See Matthew 5:14-16, above, and Ephesians 4:17, 24, and 5:1-2, below). The Apostle Paul had Christ-like witnessing in mind when he wrote,

> *This I say, therefore, and affirm together with the Lord, that you* **walk no longer just as the Gentiles also walk**, *in the futility of their mind...* **And put on the new self**, *which in the likeness of God has been created in righteousness and holiness of the truth (Ephesians 4:17, 24).*

> *Therefore be imitators of God, as beloved children; and* **walk in love, just as Christ also loved you**, *and gave Himself up for us, an offering and a sacrifice to God as a fragrant aroma (Ephesians 5:1-2).*

When Jesus declared that we are the light of the world, He was saying that our way of living would bear testimony to the world of the glory of God. The way we love our spouses, treat and train our children, work on the job, relate to our neighbors, and order our lives testifies to others of Jesus' presence in our lives. Such testimonies should be good news to a dark world, declaring to them, "There is hope!"

[handwritten: Be the news, and hope and light in the dark depressed world]

God "Calls Out" Through His People

The second kind of witnessing is the one I think people typically understand: the kind that means "proclaiming the gospel to a lost world." God gives us opportunities to share what God has done in Christ with those around us who ask us why we live the way we do. We're to be ready to give a defense for the hope lying within us. Here are some scriptural examples of this kind of witnessing:

[handwritten: Most all the accounts of proclaiming the gospel come from after there is relationship and others. See/since the difference.]

*And Philip opened his mouth, and beginning from this Scripture **he preached Jesus to him** (Acts 8:35).*

*And they said, "Believe in the Lord Jesus, and you shall be saved, you and your household. And **they spoke the word of the Lord to him,** together with all who were in his house" (Acts 16:31-32).*

*For since in the wisdom of God the world through its wisdom did not come to know God, God was well pleased **through the foolishness of the message preached to save those who believe.** For indeed Jews ask for signs, and Greeks search for wisdom; but **we preach Christ crucified,** to Jews a stumbling block, and to Gentiles foolishness, but to those who are the called, both Jews and Greeks, Christ the power of God and the wisdom of God (1 Corinthians 1:21-24).*

This form of evangelism ought to include not only the call to trust Christ for salvation, but also the call to obedience and discipleship. It is not uncommon to hear ministers present the good news of forgiveness of sins without preaching the importance of repentance and obedience. God's promises of forgiveness and salvation come with a condition of turning from our futile way of living according to the course of this world. The following verses underscore this call to repentance and discipleship:

Now when they heard this, they were pierced to the heart, and said to Peter and the rest of the apostles, "Brethren, what shall we do?" And Peter said to them, "**Repent**, and let each of you be baptized in the name of Jesus Christ for the forgiveness of your sins; *and you shall receive the gift of the Holy Spirit. For the promise is for you and your children, and for all who are far off, as many as the Lord our God shall call to Himself.*" And **with many other words he solemnly testified and kept on exhorting them**, saying, "Be saved from this perverse generation!" (Acts 2:37-40).

Or what agreement has the temple of God with idols? For we are the temple of the living God; just as God said, "I will dwell in them and walk among them; and I will be their God, and they shall be My people. **Therefore, come out from their midst and be separate**," says the Lord. "**And do not touch what is unclean**; and I will welcome you. And I will be a father to you, and you shall be sons and daughters to Me," says the Lord Almighty. Therefore, having these promises, beloved, let us **cleanse ourselves from all defilement** of flesh and spirit, perfecting holiness **in the fear of God** (2 Corinthians 6:16-7:1).

What Is Effective Evangelism?

For effective evangelism to take place, three ingredients are necessary. If one of these is missing, our evangelism will fall short of producing eternal fruit.

The Entire Godhead

The first "ingredient" almost goes without saying, but it is the entire Godhead. True evangelism cannot take place if God is not at work in the hearts of both the evangelist and the one listening. I mention this first because all too often, our modern methods and messages are designed to work *without God*. For many decades now, countless people have been led to pray a prayer of acceptance and ask for forgiveness when there was no sign of God's Spirit at work in their lives. Through this practice, much of the church has come to believe that if a person prays "the prayer," then evangelism has been successful. But God's Word reveals there's more to salvation than one's repeating a formulaic prayer.

Jesus astounded His own disciples when He told them the heavenly Father must draw someone to the Son. It is good for us to remember that the Father's part in salvation is *drawing those whom He has chosen to Jesus.*

[*No one can come to Me, unless the Father who sent Me draws him;*]*and I will raise him up on the last day. It is written in the prophets, "And they shall all be taught of God." Everyone who has heard and learned from the Father comes to Me (John 6:44-45).*

The Son's role in redemption involves His *removing the wrath of God* through His substitutionary death. Then He also continues the saving process through His *ever-living intercession:*

> *Much more then, having now been justified by His blood,* **we shall be saved from the wrath of God through Him.** *For if while we were enemies,* **we were reconciled to God through the death of His Son,** *much more, having been reconciled, we shall be saved by His life (Romans 5:9-10).*

> *Hence, also, He is able to save forever those who draw near to God through Him, since* **He always lives to make intercession for them** *(Hebrews 7:25).*

The third person of the Holy Trinity, the Holy Spirit, *regenerates and renews those whom the Father has chosen.* Without the work of conversion and new birth accomplished by the Holy Spirit, the prayer of invitation or acceptance is useless and ineffective. The following verses stress the importance of the work of the Holy Spirit in evangelism:

> *Jesus answered, "Truly, truly, I say to you,* **unless one is born of water and the Spirit,** *he cannot enter into the kingdom of God. That which is born of the flesh is flesh, and that which is born of the Spirit is spirit (John 3:5-6).*

> *He saved us, not on the basis of deeds which we have done in righteousness, but according to His mercy, by the washing of regeneration and* **renewing by the Holy Spirit,** *whom He poured out upon us richly through Jesus Christ our Savior (Titus 3:5-6).*

If our evangelism is going to be effective, the entire Godhead must be at work. In fact, if God is not building the house, they labor in vain who build it (Psalm 127:1). When we evangelize, we want to do so in the power of the Holy Spirit. If we know what God is doing in the heart of someone we're talking with, we can be more cooperative by sharing scriptures and explaining to him what God is doing so that his confidence may be in God instead of himself.

The Word of God

The second ingredient necessary for effective evangelism is the Word of God. Faith must have words of authority to stand on. When we give someone God's Word, we're giving the Holy Spirit something to work with in that person's heart. There are tremendous encouragements from the Bible in this regard. This ought to inspire us to memorize and meditate on great passages of Scripture like these containing the gospel promises and hope:

> *For I am not ashamed of the gospel, for it is the power of God for salvation to everyone who believes, to the Jew first and also to the Greek (Romans 1:16).*

> *For you have been born again not of seed which is perishable but imperishable, that is, through the living and abiding word of God (1 Peter 1:23).*

The Believer in Step With the Spirit

The third ingredient is the obedient, Spirit-following believer. Our job as evangelists is not to complete a predetermined presentation, but to keep in step with the Spirit of God who is at work to save the individual. Remember, if God isn't at work to save someone, you're not going to be able to save him. But if the Holy Spirit is at work convicting him of sin, then the scriptures you share need to address those issues. If he has already come under conviction and is in need of hope, then it's time to share the hope of the gospel.

All too often, we share the hope of the gospel long before the individual is ready. If the Holy Spirit hasn't convicted him of sin's presence, power, and penalty, then he is not ready to hear about God's forgiveness. The natural heart can't understand why forgiveness and repentance are necessary unless the Holy Spirit grants enlightenment. Jesus told Simon the Pharisee that a man who has been forgiven of much sin loves much, and the person forgiven of few sins loves little (Luke 7:47). If a person does not understand the magnitude of his sin and his great need for forgiveness, he cannot love God much. And if the convicting work of the Spirit has not occurred, then the message of God's forgiveness has little life-changing effect.

Read the following scripture passage in light of its context, and you'll notice that the evangelist did not follow a predetermined method of evangelism, but shared what was needed in light of the obvious work that the Spirit of God had already done. *That's where I want to go*

> *... behold, there was an Ethiopian eunuch, a court official of Candace, queen of the Ethiopians, who was in charge of all her treasure;* **and he had come to Jerusalem to worship.** *And he was returning and sitting in his chariot,* **and was reading the prophet Isaiah. And the Spirit said to Philip,** *"Go up and join this chariot." And when Philip had run up, he heard him reading Isaiah the prophet, and said,* **"Do you understand what you are reading?"** *And he said, "Well, how could I, unless someone guides me?" And he invited Philip to come up and sit with him (Acts 8:27-31).*

Philip explained the words of Isaiah to the eunuch because God was using that passage at the time in the man's life. As they continued riding together, the man's response indicated that God's Spirit was at work.

work the tie to the man caught Philip.

> *... The eunuch said, "Look! Water! What prevents me from being baptized?" And Philip said, "If you believe with all your heart, you may."* **And he answered and said, "I believe that Jesus Christ is the Son of God."** *And he ordered the chariot to stop; and they both went down into the water, Philip as well as the eunuch; and he baptized him (Acts 8:26-40).*

As you read through the book of Acts, you'll see that in every case when the gospel was presented, the evangelist gave the message needed in light of what the Holy Spirit was doing in the hearts of the listeners. Our gospel presentation should not be "canned," but rather one that addresses the same issues the Spirit of God is dealing with in their lives. *Being in tune with the Spirit is key.*

Here is an illustration. If you are speaking with someone whose life is in shambles, then the Spirit of God may be working. God is giving them over to the sinful tendencies within them so they may learn firsthand the power and character of sin. With such a person, the scriptures about man's sinfulness will strike the heart with power because he or she is actually experiencing it. Our evangelism in such a case has power because it is relevant to life. *# relatable*

When the same person begins to see how sin has been the cause of his problems, and the Spirit of God is pressing guilt and responsibility upon his heart, then his heart is prepared for verses about repentance and what God has done in Jesus Christ.

When a person cries out, "What must I do to be saved?" *then* perhaps the words of Peter in Acts 2 or Paul in Acts 16 are relevant and timely. "Believe on the Lord Jesus Christ, and you shall be saved."

God's way of evangelizing involves, therefore, these three ingredients: God (the Father, Son, and Holy Spirit), the Word of God, and the believer who is keeping in step with the Spirit of God as he witnesses.

We Have One Motive—LOVE!

What should be our motive in evangelism? Our goal should not be another person's salvation because salvation falls under God's jurisdiction. Instead, we should aim to be God's agents of love toward His enemies, keeping in tune and in step with the Spirit of God as He is at work in their lives. God has not called us to save the lost, but to proclaim His excellencies—His working in their lives. The Apostle Paul wrote in 1 Corinthians 14:1 that we are to pursue love. We can do that! If people recognize that the reason we are sharing with them is to love them, and they are confident that we would love them whether they believed in Jesus or not, they are more likely to be receptive to our witness.

However, when we have the goal of leading a friend, co-worker, or neighbor to a "decision for Christ," or of getting them to come to church, they will discern a spirit of striving and put up their defenses. Even though they are not yet alive to God, they are aware deep down in their hearts that God is not speaking to them and that they are being manipulated. They understand that if someone can talk them *into* a decision for Jesus, someone else can talk them *out of* the decision. They intuitively know that the results won't be any different from anything else they've tried in life. However, when we are motivated by love for them, they don't detect a fleshly, striving spirit and are more open to listen with their hearts.

The Spirit of God is holy. There is no other spirit like Him. He is love, and He comes with wisdom and peace, even though His message may strike fear and cut deeply into their hearts. When we evangelize from the motivation of love for God and others, we are free to tell the person the truth about God and about sin. We won't hold anything back because we trust in God and the truth rather than our persuasiveness and a flesh-appealing message.

When we evangelize God's way, we purpose to love those around us with His love. We don't engage people in a conversation just so we can convert them; we do so to love them. Sometimes the loving thing at the moment isn't to share Jesus verbally, but to "live Jesus" in action. At other times, the loving thing to do is to share the truth of God, which exposes sin for what it is—hatred and rebellion against a holy God.

Perhaps you have participated in an evangelistic team going door-to-door, and wonder how what we have studied integrates into such evangelistic methods. Certainly God has used such methods to facilitate the new birth of many. The important thing to remember as you interact with people is that God has brought you to that door for a purpose. If all you do is quote a canned gospel presentation, you may only be effective with a few who are *ripe* by the previous work of God's Spirit. However, if you keep in mind the ideas in this chapter, you will wisely discover what God is doing in their lives currently so you can evangelize in His power and love!

Keep in Step With the Spirit of God

How does one keep in step with the Holy Spirit? If we are to follow the work of the Spirit of God, we want to help people see what God is doing in their lives—to interpret the events of life by using the Scriptures. There are times in people's lives when they are more "ripe for harvest" than at other times. For instance, times of crisis (death in the family, birth of a child, personal trials, divorce, etc.) are instruments God uses to make a person feel his or her need and emptiness.

You want to discover what the Holy Spirit is doing in a person's life before you share Jesus Christ, the Scriptures, or a testimony with him. God usually works through circumstances and relationships, so you might ask questions inviting him to share with you regarding these areas of life. Then determine to listen carefully, both to what he says and to how the Holy Spirit is leading you.

The next few pages present a diagram and a set of three tables showing the different aspects of God's saving work. These might help to make a good study tool because they will help you discern as you are talking with a person where he is in the process of conversion.

The diagram shows an overview of the process of God's saving work. By first referring to the diagram and estimating where you think the person is in the process, you can then refer to one of the three tables that provide scripture references for discussion. The three tables correspond to the three different "heart conditions" illustrated in the diagram.

it's all about the heart

Memorizing the scriptures and where they fall in the process of a person's conversion will make for the most spontaneous conversations. But whether or not you memorize them, if you have them easily available you can share the appropriate scriptures with whoever in confidence that the Holy Spirit will apply them in power to their life.

The table below deals with the topics that are common to the three heart-condition tables used with the diagram. Consider each of the questions carefully. The answers to these questions will help you understand the scripture references in each table and how to apply them in discussion to the person with which you are witnessing.

study this in detail.

Topic	Key Question
Doctrine	What is the most important doctrine I can share with this person?
Life Principle	What kind of life is reigning in him?
Experience	What is he experiencing in his life that demonstrates the truth about the kind of life reigning in him now?
Will's Ability	What is he able to do by the power of his will?
Heart Condition	What is the condition of his heart in the kind of life that is reigning in him now?
Power Principle	*Something* has power over this man that actively determines how he lives; what is it?
Revelation	What is revealed to the man about God and about himself in the life that is now reigning in him?
Sin Principle	What power does sin have in the man's life at this time?
Examples	What Bible characters can I think of whose lives or experiences demonstrated the topics defined in the tables?

QUESTION: WHAT IS THE SPIRITUAL STATE OF THE PERSON I AM TALKING WITH?

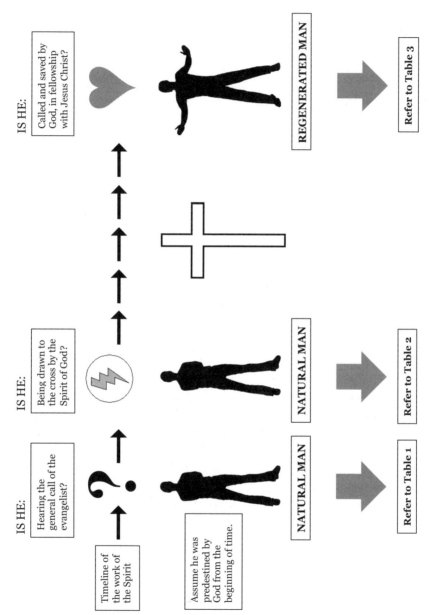

God's General Process of Conversion Diagram

Table 1: The General Call of the Evangelist to the Natural Man
Matthew 22:14

Topics	Scriptures	
Doctrine	Depravity Romans 1:18-32 Genesis 6:5 Romans 3:9-19	
Life Principle	Old Man Romans 6:6	
Experience	**Selfishness** 2 Timothy 3:2	**Lust/Covetousness** Ephesians 2:1-3 Romans 7:7-8
Will's Ability	**Enslaved to Sin, Unable to be Righteous Before God** Romans 6:16-17, 20	**Sins** Romans 7:9, 14
Heart Condition	**Unregenerate and in Darkness** Genesis 6:5 Romans 3:9-12	**Under Law** Romans 3:19 Galatians 3:23-24
Power Principle	**Flesh Rules** Romans 7:14	**Flesh Strives** Joshua 24:16-22
Revelation	**God's Attributes, Power, Nature** Romans 1:19-20 **Man's Hypocrisy** Matthew 7:21-23	**Man's Pride** Philippians 3:1-6
Sin Principle	**Sin Reigns in the Body, Empowered by Flesh Under Sin** Galatians 3:22 Romans 3:9 **Bondage to Sin** Romans 7:14	
Examples	**Hypocritical Judas** John 6:64-71	**Proud Saul (as a Pharisee)** Philippians 3:1-6

The first kind of "calling" the natural man receives is illustrated best by the call or preaching of the evangelist, often referred to as the "general" call. Through this calling, the unregenerate, natural man receives the truth about the gospel of Jesus Christ. This truth is often given in the form of scripture—the Word of God *(logos)*. It is necessary information, but without the work of the Holy Spirit drawing the man and supernaturally transforming his heart, he will only receive it as *knowledge*. He may either accept or reject the truth being offered, but the main thing you will see is that he feels little sorrow for his sins and no great need for the mercy of God. He may be attracted to religion as a means of self-improvement, but only if he can practice it on his own terms, and he will be motivated by self-interest rather than love for Christ.

This table will help you learn appropriate scriptures to present to a person who still needs to discover his bondage to sin, his guilt before God, and his need for salvation.

Table 2: God Draws the Natural Man
John 6:44

Topics	Scriptures	
Doctrine	Repentance 2 Corinthians 7:9-11 Acts 11:18	
Life Principle	New Man Conceived Romans 7:14-17	
Experience	Awakening Romans 7:7-14	Powerlessness, Fear, Destruction Acts 16:29-30
Will's Ability	Meditate and Mourn Matthew 5:4 2 Corinthians 7:7, 9-10	Cry Out Romans 7:24 Romans 10:13 James 4:9
Heart Condition	Awake to Sin Through Law Romans 7:9 1 Timothy 1:8-11	Conviction John 16:8 Romans 7:7-24
Power Principle	Flesh Fails Romans 8:3	Flesh Gives Up Romans 6:6 Romans 8:13
Revelation	God's Wrath Romans 1:18-32	God's Judgment John 16:8 Romans 2:2-3
Sin Principle	Sin Reigns in the Body, Empowered by Flesh Under Sin Galatians 3:22 Romans 3:9 Bondage to Sin Romans 7:14	
Examples	Saul (Life Change at Damascus) Acts 9:3-9	Saul (Flesh Unable to Glorify God) Romans 7:14-25

The next kind of "calling" the natural man receives is the drawing of the Holy Spirit of God. God begins to open the heart of the man and draws him to Christ (John 6:44). The man begins to see his own sinfulness and accountability before God. He becomes increasingly fearful of the judgment of God and sees the failure of his own attempts to keep God's commandments through the power of the flesh. Awakened by God to his guilt and need for God's mercy, the man begins to cry out for God to grant him repentance. Aware of his bondage to sin, he is no longer satisfied with the "appearance" of religion. He wants to receive mercy and real salvation from God.

This table will help you learn appropriate scriptures to present to a person who has discovered his bondage to sin, his guilt before God, and his need for salvation through the finished work of Jesus Christ.

Table 3: God Calls and Saves the Regenerated Man
2 Timothy 1:9; Romans 8:30, 9:29; Hebrews 9:15; 2 Peter 1:10

Topics	Scriptures			
Doctrine	Justification Rom. 5:1-2 Rom. 8:30	Sanctification Rom. 6:19 1 Thess. 4:3, 7	Repentance 2 Cor. 7:9-11 Acts 11:18	Glorification Rom. 8:30 Col. 3:4
Life Principle	New Creation and New Birth 2 Cor. 5:17, 1 Pet. 1:3			Perfect Creation Phil. 1:6
Experience	Peace and Power Rom. 5:1 2 Pet. 1:2-3	Love Gal. 5:6 1 John 2:9-10	Joy 1 Pet. 1:6-8	Glory Rom. 5:2
Will's Ability	Obey Jesus 1 Pet. 1:2 Rom. 6:17	Put Sin to Death Rom. 8:12-14 Col. 3:5-8	Worship Rom. 12:1-2 Heb. 13:15	Reign With Christ 1 Cor. 6:2 2 Tim. 2:12
Heart Condition	At Peace by Faith Gal. 3:23 Rom. 5:1-2	Faith Works Gal. 5:6 1 Pet. 1:22	Hope Comes Rom. 5:3-6 Rom. 8:23-25	Hope Realized Rom. 8:25 Gal. 5:5
Power Principle	Spirit Washes Acts 15:8-9 1 Pet. 1:2	Spirit Fills Gal. 5:16, 25 Rom. 8:9-11	Spirit Seals Eph. 1:13-14 2 Cor. 1:21-22	Spirit Transforms Phil. 3:21 2 Cor. 3:18
Revelation	Union With J.C. Rom. 10:17 Rom. 6:2-6	Relationship Eph. 1:17-20 Matt. 16:16-17	Christ With Us Gal. 2:20 Col. 1:26-27	Union With God Col. 3:4 Rom. 6:5
Sin Principle	Grace Reigns Over Sin Still in the Body Rom. 6:6 Sin Is Powerless Against the Spirit Rom. 8:13 In Christ, We Die to Sin (Not Sin Dies) 1 Pet. 2:24, Rom. 6:11 We're Freed From Sin's Penalty and Power to Kill Rom. 8:1-2			Sin Is Destroyed 2 Pet. 3:10-13 Righteousness Reigns Rom. 5:21 Gal. 5:5 2 Pet. 3:13
Examples	Paul (As Saul) Acts 9:15-19	Paul 2 Tim. 4:7	Paul Rom. 8:15-17	Jesus Rom. 6:4-5

The next kind of "calling" is the effectual call of God to salvation through Jesus Christ. The man (or woman) is experiencing a spiritual rebirth and the peace of God as God grants him repentance and forgiveness for his sins. He begins to see the power of the Holy Spirit reigning in him and delivering him from sinful practices that formerly kept him in bondage. The Holy Spirit is now writing the Word of God (*rhema*) into his heart. He is coming to love God and know the love of God. He is becoming interested in discipleship, in obedience, in putting to death the deeds of the flesh, and in holy living for the glory of God.

This table will help you learn appropriate scriptures to present to a person who has been drawn by the Holy Spirit to salvation and is experiencing the spiritual rebirth through the finished work of Jesus Christ. These scriptures will help the person see himself as a new creation in Christ and to grow in the knowledge of the truth and in living a life that pleases the Lord. An overview of all of the tables appears next.

God's General Process of Conversion

Topics	General Call of God Matthew 22:14		God Draws John 6:44
Topics	**Natural Man**		
Doctrine	Depravity Rom. 1:18-32; Gen. 6:5 Rom. 3:9-19		Repentance 2 Cor. 7:9-11 Acts 11:18
Life Principle	Old Man Rom. 6:6		New man conceive Romans 7:14-17
Experience	Selfishness	Lust/Covet Eph. 2:1-3	Awakening Rom. 7:7-14
Will's Ability	Enslaved to sin	Sins Rom. 7:9	Meditate/ Mourn Matt. 5:4 2 Cor. 7:7, 10
Heart Condition	Unregenerate darkness Gen. 6:5 Rom. 3:9-12	Under law Rom. 3:19 Gal. 3:23-24	Law "comes" Rom. 7:9 1 Tim. 1:8-11
Power Principle	Flesh Rom. 7:14	Flesh strives	Flesh fails Rom. 8:3
Revelation	God with us Rom. 1:19-20 Matt. 7:21-23	Man's pride Phil. 3:1-6	God's wrath Rom. 1:18-32
Sin Principle	Sin reigns in the body empowered by flesh under sin. Bondage to sin. Gal. 3:22; Rom. 3:9; Rom. 7:14		
Examples	Judas John 6:64-71	Saul (Pharisee) Phil. 3:1-6	Saul (Damascus) Acts. 9:3-9

God Calls and Saves
2 Timothy 1:9; Romans 8:30, 9:29; Hebrews 9:15; 2 Peter 1:10

Regeneration

	Justification Rom. 5:1-2 Rom. 8:30	Sanctification 1 Peter 1:1-2 1 Thess. 4:7	Repentance 2 Cor. 7:9-11 Acts 11:18	Glorification Rom. 8:30 Col. 3:4
	New Creation New Birth 2 Corinthians 5:17			Perfect Creation Phil. 1:6
Powerlessness, fear, destruction Acts 16:29-30	Power, peace Romans 5:1 2 Peter 1:2-3	Love Gal. 5:6 1 Jo. 2:9-10	Joy 1 Pet. 1:7-8	Glory Rom. 5:3
Cry out Romans 7:24 Romans 10:13	Obey Jesus 1 Peter 1:2 Romans 6:17	Put sin to death Rom. 8:12-14 Col. 3:5-8	Worship Rom. 12:1-2	Reign with Christ 1 Cor. 6:2
Conviction John 16:18 Romans 7:7-24	Faith comes Galatians 3:23 Romans 5:1-2	Faith works Gal. 3:23 Rom. 5:1-2	Hope comes Rom. 5:3-6 Rom. 8:23-25	Hope real-ized Rom. 8:25 Gal. 5:5
Flesh gives up Romans 6:6 Romans 8:13	Sprit washes Acts 15:8-9 1 Peter 1:2	Spirit fills Gal. 5:25 Rom. 8:9-11	Spirit seals Eph. 1:13-14 Rom. 5:3-6	Spirit transforms Phil. 3:21
Judgement John 16:8-9 Romans 2:2-3	Union w/ J.C. Romans 10:17 Romans 6:2-6	Relationship Eph. 1:17-20 Matt. 16:16-17	Christ with us Gal. 2:20	Union with God Col. 3:4
	Grace reigns over sin still in the body, but powerless against the Spirit. In Christ, we die to sin (not sin dies). We're freed from sin's penalty and power to kill. Rom. 6:6; 8:13			
Saul Romans 7:7-12	Paul Acts 9:15-19	Paul	Paul Rom. 8:15-17	Jesus Rom. 6:4-5

It is also helpful to know that God usually works *progressively* in revealing Himself. For instance, a person first needs to understand what and who God is. If he has one wrong idea about God, then many of his ideas about God are going to be deficient, and his responses to God and the circumstances of his life will be unfruitful. When I am presenting Christ to someone, I've found it is wise to discover what he knows and thinks about God. He may have created a god of his own imagination that has very little resemblance to the true God.

Experience has shown me it is not wise to assume that because a person goes to church, he knows the truth about God. The Christian sub-culture in America has created a very materialistic and sensual idea of God.

If you're going to give someone a good foundation for faith, you'll want to show him scriptures revealing what kind of God the true God is and who He is. That's why the chapters, "What Is God?" (Chapter 16) and "Who Is God?" (Chapter 17) come first in this book after dealing with the scriptures that have been abused. I wanted us to be grounded firmly in the nature and character of God so our faith might be anchored in truth.

Once someone understands the truth about God, the Holy Spirit can then teach him about his sinful condition. Sin can only be defined in light of God's righteousness. Once God's righteousness and justice are established in his mind, his own unrighteousness and rebellion against God will be exposed. It is wise to also discover what he thinks about sin and his condition before God. Most people think they are good people whom God would certainly allow into heaven. This reveals how low their view is of God and how high their view is of themselves!

When a person grasps the nature and character of God, he is ready to understand the effects of the Fall on mankind, his own enmity against God, and his helplessness to justify himself. God gives a person over to his sin in order to teach him these things. Our role is to use the Word of God to explain his condition of sin and enmity against God. When one understands that God hates sin, that He must be just in punishing all sin, and that He cannot simply dismiss it, the sinner is called to account. Then from his heart he will be asking, "What is to be done?"

Most people who are under conviction will ask, "What can I do?" We must be careful not to respond to the question by giving them something *to do*. The flesh is always looking for some way to justify itself before God. If we tell them to pray a prayer or read their Bible or go to church, they'll do it! But they won't do it for the glory of God. They'll do it for "fire insurance" and to lighten the weight of guilt. *Instead of telling them what they can do, the wise evangelist tells them what God has done in Christ.* The atoning work of Jesus Christ on the cross will be music to the ears of those who are deeply convicted and feeling their helplessness before God. Sharing the scriptures about how God has reconciled His people to Himself through Jesus' blood and substitutionary death gives them a basis for unshakable faith in Christ instead of in the works of the flesh.

If the Spirit of God is granting them repentance and faith in Christ, then it is time to take them to the scriptures teaching that such a work is the gift of God. Repentance and faith are evidence that God has forgiven them their sins and has known them from all eternity. Now, that is GOOD NEWS! Their faith will rise up and cling to Jesus with gratitude and joy unspeakable. Sinners need to see that God is giving them repentance and faith before they can know His forgiveness and live with assurance and hope.

It is helpful to remember that faith is not something *we do*, but is evidence of what *God is doing*. It is a work of God, cleansing the heart from a guilty conscience. Praise God for His glorious grace in our salvation! His grace saves us through faith in Jesus Christ. As evangelists, we want to exalt God's work through Christ so that faith has a broad plain upon which to stand for eternity.

Discover What the Holy Spirit Is Doing   *Relationship*

One way to know where the Holy Spirit is at work is to build relationships with people in your "network" or "world." When these people are "ripe for harvest," the Holy Spirit may bring you to mind as someone who cares and can help. In other words, you want to give Jesus a name. His name to your friends will be your name! When they are hurting and in trouble, God will lead them to you for help, and in so doing, will be leading them to Himself. How can you build the relationships God has put in your life?

1. Take an interest in them as people, not as potential converts. You're there to love them. Ask questions, listening for signs of their idols and of how God is working: *Be genuine, but not forceful*

   • *Do you have an interest in spiritual things?*

I don't think we should really follow a specific format, or have a list of quest... [handwritten]

• *Tell me about yourself.*

   • *Have you ever wondered why that is occurring? The Bible says...*

   • *Has your relationship with God been satisfying?* If they say yes, ask them to tell you about it. If they say no, ask them if they would like to hear how it could be.

2. Make comments or mention something you are going to attend, in order to see if there is openness to spiritual things.

3. Invite them to a worship service, Bible study, or fellowship event. Be honest and up front about what is going on there. For example: *The pastor is leading us in a study on gaining stability and security in our lives from the book of 1 John in the Bible. It has really been meaningful to me and I think it could be helpful to you. Would you like to come?*

4. Give the Holy Spirit time to work with the truth or scriptures you've given to them. Schedule another time to meet with them in order to test if the Spirit of God is really working or if they are just being cordial. If God has chosen them, you can know He will keep them until you meet again. There's no need to rush the work of God. Love them and build relationship with them. *I also don't think Just has to be when you meet with them until that's what they want. But live out this now + when they're ready for that closer building* [handwritten]

Remember: Evangelize God's Way

   Obviously, a great deal more can be said about evangelism. I've wanted to answer some common questions that arise regarding evangelism in light of the doctrine we have studied thus far. Also, it is important that when we share the gospel, we share with the right motive and a clear understanding of how God uses us to facilitate the salvation of His people. Let's remember:

1. We witness because we've been commanded and have the filling of the Holy Spirit to witness.

2. Evangelism is being God's instrument of light in the darkness. Our lifestyles are what make our proclamation of the gospel powerful.

3. For true evangelism to take place, God must work, His Word must be used, and we must follow the Spirit's leading.

4. Our motive for evangelism is love, not the person's decision for Christ.

5. Learning God's order of salvation will help us discern what God is doing in people's lives.

I hope this chapter has helped set you free from guilt if you have thought *you* were responsible to "get people saved." My goal has been to implant a vision for sharing the gospel through your life and message that is consistent with the truth about God, man, and the new birth by the Holy Spirit. Perhaps there's no one we're more concerned about coming to Christ than our children. In the next chapter, I would like to encourage you in how God may use you to lead your children to Jesus Christ.

'the weight is not on us to "get people saved".'

Twenty-eight

Leading Your Children to Christ

As responsible parents, we have many goals and dreams for our children, the highest of which is probably their conversion to Christ. In this chapter, we are going to think through the idea of leading our children to Christ in light of what the Bible says about the spiritual condition of the hearts of our children and the preparatory work of the Holy Spirit to lead them into the kingdom of heaven. I hope to approach this subject in an orderly, organized, and logical fashion.

First, let's review the applicable truths we've studied thus far.

1. Salvation is a matter of the heart.

2. The heart of a child is bound in the darkness of sin. It is deceitful and at enmity with God. The spirit is dead in sin.

3. If a child has been known in Christ and is to be saved, God must give him repentance and faith; he cannot create faith within himself.

4. If he is to be born again, he must first be prepared for relationship with God by a healthy fear. This fear comes from knowing and applying the truth about the nearness of the kingdom of the heavens.

5. In God's timing and according to His purpose, He will teach them about their sinful, helpless state before Him.

How does God reveal one's sinful, helpless state? He gives him over to his sinful heart's lusts and pride to teach him about his need for a savior and a new heart. This process is not a comfortable one! A parent's tendency when confronted with a child's sinful actions is to discipline him and teach him not to behave that way. Although this is important, if the parent doesn't explain *what God is revealing about the heart*, a child may think that life is all about managing sin and not letting anyone catch him when he misbehaves or sins.

Your mission is to teach your child the foundational truths about God. Lead him through the ideas you've learned in this book, beginning with God's purposes, the Fall, and sin. Help him to understand the nearness of God's presence, the judgment of God, and God's redemptive work through Jesus Christ. Teach him to look for the Holy Spirit's preparatory work in his heart in the midst of his relationships and daily circumstances, and when he reads God's Word. Finally, present to your child the gospel promises upon which repentance and faith rest. Keep before him his responsibility to repent and turn to Christ. It is imperative that you lead him to the appropriate scriptures describing the work of God in his life as you keep in step with the Spirit of God at work in him.

God Works Through Circumstances and Relationships to Expose and Reveal the Motives of Our Child's Sinful Heart

All the ways of a man are clean in his own sight, but the Lord weighs the motives (Proverbs 16:2).

I, the Lord, search the heart. I test the mind, even to give to each man according to his ways, according to the results of his deeds (Jeremiah 17:10).

Every time we need to correct our children, we should explain to them what God is teaching them about themselves. It's one thing to read a Bible verse about our being sinners, but it's quite another thing for the heart to understand such a truth and act upon it. Sad to say, we must learn about our sinfulness through experience. Is this not common to all who have come to faith in Christ?

I've heard many testimonies of people who say they "accepted Christ" when they were children. But then they confess about a time when their lives *really* changed—later in their teen or young adult years. What brought about the change? Without exception they share about a time when they fell into sin and saw the reality of their sinful, helpless condition and their need for Christ. Without realizing it, they were describing the time when God taught their hearts about those things which then led to their repentance and a deeper faith in Christ.

When God works to expose and reveal the motives of the heart, He gives us over to ourselves! That's a scary thought, isn't it? If it isn't, it should be. However, when He does so, we see what God sees—a selfish, ambitious, and proud heart. When God is leading us to Christ, He gives conviction of sin. This time of instruction to children by the Father is an uncomfortable time for their parents. In fact, it can be heartbreaking, embarrassing, and overwhelming. If we're not careful, our reaction to a child who is under the hand of God may be self-protective. Instead of grieving over the sin, having compassion on them, and teaching them what God is doing, parents sometimes threaten their children by shaming them. The parents' hope is that the children will quit embarrassing them, straighten up their behavior, and do whatever it takes for the parents to maintain a good reputation.

Remember this: If your children are to be saved, God must teach them about the power of sin in their hearts and bodies. This will not be a comfortable time for anyone; nevertheless, it must not be short-circuited. Before they can be saved, life *must* get difficult. They will be given over to their sinful hearts' desires. But take heart; this is God at work!

God Works to Prepare Them for Faith in Christ

God works in the hearts of our children to prepare them for faith in Christ as they consider the nearness of the kingdom of heaven. It is our privilege to teach them about God's nearness, His watching and recording every word and action in order to judge them in the final Day, their need to rethink how they live in light of this truth, and the promise of God to those who apply the truth to their lives. In short, it leads to eternal life and faith in Jesus Christ.

Children should learn that they cannot please God in their own strength. They can't "work up" repentance, faith, love for God's Word, and fellowship with God. As you teach them these things and they watch your own relationship with God, they become disciples of the kingdom of heaven, learning these truths firsthand through their experiences. As they think about the Day when the sky unfurls and Jesus stands ready to judge every word and deed, they come face to face with what God sees and knows about them. Be sure to remind them often about the many promises of God in Christ. This prepares the way for faith to come.

When they see the truth of their inability to save themselves, the time is nearing for them to give their lives to God, trusting and submitting themselves to His will. As God gives them understanding and opens their hearts to believe His Word, He will call them to follow Him, and you can encourage them to do so. They will be filled with hope to know that an open heart—a teachable attitude—is evidence of God's mercy toward them.

God Uses His Law

Although adherence to the Laws of God cannot save us, they play an important part in teaching us about our hearts' enmity against God, and about our need for His mercy and righteousness. We lay the foundation for our children to learn these lessons by consistently providing righteous standards of living, both by our own example and from the Scriptures. The Apostle Paul wrote this to Timothy about the use of the Law:

> But we know that the Law is good, if one uses it lawfully, realizing the fact that law is not made for a righteous man, but for those who are lawless and rebellious, for the ungodly and sinners, for the unholy and profane, for those who kill their fathers or mothers, for murderers and immoral men and homosexuals and kidnappers and liars and perjurers, and whatever else is contrary to sound teaching, according to the glorious gospel of the blessed God, with which I have been entrusted (1 Timothy 1:8-11).

Some evangelists call this ministry of the Word of God *the Law work*. God has a purpose for the Law. It works upon our hearts, teaching us about God, ourselves, and the character and power of sin. From the Scriptures we learn God's purposes for the Law:

1. God's law reveals the character of God.

2. God's law reveals the powerlessness of the flesh.

3. God's law reveals sin's power over the flesh.

4. God's law defines sin as God sees it.

5. God's law exposes our enmity and hostility toward God.

6. Thus, God's law reveals our need, and in our need we find a basis for repentance.

This idea is worth repeating: we must teach our children that keeping the Law of God doesn't put us in favor with God. Yes, we must teach them what God requires of man, but we must also balance that truth with what God has provided for man in Jesus Christ.

The Rod and Reproof

One aspect of applying the Law to your children is *consistent discipline*, using "the rod and reproof" in the early years of life (see Proverbs 29:15). The idea of spanking children has been greatly discussed among child psychologists and parenting specialists since Dr. Benjamin Spock discouraged the practice. Some consider the use of the rod to be the same thing as beating a child. Their experiences with their own parents and the testimonies of others who were beaten with belts, boat oars, boards, hands or fists, and other unbiblical means have convinced them that spanking can only be destructive and detrimental to effective childrearing. It seems clear that such destructive means of discipline are not what the Scriptures intend to teach us as parents who are working to lead our children to Christ. After all, God does not treat us with such severity, especially when we are just coming to faith. *The rod should never be used in anger.*

What exactly is a "rod"? I think the rod should never be something associated with your person, like your hand or your belt. I also do not suggest using something like a wooden spoon because children sometimes associate such an object with chastisement and then wince when it is pulled out for its normal use. A biblical *rod* might best be understood as a *switch*. It needs to have some flex in it and be thick enough to be effective and not break—perhaps a half inch in diameter at the most. I've seen parents use a flexible plastic rod, about a quarter inch in diameter and about 24 inches long. It makes sense to use a smaller, narrower, lighter rod for younger children and a more substantial one for older children.

What is the purpose of using a rod? The Apostle Paul demonstrated that the goal of instruction should be *love from a pure heart, a good conscience, and a sincere faith* (1 Timothy 1:5). A parent who doesn't have such a goal should not employ the rod. It is an instrument of discipline to be used as *part of the process* of training your children in various matters of obedience. Another purpose of the rod is to teach children that sin has consequences, and it is a forewarning of the greatest punishment of eternal death. When used consistently and lovingly with instruction, the use of the rod serves to remind the child of the importance of learning a particular behavior or *not* practicing a sinful, destructive action.

Contrary to what some may think, the purpose of the rod is not for breaking the will. That's God's job. Nor should the rod be used as an idolatrous "carving tool" to make your child "into your own image" so that he will do what you want, when you want, like you want. If you use the rod in these ways, you will alienate your children. They can tell if the rod and reproof are being used to do what only God can do— produce a work of repentance in the heart. Children know you don't trust God when the severity of the spanking changes with the offense. When parents use the rod to *get a sense of satisfaction or justice for themselves*, children cannot perceive that discipline as being motivated by love because it isn't. It's motivated by idolatry. [If you are interested in learning more about idolatry, how it works, and how to address it, I have written about the subject in more detail in *Equipped to Love: Idolatry-Free Relationships*. Refer to the Resources page at the end of this book for more information.]

The Christian parent strives to lovingly *train* his children in proper behavior and obedience. It was a helpful lesson to me as a father to learn about using the rod. I found it effective to clearly teach my children that their being spanked with the rod wasn't for *punishment* as much as it was for *training*—to remind them how to behave the next time. We determined ahead of time how many swats would be given when we used the rod. Consistency is also important. When your children transgress God's law and your word, explain how disappointed you are that they have chosen to act in such a way that the rod is necessary. Lovingly explain that their sin reveals how God gave them over to sin in their hearts so they might see how powerful and terrible sin is. Then patiently and without anger, obey God's Word and administer the use of the rod with enough force to cause pain.

It should go without saying that your goal is not to inflict marks or to beat your children. I encourage you to spank with the same amount of strength every time. Pray for them and give them an opportunity to express both their sorrow to God for disobeying Him and gratefulness for the lesson regarding sin and their hearts. You might also tell them that the reason you are using the rod is to remind them of how to behave the next time this situation arises, as well as of God's judgment in the future.

There may be times when you can tell that your child is teachable. I urge you to seize these opportunities and teach him or her about Jesus having taken our stripes and having been wounded for our transgressions so that we might have peace with God.

> **Surely our griefs He Himself bore, and our sorrows He carried;** *yet we ourselves esteemed Him stricken, smitten of God, and afflicted. But* **He was pierced through for our transgressions, He was crushed for our iniquities; the chastening for our well-being fell upon Him, and by His scourging we are healed.** *All of us like sheep have gone astray, each of us has turned to his own way; but* **the Lord has caused the iniquity of us all to fall on Him.** *He was oppressed and He was afflicted, yet He did not open His mouth; like a lamb that is led to slaughter, and like a sheep that is silent before its shearers, so He did not open His mouth (Isaiah 53:4-7).*

Another excellent training tool is *reproof.* This word primarily means "criticism for a fault." Reproof may be a sharp rebuke, but in the Scriptures the word carries several meanings that include *conviction* or *convincing* or *persuading.* It implies a kindly intent to correct a fault. Both the rod and reproof are important instruments to use if your children are to come to understand their responsibility before God. If you are faithful to obey God's Word in the early years, God will not need to use His rod (often in the form of civil government) in the later years. The following verses from Proverbs reveal the value of the rod and reproof:

> *The rod and reproof give wisdom, but a child who gets his own way brings shame to his mother (Proverbs 29:15).*

> *He who spares his rod hates his son, but he who loves him disciplines him diligently (Proverbs 13:24).*

> *Foolishness is bound up in the heart of a child; the rod of discipline will remove it far from him (Proverbs 22:15).*

> *You shall beat him with the rod, and deliver his soul from Sheol (Proverbs 23:14).*

Several verses in Proverbs 1 indicate that personal calamity may be another "rod" God uses if a child responds improperly to the reproof of a parent. In that chapter, a parent stands in the place of Wisdom calling out to the child in order to protect him. Part of training includes teaching your children the importance of *listening to, heeding, and valuing* your reproofs so they will not need the harder discipline of personal devastation that often results from an independent spirit. Help them to see that a child who will not listen to his parents' counsel may one day feel the sting of lonely humiliation:

> *Turn to my reproof; behold, I will pour out my spirit on you; I will make my words known to you. Because I called and you refused... and did not want my reproof, I will also laugh at your calamity" (Proverbs 1:23-26).*

Reproving and punishing your children according to God's Word is a constant testimony that your heart is turned toward them. If you are inconsistent or neglect the rod and reproof, they will conclude that you really don't care about them. Their hearts will turn to the world and their peers, and you'll lose your basis for effective discipline. Dads, I think it is wise to communicate to your children that *you* are the source of discipline for your children, not Mom. When you aren't at home, they need to know that she acts in your place. Their response to her is a response to you! Moms, it is wise for you to remember also that the way you discipline your child is a representation of your husband's heart for the child.

Maintain Their Hearts' Direction Toward You

One of the other means of preparing the hearts of children for a relationship with Jesus Christ is the father/child relationship. This is discussed at length in my audio and video series, *Equipping Men: Practical Tools for Life's Issues*, in the message entitled, "*Heart Maintenance.*" A child will respond favorably to instruction and discipline if he knows the heart of his father is turned toward him. Your child's open heart toward you is an open heart prepared for the Lord. The Spirit indicated this in Luke 1:17 when He spoke of John the Baptist. Just as John was a forerunner to the people of Israel for the Lord Jesus, so is a father the forerunner to his children for the Lord Jesus. Notice what the Spirit said of John the Baptist:

> *And it is he who will go as a forerunner before Him in the spirit and power of Elijah, **to turn the hearts of the fathers back to the children,** and the disobedient to the attitude of the righteous, so as to make ready a people prepared for the Lord.*

As a general rule, children whose hearts are soft and turned toward their fathers are also soft and open to the Lord. If children's hearts are closed to their fathers, they generally are closed to the Lord. Parents who value highly their relationships with their children, keep their hearts turned toward their children, and work at maintaining heart connections with their children are leading their children to Christ in an indirect yet powerful way.[38]

Place Godly Examples Before Your Children

Exposing your children to men and women of faith greatly contributes to their heart preparation for relationship with God. Through books, you can introduce great men and women of God to your children. Family reading times, school assignments, and personal private devotional reading may enable them to learn from others.

We found the ministry of hospitality to be a wonderful means for allowing our children opportunities to rub shoulders with faithful men and women. Much wisdom and passion for Christ may be shared around a dinner table or dessert. Guest speakers, missionaries, elders, and other ministers have stories to tell about their relationships with Christ. I learned to simply ask our guests to tell us "their story." As each of them shared about their lives, our children were being exposed to how God works and faithfully takes care of His people.

Of course, there's no one better to provide a Christ-like example than you—the parents! The testimony of your lives speaks much more loudly than your words. Children cannot deny the reality of God when they have grown up watching God live in their parents. It gives the gospel validity and vitality in their sight. The marriage relationship of the parents is a testimony of Christ and His church and should be a powerful attraction for the child to come to Jesus.

What if your marriage is not what you would like it to be? What if your spouse is not a believer, or has abandoned you and your children, or is absent for reasons beyond your control? Perhaps he or she is hostile to God, or is indifferent to the responsibilities of parenting. Maybe you don't share the same vision for your roles as parents or for your children's future. There is still a basis of hope for you and your children. That basis is His promises to you as you humble yourself before Him. God will finish what He has started in you and your children.

You also have hope because He has given you access to Himself through prayer. However flawed and ineffective your life seems to have been so far for your children, keep going to Him, and rely on His promises to you. Determine to keep doing your best as a parent, for His glory and your children's good. Remind yourself as you do so that He will live through you, and your life will reflect Him. Talk with Him and trust Him even if you feel unqualified. If you have a teenager whose heart is hard, and you must either deny him some privilege or require some act of him that you know is likely to cause strife, then pray, "Lord, help me do this the right way, and soften his heart toward You and me." If he responds rebelliously, keep trying to win his heart. Thank God each time you are able to work with him without losing your quietness and confidence in the Lord.

Repeat the Promises of God in the Gospel and Our Confession Regarding Jesus Christ

Have you recognized the relationship of hope to your faith and love for Jesus Christ? According to the Apostle Paul, faith and love come because of the hope of the gospel:

> *We give thanks to God, the Father of our Lord Jesus Christ, praying always for you, since **we heard of your faith in Christ Jesus and the love which you have for all the saints; because of the hope laid up for you in heaven**, of which you previously heard in the word of truth, the gospel, which has come to you, just as in all the world also it is constantly bearing fruit and increasing, even as it has been doing in you also since the day you heard of it and understood the grace of God in truth (Colossians 1:3-6).*

The promises of God have the power to produce hope in the hearts of your children, just as a father's promise to take his children to their favorite amusement park would inspire hope in them. From the time the father makes the promise, the children begin to hope and believe they are going to enjoy the experience. Love for their father swells in their hearts as they think about his fulfilling his promise. When the day comes and the family goes on the excursion, a deeper love for their father grows as they realize his faithfulness to his word. The gospel promises repeated to your children may have the same impact. *Hope produces faith, which works through love.*

Here are some promises worth repeating to your children:

God Promises Eternal Security to Those Who Come to Jesus

Jesus said to them, "I am the bread of life; he who comes to Me shall not hunger, and he who believes in Me shall never thirst.... All that the Father gives Me shall come to Me, and the one who comes to Me I will certainly not cast out" (John 6:35, 37).

God Promises to Be a Father to Those Who Turn to Him from the Idolatry of the World

"Therefore, come out from their midst and be separate," says the Lord. "And do not touch what is unclean; and I will welcome you. And I will be a father to you, and you shall be sons and daughters to Me," says the Lord Almighty (2 Corinthians 6:17-18).

God Promises Satisfaction to Those Who Trust in Him for the Salvation of Their Souls

For the Scripture says, "Whoever believes in Him will not be disappointed." ... For "Whoever will call upon the name of the Lord will be saved" (Romans 10:11, 13).

God Promises the Holy Spirit to Those Who Ask

*And I say to you, ask, and it shall be given to you; seek, and you shall find; knock, and it shall be opened to you. For everyone who asks, receives; and he who seeks, finds; and to him who knocks, it shall be opened. Now suppose one of you fathers is asked by his son for a fish; he will not give him a snake instead of a fish, will he? Or if he is asked for an egg, he will not give him a scorpion, will he? If you then, being evil, know how to give good gifts to your children, **how much more shall your heavenly Father give the Holy Spirit to those who ask Him?** (Luke 11:9-13).*

Of course, there are many more promises. I imagine you have some favorites. Remind them often to hold the promises of God tightly, trust in God to assure them, and give their lives to Him as disciples.

You might try this demonstration with one of your children. Holding the end of a dowel rod, representing the promises of God, extend the "promises" (the rod) to your child. Then ask him, "Do you want what God promises? If so, lay hold of them." He will probably take hold of the other end of the dowel. Don't give the rod to him immediately. Ask him another question: "How badly do you want to receive what God promises?" More than likely he will begin to pull on the other end. Continue to hold on and refuse to give it to him. At this point you may explain the value of God's timing in fulfilling what He promises. It is during the time of waiting that true faith is born out of hope and fleshly unbelief is purged.

If he is attempting to pull the rod out of your hand, then what you are feeling on your end is not faith, but his reliance on *his* fleshly efforts to *make you* fulfill the promise. He must learn to lay hold of the promises without demanding fulfillment, trusting God to give what He promises at the perfect time. Explain to him that God delays the fulfillment in order to produce faith in us, and this faith comes from the hope of the promises.

You see, while the child waits, he must ask himself if he really believes God when God says He will give life to those who are disciples of the kingdom (John 7:37-38). As he waits, he must lay aside unbelief and purify his faith as he thinks about God's character and His ability to keep His Word. In this way the child learns how faith is built because of hope. He may be assured that no true disciple of the kingdom of heaven who has endured to the end has ever been disappointed!

Lead Them to Live in Relationship With Him

Living in relationship with God is another way of describing being a disciple in the kingdom of the heavens. Your children need to be aware that they are living in His sight at all times. He is as near to them as the air they breathe. Although they cannot see Him, He is there watching, listening, and interacting with them. God is first *with them* before He is *in them*. The promises of God are to those who follow Him, give their lives to Him, and enter into a lifetime of discipleship. This was beautifully exemplified in the lives of the disciples of Jesus Christ. Discipleship will involve prayer and study of God's Word, with application. This is how we practice being disciples of Jesus Christ today.

Again, I don't want you to misunderstand me. I'm not saying that being a disciple of Jesus Christ and obeying His Word will justify anyone before God. In fact, we want to be sure to teach our children this truth.

What I am emphasizing, though, is the vital place discipleship plays in putting one on the road to life where he will be taught by God, be born again by God's Spirit, and will eventually enter into eternal life.

In our family, I think it was important in the lives of our children that before they were born again they talked with God on an event-by-event basis as they went through their days. They were "practicing the presence of God," much like Brother Lawrence wrote about in the classic book, *The Practice of the Presence of God*.[39] It is wise for our children to realize that *everyone is in relationship with God all the time*. The question is: Is their relationship one of enmity because of sin, or one of peace through Christ?

We should not overlook the importance of prayer as an expression of living in relationship with God. God has ordained prayer as well as the gospel as a means by which salvation is administered. It may be in a time of prayer and meditation that God will reveal Christ to them. The prayers of your children demonstrate the first kind of natural faith that precedes saving faith. It is one of the ways they can practice relationship with God before they are born again.

Consider These Dangers

Leading children to Christ has some challenges, as any experienced parent knows. Children are easily impressed and persuaded by fear of death, punishment, and displeasure. Adults can usually influence children to do almost anything, using various methods that involve these dynamics.

Children are very impressionable, making them easy targets for an evangelist's emotional appeal to trust in Christ so they will not spend eternity separated from those they love. If the evangelist makes his appeal with tears, emotionally manipulative music, or some other similarly powerful device, children may easily become afraid for themselves and so raise their hands or go forward to "receive Jesus." If a child is in a group, and a tearful appeal is being made to receive Jesus or else risk being left out (or "left behind"), he may feel pressured to join with his peers on the "salvation bandwagon."

The softness of heart in many children makes them vulnerable to an evangelistic presentation that simply makes them feel guilty and fearful. Young children especially may be made to feel guilty for not "accepting Christ," who has loved them so much as to die for them. Not wanting to feel guilty or condemned to hell, a child may do whatever someone suggests for his salvation—pray or repeat a "sinner's prayer," raise a hand, or be baptized. However, the question is: Has the Spirit of God regenerated the heart of the child? It's hard to know in light of his natural desire to avoid guilt, condemnation, and separation.

If their hearts are focused on themselves, children are also very susceptible to being motivated by the promises of reward and happiness. This makes them vulnerable to another common pop-church evangelistic approach: the "happy" tactic. The theme of this method is, "We're so happy in Jesus; won't you join us so you can be happy, too?" If we tell a child about God's promise of a reward for those who believe in Christ and the hope of eternal joy and happiness with Christ, the child naturally will be interested. Then even though there may be no work of the Spirit in his heart, a child may be convinced that "deciding for Christ" is in his or her best interest, because "God loves him and has a wonderful plan for his life." Yet, without the work of God by His Spirit preparing their hearts, many children—and their parents—may be falsely assured of salvation when nothing has occurred except a natural response to an emotional appeal.

Most children have a strong motivation to please their parents or leaders. Desiring the approval of parents, a pastor, a Sunday school teacher, or a friend may be enough motivation for a child to say he has accepted Christ and wants to be baptized. Consider what occurs naturally in the mind of a five-year-old when an older sibling trusts in Christ. The child sees the wonderful joy and approval from the parents directed toward the older brother or sister. Without any work of the Holy Spirit in his own heart, the child figures out how to get the same approval—by mimicking the older sibling! So watch for imitative spiritual behavior in younger children.

Children reared in Christian homes must be taught the difference between hearing truth with their heads and hearing truth revealed to their hearts. Jesus taught a foundational lesson in the Parable of the Sower in Mark 4 and Luke 8. Children should learn that listening requires more than *hearing about* Jesus and truth from God's Word. Until one is *doing something* with what he hears, he hasn't really heard. I'm not talking about salvation by works here, but discipleship requires attentiveness to the things that please and displease God. Children, therefore, must be taught to memorize and meditate on Scripture and to trust God to show them what they are to do with the truth they have learned. Although their doing good cannot save them, their learning what pleases the Lord and acting on it is what identifies them as His disciples. Being disciples in the kingdom prepares their hearts for faith in Christ. If you wish to know more about the importance of listening, I encourage you to listen to the first message, *"Having Ears to Hear"* in my series, *Rising to the Call*.[40]

Beware of Leading Them to Pray "The Sinner's Prayer"

What I'm about to say may sound strange to you if you have attended churches where altar calls are a part of the weekly worship service. *I advise caution in leading your children to think that if they pray a prayer of invitation to accept Jesus Christ as Savior, they are saved.* In a desire to please a parent or minister, to be rid of guilt, or to gain the praise of their fallen conscience, many children have prayed what has become known as "The Sinner's Prayer." Many of these children think they are saved, and only after many years of frustration and disillusionment discover they were never saved in the first place. The terrible loss these have suffered may be remedied with prayer and with careful and patient teaching, but an even worse tragedy is the number of those who think they are saved but are not and do not realize they need a remedy. Many have died in their sins because of the deception.

Beware of the Influence of the Spirit of Idolatry

Without realizing it, a child may use the prayer as a "carving tool" on God to get Him to save the child instead of simply coming to God to give Him his or her life. What do I mean by this? We are all born idolaters and tend to manipulate people in relationships by using what I call *positive carving tools*. These are words and actions that we use on other people to get them to do something that benefits us.

For example, one young lady admitted that she used smiles to get her boyfriend to do what she wanted, when she wanted it. Neither the young lady nor the young man was aware of their idolatrous manipulations. She thought she actually *loved* the young man when she smiled at him to get him to do something for her! In the same way, people may use "The Sinner's Prayer," thinking it pleases God. Then, because they have "pleased God," they think they love Him. The truth is revealed when God doesn't do what they want, when they want, like they want. The enmity against God in their hearts surfaces. What happens? You may have heard someone who has experienced this disillusionment say, "I've tried Jesus, but He didn't work for me."

It is important to teach your children about the spirit of idolatry, its characteristics, and its fruit. One goal I had when I wrote the book, *Equipped to Love: Idolatry-free Relationships*, was to assist parents in teaching their children about God's kind of love. True love for God must be free from idolatry. We should not go to God to get something for ourselves, but to get from Him *what we need to love and serve others, and to glorify Him.* He made us to be filled with Him, not to use Him.

You Want the Holy Spirit to Do the Work

One of the dangers facing parents is the temptation to persuade our children to make a decision for Christ as early as possible. As I said earlier, it is easy to impress and move a child to "invite Jesus into his heart." However, we need to remember that if someone can talk a person into "accepting Christ," someone else can just as well talk him into rejecting his profession of faith. Let's remember that if God changes the heart and gives repentance and faith, no one can talk him out of his confession.

I admit that it is an exercise in self-control for parents to wait on the Lord for the salvation of their children. My children were not born again until they were in their mid to late teens! We all learned to wait patiently on the Lord in hope. We reminded them of the importance of waiting on God to do the work in their hearts by assuring them that God would reveal Himself to them and give them His Holy Spirit. We encouraged them further with the hope that when He did reveal Himself and His Son in them, they would never be the same!

Ugh! We Didn't Know These Things and Now Our Children Are Grown!

God gives grace to the humble! There is always a hope for God's people who repent, admit their failures, and turn to the Lord. I'm always encouraged by the testimony of the Apostle Paul, whom God used in tremendous ways late in his life after having been a "blasphemer and a persecutor and a violent aggressor." I've heard wonderful testimonies from men who humbled themselves before their wayward young adult children, asked their forgiveness for their parenting failures, and prayed for God's mercy upon them. The principles found in the message "*Heart Maintenance*" from the *Equipping Men* series may also be applied to young adults whose hearts have been lost due to negligent or wrong parenting. Take heart! Ask the Holy Spirit to emphasize what you can use now in your relationships with your children as you read this chapter. The Lord will give you grace as you humble yourself and trust in Him.

Trust in the Lord!

I hope these suggestions encourage you that God can use you to lead your children to Christ. I think God's plan is for His people to have godly offspring. If God has turned a father's heart toward his children, then the father may be assured that he is an expression of *God's* heart for his children. May God lead you by His Spirit as you lead your children to the Lord Jesus Christ. There's no greater joy than to see your children walk in the truth.

Twenty-nine

Our Confession

Do you sometimes feel like the storms of life are going to obliterate your faith and smash it upon the rocks of perilous circumstances and disappointments? Or do you feel that you have an unshakable faith? As parents and leaders of your family, your faith in God sets the standard for the next generation. The timeless message from the book of Hebrews provides what we need to live anchored in Jesus Christ. Let's humble ourselves before the Lord and request strength and anointing as we receive from God's Word this wonderful encouragement to draw near to God and hold fast our confession in Jesus Christ. *you have said in Your word"

Our Father in heaven, who sits on the throne above all creation, and Lord Jesus, who sits on the right hand of the Majesty on high as our high priest, and Holy Spirit, who teaches us and guides us, we worship You and praise You. We ask as we look into Your Word, in the book of Hebrews, that You would anoint the teaching, You would anoint Your Word, and You would pour out Your Spirit on us so we would have understanding. Open our minds to understand Your will and Your purpose and Your plan; reveal in us an unshakable faith. Lord, You have said in Your Word that You have given us an unshakable kingdom, and we thank You for it. I pray You would enable me to articulate and communicate this glorious truth so we might be anchored in Jesus Christ our Lord. In His name we pray. Amen.

The message of this chapter will be especially helpful to the men. God intends for us to be strong in faith. We are to be the anchors and towers of stability for our families as they endure the storms of life. Our faith should be a contagious faith, an unwavering faith, a vibrant faith, and an enduring faith. I hope there are young men reading this book. You should be building the foundation for becoming leaders of the next generation of families. The teen years are the time to build your faith, grow in faith, and be strengthened in your relationship with God. When you become husbands and dads, you'll be towers of strength for your families.

Although we know we ought to be examples of stability, sometimes we're not. Right? There are reasons that we are not the bastions of faith we want to be. I think one of the main reasons is that we have not understood the importance of our confession.

What Is Your Confession Regarding Jesus Christ?

Do you understand or do you know what you confess to believe about Jesus Christ? Your answer to this question is important because your confession is the foundation for your faith. Another important question is: *Are you sure your confession is scriptural and grounded in the essential truths regarding Jesus Christ?* For instance, if your confession merely acknowledges Jesus as a prophet, as the Islamic faith does, it lacks the essential truth that Jesus was the Son of God incarnate.

Our confession regarding Jesus Christ is also vital because it provides a basis and a confidence for leadership and relationships. Living by our confession establishes a security that is able to weather any storm. In studying the book of Hebrews we find repeated truths about Jesus Christ, which form the basis of our confession. I've put it into a summary statement so we can memorize it and apply it to the events of life:

Jesus Christ is God's son (1:1-2),

And He is our high priest (1:3; 8:1).

After making purification for sins, He sat down at the right hand of the Majesty on high (1:3)

Where He intercedes for us (7:25)

And runs all things by the power of His spoken word (1:3).

He will preserve and save us through suffering, trials, and temptation (10:39, 4:16)

By giving us mercy and grace (4:16)

IF we will draw near to Him and hold fast our confession (4:14-16, 10:23).

I hope you will study the confession carefully. Perhaps you might read it again—maybe read it a couple of times. Every phrase, every truth about our Lord is important. I am sure more could be said about Jesus Christ, but I sought to include the most foundational truths that provide an anchor during the storms of life. There is value in understanding the importance of each truth in this confession, so let's look carefully at each phrase.

Jesus Christ Is God's Son

Let's begin by noticing what was written in Hebrews Chapter 1, verses 1 through 3:

> *God, after He spoke long ago to the fathers in the prophets in many portions and in many ways, in these last days has spoken to us in His Son, whom He appointed heir of all things, through whom also He made the world. And He is the radiance of His glory and the exact representation of His nature, and upholds all things by the word of His power. When He had made purification of sins, He sat down at the right hand of the Majesty on high.*

The identity of the person of Jesus Christ is foundational to our faith. Who is He? He is God's Son. Why is this important? When we confess Jesus as the Son of God, we are acknowledging His ownership of all things. We are also declaring His incarnation and all it entails. As the Son of God, He is the Messiah, sent by God to accomplish redemption and to reveal the glory of God. God has identified no other man as THE Son of God. God bore witness to the identity of Jesus of Nazareth numerous times in Christ's earthly life through miracles and through audible words from the kingdom of heaven, all of which were seen and heard by witnesses who testified to the veracity of the events. God the Father has given jurisdiction over all things to Christ because He is the Son of God. The Father will honor His Son when Christ judges all things at the end of history.

[handwritten margin note: It's all about Jesus, don't you think?]

[handwritten note: everything is about Christ. The beginning was christ, the middle was/is Christ, + the end will be Christ]

What use is this to us? If we know Jesus Christ and He lives in us, then we have a relationship with the living God who is acting in ALL of the events and affairs of history. We can talk with Him about everything.

[handwritten note: because He cares for you, loves you, and His purpose for you is to glorify Him. Cast ALL your cares on Him,]

Jesus Christ Is Our High Priest

Another vital truth to our faith is the ministry of the Lord Jesus on our behalf. The role of the high priest was to enter into the Holy of Holies on behalf of man and to represent the Holy One to man. You may recall that one of the signal events at the death of Christ was the tearing of the partition between the Holy Place and the Holy of Holies in the temple. This testified on earth to the priestly function accomplished by our Lord. He has brought God to man and man to God in a glorious ministry of reconciliation. Therefore, the veil that separated God's people from encountering Him personally was torn apart. Jesus was the fulfillment of the sacrifices and offerings that had been made by the priests in the tabernacle and temple under the Old Covenant. Even now, as you read this book, Jesus represents you before His Father and is the source of your presence and standing before God in grace. For us as believers, Jesus is not simply a high priest—He is our high priest. *Through Him, we can approach our Father at any time!*

After He Made Purification for Sins...

[handwritten: It is His righteousness not our own goodwork]

What did Jesus Christ do as our High Priest here on earth? In that role, He accomplished what we could not accomplish: He removed our sin far from us. He has presented us blameless and righteous in His own righteousness before our Father. Often what shakes our faith is our own sinfulness. *We must remember that God has dealt once for all time, through Jesus' death, burial, and resurrection, with the separation and corruption that our sins have made between us and our Father.* The great truth the Apostle Paul penned to the Corinthians secures our faith when the storm winds blow:

[handwritten left margin: now because of Jesus, when we stand before God, we are presented holy and blameless]

[handwritten: on for all much Dei bee Pau]

[handwritten: Its all paid for we don't have to live in guilt.]

> *God made Jesus to be sin on our behalf, that we might become the righteousness of God in Him (2 Corinthians 5:21).*

... He Sat Down at the Right Hand of the Majesty on High...

This part of the confession indicates what we believe about Jesus' present position of power and authority. Because of what He did on earth as High Priest, He has been rewarded, exalted, and given a name above every name. He has conquered sin, death, the devil, and everything hostile to our being in right relationship with God. He who is our Advocate is in the most powerful position possible—seated at the right

[handwritten: as a result of the cross]

hand of God, Most High. This should comfort us when we are afraid and anxious in the midst of trials, suffering, and temptations. The instant we remember that He is our Advocate, our hearts may rejoice, rest, and abide in Him. *Remembering also that we are seated with Him in the heavenly places, where there is peace and authority over all things, we are reassured that nothing can come our way except through the approval of Jesus Christ, who is before all things and through whom all things hold together.* This is truly an anchor for our faith!

all things, not some, all

First place, before all other things that aren't Him.

... Where He Intercedes for Us...

In Hebrews 7:25, Jesus ever lives to intercede for us. Paul explains that we shall be saved from the wrath of God through Him (Romans 5:9-10). We can be comforted when our faith is shaken to know that Jesus never ceases to intercede for us. I'm not saying He prays for every single person every moment of every day. I don't know that. However, we can be sure that we, as the objects of His love and atonement, are not out of His thoughts. Interceding for our deliverance through the storms of life is one of the purposes of His prayers! Let's take this faithful intercession of Christ further in a way. Consider this: *One hundred percent of His prayers are answered because He always prays according to the will of the Father.*

What does this mean to me personally? It means that whatever event that may be shaking my faith has come as an answer to Jesus' prayer for me. In the midst of a trial or affliction, I might be tempted to doubt Jesus' prayer request. But if my faith is to be anchored in the power of Christ, then this truth of His intercession for me is vital. I am assured that God is for me (Romans 8:31), and that Christ's intercession focuses on my being conformed to His image and values. He wants me to know Him more intimately, so He has designed particular trials to draw me into deeper relationship with Him, and Jesus is praying for me that I will rely on God for all that I need in the midst of those trials. The results of each trial are that I am more conformed to the image of Jesus, and God is more glorified through my life.

... And Runs All Things by the Power of His Word

My confidence is also bolstered by another truth. Not only does Jesus intercede continually, but also *He has complete, absolute control of every person and every event at all times.* This is not to say He *makes* people do what they do, but we confess that Jesus *uses everything and everyone for His purposes.* Numerous scriptures serve as the basis for this aspect of our confession, but the verses below confirm the truth stated in Hebrews 1:3, that Jesus "upholds all things by the word of His power."

What does this mean? I don't think the author had the inspired written word of God in mind as the source of power to uphold all things. Rather, he knew that all things exist and function according to the spoken word of Jesus Christ. It's another way of saying Jesus has jurisdiction or authority over everything. He merely needs to speak, and all things exist and respond. Jesus' disciples witnessed this power numerous times as He spoke and the dead were raised, the winds and waves were quieted, the sick were healed, and plants shriveled. This tremendous truth echoes through the Scriptures, especially in Paul's writings:

> *For by Him all things were created, both in the heavens and on earth, visible and invisible, whether thrones or dominions or rulers or authorities—all things have been created by Him and for Him.* **He is before all things, and in Him all things hold together** *(Colossians 1:16-17).*

> *Yet for us there is but one God, the Father,* **from whom are all things***, and we exist for Him; and one Lord, Jesus Christ,* **by whom are all things***, and we exist through Him (1 Corinthians 8:6).*

> *For as the rain and the snow come down from heaven, And do not return there without watering the earth, and making it bear and sprout, and furnishing seed to the sower and bread to the eater; so shall* **My word** *be which goes forth from My mouth; it* **shall not return to Me empty, without accomplishing what I desire, and without succeeding in the matter for which I sent it** *(Isaiah 55:10-11).*

When something happens to shake our faith or upset our plans, we have a tremendous confidence that things are not out of God's control and purpose. We know He has good intentions toward us, and we are never out of the center of His plan to use all things for our ultimate benefit. However, we may not see the benefit or understand God's ways. We may have to go through pain and anguish in order to learn not to fear but rather to seek Him. Although Paul was referring to God's gospel and His plan of salvation in Romans 11:33-36, these words are also true concerning all the events in our lives:

my mind runs wild to comprehend

> *Oh, the depth of the riches both of the wisdom and knowledge of God! How unsearchable are His judgments and unfathomable His ways! For who has known the mind of the Lord, or who became His counselor? Or who has first given to Him that it might be paid back to him again? For from Him and through Him and to Him are all things. To Him be the glory forever. Amen (Romans 11:33-36).*

Lew Sterrett, a horse trainer from the Miracle Mountain Ranch in Spring Creek, Pennsylvania, has a series of lessons entitled, "Sermon on the Mount." In the lesson on self-control, Mr. Sterrett, while training an unbroken filly, made a very insightful comment. He said that fear is a sign of someone who has not relinquished control and ownership of his or her life. He said this while he was training the horse to seek him when she was being introduced to the rope around her middle. He was teaching the horse to be peaceful in the midst of pain, confusion, and new pressures by focusing on the trustworthiness of her trainer rather than on the cause of the conflict.[41]

Like the horse, we have to be trained to look to the trustworthiness of our God and Savior who has purchased us with His blood. When He wisely applies a new pressure to train us to seek Him instead of succumbing to fear, our tendency is to strive to escape what we view as a problem. We may doubt His love, question His purposes, and feel like we deserve better treatment from His hand. As long as we do any of these things, we find that we have no peace or grace in the situation. However, the moment we remember that *God runs all things by the power of His word*, in accordance with Christ's intercession for us, we find that the fear leaves us and His peace floods our souls. This is because of the truths outlined in the rest of our confession.

He Will Preserve Us Through Suffering, Trials, and Temptation...

Our faith is tempted to shake when various trials come our way. Sometimes we *suffer* from sickness or the loss of a loved one. There are times when we are tried by circumstances and relationships, which I will call *trials*. Then *temptations* provide more opportunities for us to be preserved by our Savior and demonstrate our faith in Him. However, God's Word tells us we should not be surprised by them (1 Peter 4:12). In fact, James writes in the beginning of his letter that we are to *count it all joy* when we encounter various trials! We can do this if we will believe that

God has *designed* these trials for our good and will preserve us through them as we look to Him for the power to embrace them with grace. The faith God has given us is a tremendous encouragement in the midst of all kinds of troubles. Look at what He has said about those of us whom He has called to be His sheep, and the promise to us of His preservation:

> *But we are not of those who shrink back to destruction, but of those who have faith to the preserving of the soul (Hebrews 10:39).*

... By Giving Us Mercy and Grace...

How is it that we do not shrink back and that our souls are preserved? We walk with Him in hope and confidence. When our faith is assaulted, and we cling to Him, He is the anchor of our souls. God has provided everything we need for an unshakable faith in Jesus Christ. When we hold fast *to Him*, we find He pours out mercy and grace that preserves our souls in the midst of the trial.

> *... so that we may **receive mercy and find grace** to help in time of need (Hebrews 4:16).*

Sometimes we don't respond immediately to trials by applying our confession. The result: we sin. When we sin and then draw near to God, we can be confident that *we will receive mercy.* He is acquainted with our weaknesses and knows what it is like to suffer, to be tried, and to be tempted. That's one of the reasons He came to earth in a body—so He could know what we experience firsthand. Since Jesus has given His life for us as the ultimate act of mercy to us in our sin, then we can be sure He will give us mercy in specific instances when we are in need.

However, when God searches us and reveals what *He sees* in us (through the suffering, trial, or temptation), and we have drifted from our confession, *we also need grace* (that is, God's power) to work in us so that we may stand anchored peacefully in the midst of the storm. When the author used the word "grace" in this context, he was not referring to the grace by which we are justified in Jesus Christ. We usually think of this grace as undeserved favor and associate it with salvation. Instead, he had in mind the powerful gift of an inner work of the Spirit of God, enabling us to be at peace and to endure to the end for His glory. But this mercy and grace doesn't come automatically. It comes only...

... *If* We **Draw Near and Hold Fast Our Confession**

If we look carefully at the words of verse 16...

*Therefore let us **draw near** with confidence to the throne of grace, **so that** we may receive mercy and find grace to help in time of need.*

... we see that *drawing near to Him and holding fast this confession is the means by which we receive mercy and grace in time of need.* Christians may delay drawing near or may timidly draw near to the throne of grace when the storms of life blow. When we do, we don't receive mercy and grace in the time of need! That's not to say we no longer are under God's saving mercy and grace. We are always in that state. However, the need of the moment is for a specific mercy and grace. When the assault is on, I need peace! I need grace to endure! Don't you? The writer has given the warning, and it is an appeal to us to exercise our faith in our relationship with God. If we drift away from our confession and don't draw near to God, we will be lacking mercy and grace in the specific situation that God has ordained for us.

But why put it in the negative? Instead, the author encouraged our hearts with what we know to be true. We need to be reminded: We can draw near to Jesus Christ by holding fast our confession and applying it to situations or relationships, and He'll be an anchor for us, a solid rock in the storms of life. Everything that could separate us from God and hinder us from drawing near has been removed. There is no reluctance on His part to pour out mercy and grace. *He's already done so!* He has given us the Holy Spirit, who works in us to do God's will and to please Him (Philippians 2:12-13). Through His Son He has spoken to us these tremendous truths into which we may anchor our faith. God has provided all we need to walk in peace through every trial, from the smallest conflict to the ultimate test of our souls—death and judgment. Our faith is stable only when we hold fast this confession, write it into our hearts, and live it out each moment of our lives.

*Therefore, since we have a great high priest who has passed through the heavens, Jesus the Son of God, **let us hold fast our confession**. For we do not have a high priest who cannot sympathize with our weaknesses, but One who has been tempted in all things as we are, yet without sin. Therefore **let us draw near** with confidence to the throne of grace (Hebrews 4:14-15).*

I think of this confession as a tool for life. Tools are made for certain situations. Some tools are used more than others. Our confession regarding Jesus Christ is to be employed on a moment-by-moment basis everyday. The more we practice with it, the better we get at living anchored in Jesus.

I encourage you to memorize this confession. Teach it to your children, and encourage them daily to apply the truth. You'll be equipping them with a tool for life! Let's look at it one more time:

> Jesus Christ Is God's Son, and He Is Our High Priest.
>
> After making purification for sins, He sat down at the right hand of the Majesty on high, where He intercedes for us and runs all things by the power of His word.
>
> He will preserve us through suffering, trials, and temptation by giving us mercy and grace IF we will draw near to Him and hold fast our confession.

Now that we've stated and explained the confession found in Hebrews, we're ready to understand the tremendous message of that book and become firmly anchored in Christ.

Thirty

Watch Out for Drifting!

[handwritten: drifting happens unexpectedly when we let our guard down]

Maybe you've heard stories of people who went over the falls on *[handwritten: guard]* the Niagara River in disabled boats. I can only imagine the terror in their hearts as their crafts drifted toward the roar and danger of the great Niagara Falls. Some stories ended in tragedy, while others told of miraculous rescues. Those rescued were saved from going over the falls because their boats became anchored in one way or another.

Have you ever been in a drifting boat when you didn't want to be? If you have, then you can relate to a common problem addressed by the author of the book of Hebrews: unbelief and drifting away from our confession and relationship with God. It can happen to the best of us before we realize what's happened, can't it? Therefore the author encouraged his readers to continually draw near to God and hold fast their confession *[handwritten: pg 289 all about Jesus]* with regard to Jesus Christ. In the remaining chapters of this book, I'd like to take you on a sort of excursion through the book of Hebrews. My goal is the same as that of the book's original author—to highlight the excellencies of Christ and to convince you of the trustworthiness of God's promises in order that you will draw near to Him in faith more and more consistently, holding fast to your confession of Christ, and becoming firmly anchored in Him through the storms of life.

In the first chapter of Hebrews we are reminded that God has spoken in the Old Testament period through the prophets, but now has spoken again in and through His Son, Jesus Christ. The author contrasts the two ways God's Word has come to man: through the messengers or prophets (the angels) and through His Son. In verse four Jesus is described as being exalted above the prophets, in the phrase, "having become as much better than the angels." Never to anyone but Jesus has God ever audibly declared, "Thou art My Son." God's pronouncement from heaven was recorded twice in the gospels: once at Jesus' baptism and again on the Mount of Transfiguration. It is important for us (the readers) to recognize that God never exalted any of the prophets with such an audible declaration from heaven.

> **To whom has He ever said,** *"Sit here at My right hand until I make Thine enemies a footstool for Thy feet"? (Psalm 110:1 and Hebrews 1:13).*

Only to Jesus Christ. I might also add, for those who have contemplated other religions, that there are no eyewitness testimonies of God ever saying such a thing to Buddha or Muhammad or Confucius. He didn't say it to any of the tens of thousands of Hindu gods. He didn't say it to anybody except Jesus Christ.

Watch Out—Don't Drift

In Hebrews Chapter 2, readers are given an important warning: You must not drift away from what God has spoken in and through Jesus Christ. Because Jesus Christ is our high priest and is the Son of God sitting at the right hand of the Majesty on high, and because He is the greatest One ever to have spoken from God to man, "We must pay much closer attention to what we have heard, lest we drift away from it" (verse 1). Here the author introduced the theme of "drifting" or "falling away." Some have mistakenly concluded from these words that a believer may fall away from eternal salvation. However, the context doesn't support such an interpretation. Instead, the author was concerned about his readers being anchored in Jesus Christ on a daily basis. The warning he gave has to do with carelessness. We cannot be careless when God speaks.

> *For if the word spoken through the angels,* [through the other messengers such as Moses, Joshua, David, Isaiah, Jeremiah, and all the prophets] *proved unalterable, and every transgression and every disobedience received the just recompense,* **how shall we escape if we neglect so great a salvation?** *After it was at first spoken through the Lord, it was confirmed to us by those who had heard, God also bearing witness with them by both signs and wonders and by various miracles, by*

gifts of the Holy Spirit, according to His own will. For He did not subject to angels the world to come, concerning which we are speaking (Hebrews 2:2-5).

Throughout Chapter 2 the author admonished his readers to pay careful attention to what God has spoken through Jesus. Why? Because He proclaimed a tremendous salvation to us, namely, that with Christ we shall be given dominion over the entire earth! This glorious promise of great salvation was prophesied in Psalm 8:6. In speaking of redeemed man, the psalmist declared,

> *"Thou hast put all things in subjection under his feet."*

Then the author of Hebrews, again referring to redeemed men, commented,

> *"For in subjecting all things to him, He left nothing that is not subject to him. But now we do not see all things subjected to him."*

In this verse, the Holy Spirit reminds us that a day is coming when the earth will be ours. As Jesus said, we will inherit the earth (Matthew 5:5). What will it take for us to be ready for all things to be subjected into our hands? We need experience and we need maturity.

how can we grow if not through suffering? [No pain] [No gain]

God's Way to Mature His People Is Through the Means of Suffering

When you are in the midst of a swirling life storm, do you find yourself asking, "Are all things really run by Christ?" or "Is Christ really sovereign over this terrible thing that just happened?" Your questions are legitimate; however, you shouldn't let them lead you to wrong conclusions. The fact that life's storms happen doesn't mean God doesn't have a good, higher purpose for them. In the rest of Chapter 2 and the first part of Chapter 3, the author informs us of God's means for strengthening our faith: <u>suffering.</u>

Christ's suffering was for our Good.

> *But we do see Him who has been made for a little while lower than the angels, namely Jesus, because of the <u>suffering</u> of death,* **⌈***crowned with glory and honor***⌉** *that by the grace of God He might taste death for everyone. **For it was fitting for Him, for whom are all things and through whom are all things, in bringing many sons to glory, to perfect the author of their salvation through sufferings.** For both*

read X5

in bringing us to glory (His glory) He uses suffering to grow us and perfect our salvation.

[handwritten: Sanctification is like "bringing many sons to glory" process]

He who underlines sanctifies and those who are sanctified are all from one Father (Hebrews 2:9-11a).

Would we design suffering into our lives if we were running all things? Definitely not! However, according to God's wisdom and goodness, He has united us with Christ. And because we are united with Christ, we will suffer also. If God the Father perfected His Son through sufferings, then we who are united with Him as sons of God may expect to be matured through sufferings. God perfects or matures the faith of Christ in and through us by means of trials, afflictions, and temptations. This is not to say that God Himself tempts, afflicts, or tries us. He uses lesser agents to accomplish these ends. As we look at people suffering, it appears to us that Jesus is not running all things by the word of His power. But the writer says He *IS* seated at the right hand and He *IS* in control of all things.

Jesus Christ Is Central to Our Confession

[handwritten: prayer] How should we respond to such a high priest as Jesus Christ who has faithfully spoken God's word to us? *We can confess that He is reigning over the world through His word.* We can also honor Him as a faithful builder. "Therefore holy brethren, partakers of the heavenly calling, consider Jesus, the Apostle and High Priest of our confession" (Hebrews 3:1). This is our confession: He is our high priest. Consider him. He was faithful. *We can confess that He is faithful.*

"He is faithful to Him who appointed Him, as Moses also was in all his house, for He has been counted worthy of more glory than Moses, by just so much as the builder of the house has more honor than the house" (Hebrews 3:2-3).

[handwritten: "a run to your high helper"] The author continues with an encouragement to honor Jesus as a faithful builder of God's house. Jesus is not making mistakes with you, in your situations and circumstances. He has not left you to find your own way out of your circumstances. As our high priest, He is not failing. He runs everything according to His word with the purpose of making you like Himself.

The warning is stated again in Chapter 3, verses 7 through 11, from the Old Testament testimony: We should not neglect the word of God when He speaks.

Therefore just as the Holy Spirit says, "Today if you hear His voice, **do not harden your hearts** *as when they provoked*

*Me in the day of trial in the wilderness, where your fathers tried Me by testing Me and saw My works for forty years. Therefore I was angry with this generation, and said, **'They always go astray in their heart, and they did not know My ways'**; as I swore in My wrath, 'They shall not enter My rest.'"*

We often have the same problem as Israel had: Their vision for their lives was not the same as God's. Their hearts went astray because their hearts' vision was to be happy and comfortable. When you recall the conflicts the children of Israel had with God as He brought them out of Egypt, you notice that their hearts were always going astray— *don't fall into that trap* always failing to believe that God had their best interest in view. They always wanted *more* or they wanted *other* than what God had provided. What are the ways of God that Israel did not know? I think there are two important ways of God's working in His people: First, God's way of maturing His people is through suffering. Second, He gives them many opportunities to practice drawing near and holding fast their confession, which will result in peace. *as you ♥ (papa) told me many times. ♥*

We see this second important lesson in God's declaration in Hebrews 3:11, *we cannot have peace in the chaos of life if we don't trust there is plan + purpose in it all.*

"As I swore in My wrath, they shall not enter My rest."
We cannot live in the rest or peace of God if we do not believe that Jesus Christ is running all things by His powerful word, and that He is doing so for our benefit. This is the point the author of Hebrews is making: *If God swore that His people would not enter into His rest when they ignored His word to them through Moses, are we to think God will let His people enter His rest if they ignore His word through Jesus, His Son? Again, this is not the rest of eternal salvation but of grace and peace in this life's trials and troubles.* *peace is not contingent w/circumstances!*

lol We should pay attention when God swears! He certainly doesn't need to swear to increase the veracity of His statements. When God swears, it must be for emphasis to His people. He means business when He says He will give no rest (no grace or mercy) to His own people who do not draw near to Him and hold fast their confession regarding the way He is running the affairs of life. *Song: "Say the Word" - Hillsong, Empires.*

Watch Out—God's People Can Be Unbelieving

> *Take care, brethren, lest there should be in any one of you an evil, unbelieving heart, in falling away from the living God (Hebrews 3:12).*

Please consider the significance of this call for caution. What is the author warning us to watch out for? First, brothers in Christ may have unbelieving hearts at some times or about some matters. Second, when unbelief prevails, true Christians fall away (drift) from their anchor (the living God). How do we fall away or drift? Well, first of all, we start thinking differently about God. We start behaving as though He were nowhere around, right? As though He were "dead," not "the living God." What is the difference between "the living God" and a dead god?

Let's think in human terms for a moment. A living person is one who is acting in life—interacting with others, relating to and communicating with them, and working out his plans and purposes. So it is with God. He is alive and active in our lives. In contrast, if we say someone isn't alive, we know he is dead because there is no action. He is not interacting, not relating, and not doing anything. So when we are worrying, grumbling, and striving to control events and people, we are behaving as though God is dead and not controlling all of life by His wisdom, goodness, power, and love. When this happens, we have "evil, unbelieving hearts." We are not holding onto our confession that Jesus is the living God and is sitting at the Father's right hand with everything subject to Him. We are, indeed, falling away from the foundational truth that God is alive and is perfectly working out His plans. The writer cautions us to take care that this does not happen.

Drifting doesn't happen in a big way all at once. We move away from God a little at a time as we fall into a pattern of thinking wrongly about God. The truth is that Jesus is sitting at the right hand of God in authority, interceding for us—but we forget this, and our hearts move away from Him. Why? *Because we are failing to apply the truth about who He is to the specific situation at hand, and we do this many times over until eventually we find ourselves "adrift" from our anchor—the truth of God and His faithful word spoken to us.* Then someone says or does something that goes against our will or desire, and in a heartbeat it seems we wake up, finding ourselves adrift from our confession and filled with anger, terror, disillusionment, or bitterness.

What better word picture is there than *drifting away* or *falling away*? He says, "Take care, be on the alert, watch out for an evil, unbelieving heart that does not believe Jesus Christ is seated at the right hand of God and is our faithful high priest." *Every time you don't believe your confession and fail to apply it to life, you reap the results: no peace or grace.* God has sworn that none will enter His rest who drift or fall away from the truth of God's good will to sanctify us through trials. If you are not careful about this, you will be a man or woman in conflict and turmoil.

[handwritten: Christ Centered Community]

We Need Encouragement Every Day

[handwritten: pivital to walk, growth and keeps us the f our walk, growth and danger of far Heb 3:13 drifting away]

Verse 13 of Chapter 3 communicates a necessary ministry in the body of Christ, and also why it is necessary. "Encourage one another, day after day." What does this say about us? I think this implies that we can all fall at any given moment. Christians must be on the alert for signs of their brothers or sisters drifting away under a trial. In fact, the danger of drifting away may threaten so regularly that we need someone to remind us every day that Jesus is praying for us and is in charge of everything.

We need someone to encourage us when we find ourselves frustrated, peaceless, and graceless because we've anchored into shifting sand. We need to hear, *"Remember, you can draw near and hold fast to Jesus and who He is and what He's doing so you can receive mercy and grace in this time of need."* *[handwritten: (lol @ that star)]*

[handwritten: There is therefore no condemnation for those in Christ Jesus.]

I'd like to give a word of caution here. If we're not careful or have been in a habit of hyper-self-condemnation we'll think the worst: "I'm toast if I don't remember my confession!" We're told in Hebrews that the Lord Jesus knows our weakness (Hebrews 4:15). We're not under condemnation (Romans 8:1). We need encouragement daily—often— that when we are in the midst of a God-ordained trial and under the consequences of unbelief, we have a channel of grace available to us. Our high priest, Jesus Christ, is merciful and gracious to every one of His brothers and sisters who will draw near to Him and apply their confession to the situation. *He is the solid rock in the storms of life!*

[handwritten: spiritual discipline]

Until we have established a habit of living by our confession, we need reminding, don't we? We need someone who will encourage us and say, "Do not worry. Enter into the rest of God. Jesus has not left the throne. He is a faithful high priest to you. You need not be troubled. Draw near to Him and hold fast your confession!"

Verse 13 also tells us that we need this encouragement because of the power of sin—it can deceive us and harden us.

[handwritten: Father of lies.]

"Encourage one another day after day, as long as it is still called 'today,' lest any one of you be hardened by the deceitfulness of sin."

How does sin harden us, and what kind of sin is the author talking about here? He is not talking about any general sin. Rather, the sin that can be so debilitating and destructive is *the sin of unbelief with regard to God, Jesus' ministry on our behalf, and our relationship with Him.* He is saying that unbelief is deceitful. Sin's presence in our own lives or in others' lives (which causes suffering or trials in our lives) argues that God is not good and cannot overcome evil. This is "the deceitfulness of sin." Some who would attempt to discredit Christianity, and others who simply do not understand, say, "God's problem is the presence of evil in the world." The truth revealed in Christ replies, "God has a purpose for the existence of evil and sin in the human experience, and He's using it for good in the lives of His people" (Romans 8:28). However, sin in us will lie and misdirect us. It will tell us that Jesus is not on the throne. It will tell us to look at a problem or at the failures and offenses of another person instead of at Jesus. *The sin of unbelief focuses our attention on anything but the truth about Jesus.* be awear

We should not make light of this important warning that comes up repeatedly in Hebrews 3 and 4. Not believing our confession with regard to Jesus Christ (see Chapter 29) means that we're adrift without an anchor in the storms of life. God has sworn there will be no peace or rest for us when we ignore what His Word has revealed to us about Jesus and our relationship with Him.

Having given us the warning of what *NOT* to do as God is maturing us through suffering, the author continued with God's tremendous promise of rest to those who will enter. We'll look into that in the next chapter.

Thirty-one

The Promise of Rest (Heb. 4)

Therefore, let us fear lest, while a promise remains of entering His rest, any one of you should seem to have come short of it.

There is a wonderful promise and hope in the first verse of the fourth chapter of Hebrews. Although the author continues his warning that we not fall short of the peace and rest of God in the midst of a trial, we shouldn't miss the hope presented in this chapter that we *may* enter God's rest. We notice the phrase, "come short of it," communicating again the same idea as "drifting away from it" and "falling away from it." We are not meant to come short of living in the peace and rest of God. We are to be men and women with an unshakable faith—a faith that cannot be shaken by life's circumstances and relational problems. God has promised this kind of rest for His people.

However, it is important to keep this is mind: His peace doesn't come from self-effort. Jesus Christ lived in the rest of His Father. He didn't strive; He wasn't troubled; He lived in peace. He was anchored in His Father's rest—He lived surrendered to His Father's will and works. As long as Jesus worked in union with His Father, there was no conflict within Him, even when He encountered opposition outwardly. He was confident that His Father was in charge and that all things were subjected to Him. He lived applying that confession to the events in His life, and so should we.

The author describes in Hebrews 4:10 what someone does who

enters the rest that God has provided for His people.

> For the one who has entered His rest **has himself also rested from his works**, as God did from His.

The reason we have an unshakable faith is that *our faith is not based on our works.* Hallelujah! If our faith were based on something we did, we would have a faith that is shakable every minute! But God has given us a true rest: faith that is resting on *His* works, not *ours*. The reason we *rest* in His works is that we know all His works are good. Psalm 145:17 boldly declares,

> "The LORD is righteous in **all His ways**, and kind in **all His deeds**."

It is for this reason that the author tells us in Hebrews 4:11,

> "Let us therefore be diligent to enter that rest, lest anyone fall through following the same example of disobedience."

The author is referring to the Israelites who refused to honor God with single-hearted trust that He was sufficient to save them and sustain them. Their sinful greed and discontentment deceived them with regard to God's promises of bringing them into their promised rest—the Promised Land. They expected the trip to be painless, void of conflict, and with a greater variety in their diet! Consequently, they failed to enter into the rest God had provided for them through His promises.

So on one hand, we should be afraid if we *don't* enter the rest God has for us. I think one of the purposes of this epistle's author was to stir up in us a strong sense of danger if we do not live in the rest of God. He was not talking about Sunday afternoon naps, but about a rest from our own works that is available to us all the time. Are we paying attention? Are we asking God for this rest? Or are we forgetting about Him and His promises, drifting little by little away from Him?

It is helpful to recognize the power of sin's deceitfulness in us and the work of the enemy against us. We are constantly tempted to believe that God is *not good* or *not kind* in all His deeds, and therefore we are tempted to turn away from God and look to other things or people for the peace and rest we desire. This is idolatry. We need to learn to face those silent charges that we make against God: *We* would not run the universe the way *He* is doing it, and because He is doing it the way He is, He is not good, not kind, not loving, not wise, and not trustworthy. This is the way the Hebrews thought in the wilderness.

On the other hand, the author encourages us to enter into the rest of God and to know this: the word by which Jesus Christ runs all things is a *living* word. It's an *active* word. What does this mean to us? It means that His word is causing everything, and it's doing everything. If our confidence is in God's *goodness* as well as His *power*, then this is extremely comforting. This assurance is, at least in part, the *way of peace* that unbelievers do not know (Romans 3:17). His goodness in running the universe is the reason Romans 8:28 comforts us: "And we know that God causes all things to work together for good to those who love God, to those who are called according to His purpose." Holding fast this confidence in His goodness enables us to rest.

The word of Christ's power is also a *penetrating* word—a word that pierces. When the word of God works in the affairs of men, it exposes the hearts of everyone involved. Motives are revealed because He can see into the heart. We're told that nothing escapes His notice.

> *For the word of God is living and active and sharper than any two-edged sword, and piercing as far as the division of soul and spirit, of both joints and marrow, and able to judge the thoughts and intentions of the heart. And there is no creature hidden from His sight, but all things are open and laid bare to the eyes of Him with whom we have to do (Hebrews 4:12-13).*

What is hopeful about these verses, and how does it connect with the promise of entering His rest? You believe God is working a good benefit in your life through all things, right? What is that good benefit? *He is sanctifying you—cleansing you of unbelief.* You may be encouraged that every affliction, trial, or temptation is carefully designed by an all-seeing God to expose those things He wants to remove and which hinder your entering His promised rest. When you're going through the trials, you must learn to not question God's goodness or promises, but determine to...

Because of Jesus we can Hold fast to our confession

Enter the Rest of God by Holding Fast Your Confession

> *Since, then, we have a great high priest who has passed through the heavens, Jesus, the Son of God, let us hold fast our confession (Hebrews 4:14).*

The author is clear! The Sabbath rest comes when we hold fast our confession. If we don't know what our confession is, how can we hold it fast? So again, what is the confession of believers, found in Hebrews?

Jesus Christ Is God's Son, and He Is Our High Priest

After making purification for sins, He sat down at the right hand of the Majesty on high, where He intercedes for us and runs all things by the power of His word.

He will preserve us through suffering, trials, and temptation by giving us mercy and grace IF we will draw near to Him and hold fast our confession.

We are encouraged to hold fast our confession, no matter what happens. Our faith stands there. Notice the truth contained in Hebrews 4:12-13 (see previous page). Our hope rests on the fact that nothing escapes God's word. Remember, at the time he wrote this epistle, the author probably wasn't thinking about the Scriptures when he mentioned "the word of God." There's been no mention of them in the context. This "word" harkens back to the word by which Jesus upholds all things. Nothing is out of control. The writer wanted us to know that everything occurring is a result of *God's spoken word*. At every given moment, in every particular circumstance, our hope rests on the facts that Jesus is our high priest, and He knows us. The author continued encouraging his readers—and us:

> For we do not have a high priest who cannot sympathize with our weaknesses, but One who has been tempted in all things as we are, yet without sin. Therefore let us draw near with confidence to the throne of grace, so that we **may receive mercy** and **may find grace to help** in time of need (Hebrews 4:15-16).

Mercy and grace are available in the midst of suffering. We may *draw near* to God, *hold fast* our confession, and apply it every single day to every single situation and every single relationship—to everything. The result is that for which we were made, and for which we long: we enter into the rest of God! *We are/were made for God's rest. To enter into it. To enjoy it.*

Jesus Is Our High Priest

Throughout Chapter 5 of Hebrews, we see that our hope rests on the fact that Jesus is our high priest. Today very few of us realize the importance of the ministry of a priest. But the first readers of this book, who were Hebrews (or Jews), were very familiar with priests and their service in the temple.

For every high priest taken from among men is appointed on behalf of men in things pertaining to God, in order to offer both gifts and sacrifices for sins; he can deal gently with the ignorant and misguided, since he himself also is beset with weakness; and because of it he is obligated to offer sacrifices for sins, as for the people, so also for himself (Hebrews 5:1-3).

Following this, throughout the rest of Chapters 5 through 9, the author revealed how Jesus Christ as high priest is far superior to the Jewish high priests. He did not need to offer sacrifices for Himself as they needed to because, although He was tempted as we are, He had no sin; and throughout His life He performed perfect righteousness. Our confession of Jesus as our high priest during times of our emotional and temporal shaking is no insignificant truth. In fact, the writer stated that this was his *main point!*

*Now, **the main point in what has been said is this: we have such a high priest,** who has taken His seat at the right hand of the throne of the Majesty in the heavens, a minister in the sanctuary and in the true tabernacle which the Lord pitched, not man (8:1-2).*

What a glorious priest we have! Of course, the most significant ministry of Jesus as our high priest was His offering of Himself as a sacrifice once for all, for all sin. He perfectly dealt with everything that could be a problem between God and us. That's why the writer of Hebrews assures us that since God has made Him our eternal high priest, we now have "hope... as an anchor of the soul... both sure and steadfast" (Hebrews 6:19). If we have "rested from our own works" (Hebrew 4:10), then because of both Christ's perfection and His sympathy toward us, we have confidence to trust Him as He runs our lives.

Consider the following aspects of Jesus' ministry to us as our high priest. First, as I mentioned above, Christ never sinned. Second, His sacrifice for us was made *once*. No more sacrifices are needed. His is perfect. It is finished. Third, He is alive forevermore, so as our eternal and perfect minister of grace, we never need to fear that what He did for us is not enough, or that a different priest may replace Him who may not do so good a job as He did in representing us before God. Fourth, He is always praying for us, and His prayers are always perfect, so His Father always answers them. Fifth, because God is answering His prayers on our behalf, we know that one day we will see Him and we will be like Him, and we will be with Him forever.

What a tremendous hope! Since God has sworn to the eternal nature of Christ's ministry as our high priest, we have every reason to rejoice with confidence under this new and better covenant.

> *The Lord has sworn and will not change His mind, "Thou art a priest forever"; so much the more also **Jesus has become the guarantee of the better covenant.** The former priests, on the one hand, existed in greater numbers because they were prevented by death from continuing, but He, on the other hand, **because He continues forever, holds His priesthood permanently** (7:21b-24).*

Jesus Is Our Intercessor

> *Therefore He is able also to save forever those who draw near to God through Him, since **He always lives to make intercession for them** (7:25).*

Who is included in this promise of salvation? *Anyone* who will draw near to God, because Jesus is able to save that person forever! The *New American Standard Exhaustive Concordance of the Bible* says that the word translated "forever" means "completely."[42] I've wondered whether the foremost concept in the writer's mind was of *eternal* salvation, or salvation from *trials, temptations, and suffering.* The context of the book causes me to lean toward the latter, not that it isn't also true with regard to our eternal salvation. Whatever he meant, the author indicated that Christ is able to save because of His intercessory ministry.

What does His intercession mean to us in the everyday events of our lives? We read that *Jesus lives to intercede for us.* We may be sure that one hundred percent of Jesus' prayers for us are answered because He always prays according to the will of His Father. Therefore we may also conclude that whatever occurs in our lives is in answer to Jesus' intercession! Both good and bad come from God's hand. As we have discussed in previous chapters, it is not that God *causes* the good and bad in our lives, but He rules over His messengers in both the jurisdiction of light and the jurisdiction of darkness, sometimes instructing and sometimes permitting them to work in our lives; and He has a purpose and use for them in conforming us into the image of His Son and in maturing our faith.

Because of Jesus' Ministry to Us, Let Us Draw Near and Hold Fast

When we get to Hebrews 10:19, we have another encouragement to *draw near* and *hold fast our confession*. The author admonishes his readers repeatedly throughout his letter to apply the truth of their confession to life. *don't just learn truth, actually apply it*

> *Therefore, brethren*, *since we have confidence to enter the holy place by the blood of Jesus, by a new and living way which He inaugurated for us through the veil, that is, His flesh, and since we have a great priest over the house of God,* **let us draw near** *with a* **sincere heart** *in* **full assurance** *of faith, having our hearts sprinkled clean from an evil conscience and our bodies washed with pure water.* **Let us hold fast** *the* **confession of our hope without wavering, for He who promised is faithful** *(Hebrews 10:19-23).*

Let's remember that *draw near* and *hold fast* are in contrast to *drift away* and *shrink back* (Hebrews 10:39). Furthermore, drawing near and holding fast are *exercises* of our faith, which contrast to the *results* of unbelief: drifting or falling short. It has been helpful to me to summarize the entire book of Hebrews with these four words: *Draw near! Hold fast!* When we read or listen to God's Word, our most important response is *what we do with it*. Mere accumulation of knowledge and mental assent to truth is fruitless if we don't do something with it. The Apostle James emphasized this when he wrote,

> *"But prove yourselves doers of the word, and not merely hearers who delude themselves" (James 1:22).*

Jesus also taught this important principle at the end of the foundational parable about listening when He said,

> *"My mother and My brothers are these who hear the word of God and do it" (Luke 8:21).*

I encourage you, therefore, to draw near and hold fast your confession so that you may enter into the promised rest of God. Then your trials will take on new meaning as you understand their eternal purpose.

Thirty-two

The Day Draws Near

Not only are _we_ to draw near and hold fast, but we are to encourage _other_ believers to do so also. After the call in Hebrews that we looked at in the last chapter, for believers to apply to their lives their confession regarding Jesus Christ, the author reminded his readers of another important doctrine: the Day of Judgment and the return of Christ:

> Let us consider how to stimulate one another to love and good deeds, not forsaking our own assembling together, as is the habit of some, but encouraging one another, and all the more as you see the day drawing near (Hebrews 10:24-25).

"As you see the day drawing near." Because of the nearness of "the day," we are to encourage each other "all the more." Evidently, the author's view of Jesus' return and the Day of Judgment were meant to be motivational to the first-century believers. As we read further in Hebrews 10, I imagine the author's reference to God's judgment of willfully sinful Christians is shocking to many today. Why? Because for most believers today, the Day of Judgment is...

Not on the Radar Screen

I've discovered that most Christians know very little about the Day of Judgment; consequently, it doesn't figure into their lives. Many people I've spoken with lack knowledge concerning the Day of Judgment because their pastors and teachers haven't taught about it. The topic is treated almost like the plague. I recently saw a church's advertisement on a huge billboard in our city. On the opposite side of the billboard from its name and address it proudly declared, "Hell and Judgment Not Included!" The attraction is clear: If you come to this church, you won't hear anything about Hell and the Day of Judgment.

At first this sounds inviting; however, on second thought, if the message of the church deletes this aspect of God's revelation to man, what else might it fail to preach that is vital to my Christian walk and future happiness? The Day of Judgment will have a profound impact on our experience in heaven for eternity. We should want to know all about it, much like we prepare for other big events in our lives.

Tragically, others are ignorant because they *want* to be ignorant of it. People have an uncanny knack for *not* finding out what they *don't want* to know. They reason in this way: *If when I push on my stomach, I feel a pain, then I won't push on my stomach. And if when I think about judgment, I feel guilty or afraid, then I won't think about judgment.* The problem with this line of reasoning is, of course, that if you feel a pain in your stomach, there's a reason it exists! If you don't discover the reason now, you may face some serious consequences later. The same is true about neglecting the pain or fear you may have when thinking about judgment. If you don't discover the truth now, you can be sure there will be serious consequences to face on that Day.

Wrong ideas about salvation by grace may further push considerations of Christians' imminent encounter with Jesus Christ on the Day of Judgment off their radar screen. Prior to their conversion, facing judgment was at least a *blip* on their screens, or maybe even a neon flashing light. But once they accepted Jesus as their Savior and were "saved," they were led to believe that being saved by grace entitled them to a "free pass" on the Day of Judgment. Their sinful actions didn't matter anymore because they thought all their sins were washed away, and they never needed to be concerned about giving an account of themselves to God. *However, most of the apostles wrote to believers about preparation for the Day of Judgment.* It wasn't a non-essential idea. It was a powerful motivational truth, especially for believers who were...

Spiritually Asleep and Willfully Sinful

Let's face it, there are true believers who are careless and willful in the way they live their lives. They have what the writer of Hebrews called an evil, unbelieving heart and are not in fellowship with other believers who will encourage them and wake them up to *who they belong to* and *where they are going*. It is easy in this generation and living in this western culture for Christians to get lulled into a spiritual sleep. They become sluggish and careless in their fight against sins such as purity, pride, fear, anger, and valuing temporal pleasures. When they are not around believers who will encourage them to pursue holiness and godliness, they soon drift away from their confession, and almost like a person who falls asleep at the wheel while driving, they lose control of their spiritual lives. It usually takes an accident or at least someone blowing a horn to wake them up. If I were falling asleep at the wheel, I would prefer a nudge from my loving wife, and her sweet voice saying, "Dear, have you noticed you're drifting into the other lane?" to wake me from my carelessness. How about you?

A Loving Brother Offers a Nudge

I'm almost sure you would prefer the sweet, loving, reminder rather than the concerned horn blast or the abrupt, screeching impact. That's why the author of Hebrews—as well as other inspired writers— warned believers about the Day of Judgment. It was a loving reminder given to wake sleeping, careless, lazy, sluggish believers into action. *The truth regarding Jesus' return and His judgment of believers is a means of grace to us*. We need it! Especially if we're falling asleep at the spiritual wheel and sinning willfully because we think grace covers everything we do.

Passages of Scripture like Hebrews 10:26-31, at which we'll look in more detail in this chapter, shake our faulty foundations and direct our attention to an eternal perspective of life. When we are awakened, we can then live in a way that contributes to our greater happiness and blessing when Jesus returns. Without the spiritual honk, we would have found ourselves surprised when we hit the "immovable object"—the Day of Judgment when we will stand before Jesus Christ. This book has focused on Jesus as a solid rock in the storms of life, but He is also a solid rock at the end of time. We can be thankful for God's gracious love for us that prepares us for the Day that is drawing near. Our hearts may be greatly encouraged by the truth that our Judge is also our Advocate. The Lord Jesus will be there with us as we go through the judgment, providing comfort as we need it. Perhaps as the tears begin to fall, He'll lovingly reach His arm around us and wipe away our tears—and His!

How Near Is It?

There's much talk in some circles about end times and Jesus' return. However, I don't want to go there. I don't think end times scenarios are primarily what the author of Hebrews had in mind when he indicated that the Day of Judgment and Jesus' return are near. The apostles didn't view time as we do today—on a sequential calendar. They broke time up into three seasons: the time before Jesus' incarnation, the time between Jesus' first coming and His second coming, and the time from Jesus' second coming and the Day of Judgment through eternity.

What did the author of Hebrews mean when he said "the Day" is drawing near? These facts help us understand why we should "all the more" live according to our confession and encourage each other:

• When Jesus returns, everyone will be judged for his deeds done in the body.

• The judgment will determine the *degrees of loss suffered* and the *degrees of reward granted* for those whose names *are* written in the Lamb's Book of Life.

• The judgment will also determine the *degrees of suffering* for those whose names *are not* written in the Lamb's Book of Life.

• Since the judgment is in reference to deeds done in the body, whether good or bad, then once a person dies or Jesus returns, nothing else can be done to contribute one way or another to the eternal result.

• Therefore, every day we live is one day nearer to the Day, and for all anyone knows, tomorrow may be the Day.

"But I Thought I Wouldn't Be Judged for My Sins!"

I'm not saying you will *pay the penalty* for your sins, which is eternity spent separated from God in torment. Praise the Lord! Those who believe what is expressed in the confession of truths taught in Hebrews have the assurance that their sins are forgiven and the ultimate penalty has been paid. If you are one of the Beloved-of-God, you have been saved from Hell and the outer darkness. However, what you have done and will do in your body matters.

Before we tackle the verses in Hebrews 10:26-31, let me establish this fact of the believer's judgment from the New Testament teaching. I encourage you to read these verses carefully and soberly because they are for your edification and preparation for this tremendous Day, which is drawing near:

> For **we must all appear before the judgment seat of Christ**, so that each one may be **recompensed for his deeds in the body**, according to what he has done, **whether good or bad** (2 Corinthians 5:10).

> But because of your stubbornness and unrepentant heart, you are storing up wrath for yourself in the day of wrath and revelation of the righteous judgment of God, **who will render to each man according to his deeds** (Romans 2:5-6).

> But you, why do you judge your brother? Or you again, why do you regard your brother with contempt? **For we will all stand before the judgment seat of God** (Romans 14:10).

> So then **each one of us will give an account** of himself to God (Romans 14:12).

> And I say to you, that **every careless word that men shall speak, they shall render account for it in the day of judgment**. For by your words you shall be justified, and by your words you shall be condemned (Matthew 12:36-37).

> Now if any man builds on the foundation with gold, silver, precious stones, wood, hay, straw, each man's work will become evident; **for the day will show it** because it is to be revealed with fire, and **the fire itself will test the quality of each man's work**. If any man's work which he has built on it remains, **he will receive a reward.** If any man's work is burned up, **he will suffer loss;** but he himself will be saved, yet so as through fire (1 Corinthians 3:12-15).

[handwritten margin note: is it built on the unshakeable kingdom HEB. 12?]

> And we know that the judgment of God rightly falls upon those who practice such things. But **do you suppose this, O man,** when you pass judgment on those who practice such things and do the same yourself, **that you will escape the judgment of God?** (Romans 2:2-3).

> For there is **no partiality** with God (Romans 2:11).

> ... **On the day** when, according to my gospel, **God will judge the secrets of men through Christ Jesus** (Romans 2:16).

> For it is time **for judgment to begin with the household**

of God; and if it begins with us first, what will be the outcome for those who do not obey the gospel of God? (1 Peter 4:17).

These verses indicate beyond a shadow of doubt the following truths about judgment:

- There is a judgment of believers by Jesus Christ.
- Believers will be judged first.
- Their deeds done in their bodies will be judged, even those done in secret.
- There will be no partiality. A sin is a sin, regardless of who does it.
- Each believer will give an account for what he has done.
- There will be losses suffered and rewards given.

But What About No More Crying?

There are a few popular verses to which people cling when they think about dying and facing Jesus Christ. It wouldn't surprise me if some of these had already come to your mind.

As far as the east is from the west, so far has He removed our transgressions from us (Psalm 103:12).

I, even I, am the one who wipes out your transgressions for My own sake, and I will not remember your sins (Isaiah 43:25).

And their sins and their lawless deeds I will remember no more (Hebrews 10:17).

It is marvelously true that because God has united His people with Jesus in His atoning work, our transgressions have been put out of God's consideration and they have no effect upon our standing before Him. God has indeed removed them from us. The following verse is also a source of comfort to us:

... And He will wipe away every tear from their eyes; and there will no longer be any death; there will no longer be any mourning, or crying, or pain; the first things have passed away (Revelation 21:4).

However, if you open your Bible to Revelation 21, you'll notice that what precedes that wonderful prophecy of no more mourning, crying, or pain is this:

*Then I saw a great white throne and Him who sat upon it, from whose presence earth and heaven fled away, and no place was found for them. And I saw the dead, the great and the small, standing before the throne, and **books** were opened; and **another book** was opened, which is the book of life; **and the dead were judged** from the things which were written in the **books, according to their deeds**. And the sea gave up the dead which were in it, and death and Hades gave up the dead which were in them; and **they were judged, every one of them according to their deeds.** Then death and Hades were thrown into the lake of fire. This is the second death, the lake of fire. And if anyone's name was not found written in the book of life, he was thrown into the lake of fire (Revelation 20:11-15).*

This passage is the end of Revelation 20, *after which* Chapter 21 begins with, "Then I saw a new heaven and a new earth..." Notice also in the passage the distinction made between "books" and "another book." We are told that the "books" have our deeds recorded in them, and that the "book" is the book of life. So just because our names are written in the book of life does not mean we are excused from the judgment of our deeds. But believers have a comfort and hope that *after* all our deeds have been judged and we have given an account of our actions in our bodies, He will comfort us. Where do you think the tears and pain came from? It isn't difficult to understand why all believers, when they see their carelessness and willfulness against their Lord and Savior, will be crying and in need of mercy and grace!

Furthermore, if you read the context of all of the verses usually used to encourage the notion that believers will escape the Judgment Day, you'll find they are all in the context of the new heaven and earth. Of course, there will be no need for God to remember our sins or transgressions any longer then, *after* they all will have been judged and we will have given an account of them. The atonement has removed their penalty, the judgment will have determined losses and rewards, and sin will have been eradicated from our resurrected bodies. At that point, God will have no reason to remember them!

However, until the judgment is over, every deed, whether good or bad, is being documented. That is what John was referring to in the phrases "the books were opened" and "the dead were judged from the things which were written in the books, according to their deeds" (Revelation 20:12).

Believers Ought to Be Awake

This doctrine of the Day of Judgment and Jesus' return is foundational, anchor-type truth. It is a gift from God reflecting His goodness that He repeatedly tells us what lies ahead. Granted, people who don't believe in Jesus have no eternal perspective at all. We shouldn't expect them to. However, the frequent occurrence in the Scriptures of references to the Day of Judgment and Jesus' return, and the way the truth was used in the epistles should be common knowledge to believers of every generation. As Paul wrote to the Thessalonians, we should not need even to be told of these things because we are informed and readying *ourselves*.

> Now **as to the times** and the epochs, brethren, **you have no need of anything to be written to you. For you yourselves know full well that the day of the Lord will come just like a thief in the night.** While they are saying, "Peace and safety!" then destruction will come upon them suddenly like labor pains upon a woman with child, and they will not escape. **But you, brethren, are not in darkness, that the day would overtake you like a thief**; for you are all sons of light and sons of day. We are not of night nor of darkness; so then **let us not sleep as others do, but let us be alert and sober.** For those who sleep do their sleeping at night, and those who get drunk get drunk at night. But since we are of the day, let us be sober, having put on the breastplate of faith and love, and as a helmet, the hope of salvation. **For God has not destined us for wrath, but for obtaining salvation through our Lord Jesus Christ** (1 Thessalonians 5:1-9).

If we are *awake*, we need not be *afraid*. A friend of mine who has been awakened to the truths of this chapter found tremendous comfort from Jesus' words to His disciples found in Luke 12:32,

> "Do not be afraid, little flock, for your Father has chosen gladly to give you the kingdom."

Our Father's great love for us has been demonstrated so we can assure our hearts before Him. The fact that God has not destined us for wrath is revealed in these things that He has done:

• Spoken to us through His Son, Jesus, who atoned for our sins and intercedes for us.

• Given us a confession about Jesus to believe and hold onto continually.

- Warned us of the sin of unbelief and drifting away from our confession and thus falling short of God's peace and grace.

- Provided the promise of rest, mercy, and grace if we will *draw near* and *hold fast* our confession to preserve us through trials, suffering, and temptations.

- Placed us in an assembly of believers who will encourage us to draw near and hold fast when they see us drifting.

However, Some Believers Are Asleep

In spite of all that God has done for His children, some have not realized the vital importance of discipleship, assembling with other believers, and putting off the deeds of darkness. Spiritual napping happens when people forsake assembling with other Spirit-filled believers, neglect the study of God's Word, and therefore, have nothing solid to anchor into. It is as if they have stripped their car of all its safety devices and warnings. They're on their own, and God never intended for His children to live that way.

Also, many simply have never gotten far enough away from the old sinful habit patterns that characterized their days in darkness. Consequently, they become spiritual sluggards whose lives fit the description of a person who is asleep in the night. They think they are saved by grace, and perhaps they are. They say they believe in Jesus and would agree with everything in our confession. However, they are ensnared by their appetites and ignorant of the truth about the Day of Judgment. They need to be awakened!

The warning of Hebrews 10:26-31 isn't for believers who momentarily and often drift from their confession. It's for those who have been drifting for a long time and have fallen asleep at the wheel—big time! They have heard the warnings and encouragements to draw near and hold fast, but are determined to fulfill their own desires and lusts anyway:

> *For if **we** go on sinning willfully after receiving the knowledge of the truth, there no longer remains a sacrifice for sins, but a terrifying expectation of judgment and the fury of a fire which will consume the adversaries (Hebrews 10:26-27).*

Lest we perilously dismiss these verses as irrelevant to *us*, comforting ourselves with the thought that they refer only to *professing but not true* believers, take note of that little word "we." Think of the children of Israel whom God brought out of the land of Egypt. The Holy Spirit always referred to them as "My people." Yet some of them were consumed because of their flagrant sin against God. The context of this passage in Hebrews gives us no reason to believe that the author had changed his intended audience from God's children to mere professing believers.

I think the author had in mind the Old Testament testimonies of God's fire destroying those who sinned against Him. Do you remember what happened to Nadab and Abihu, Aaron's sons who offered "strange fire" before the Lord? The fire of God consumed them (Leviticus 10:1-3). In Numbers 11, when God's people grumbled against God, the fire of the Lord consumed the outskirts of the camp. And shall we forget Korah's rebellion, when the earth swallowed the adversaries of Moses alive and the fire of the Lord torched 250 men? (Numbers 16:35). All of those who were destroyed were considered by the Spirit of God to be God's people. It is not wise to claim to be God's child and be determined to oppose His will.

> *Anyone who has set aside the Law of Moses dies without mercy on the testimony of two or three witnesses. How much severer punishment do you think he will deserve who has trampled under foot the Son of God, and **has regarded as unclean the blood of the covenant by which he was sanctified**, and **has insulted the Spirit of grace**? For we know Him who said, "Vengeance is Mine, I will repay," and again, "**The Lord will judge His people**." It is a terrifying thing to fall into the hands of the living God (Hebrews 10:28-31).*

Do You Know Anyone Who's Asleep?

I emboldened the words in that passage to show that the author obviously had the judgment of believers in mind. It comes directly after the verses where he told them to encourage each other all the more since they knew the Day of Judgment was drawing near. The sobering aspect of this passage is its clear reference to God's judging His own people. For many, the idea of a terrifying experience with God when they are under grace seems impossible. However, these verses refer to the Day of Judgment when God will judge the willful sins of believers—committed as an insult to His grace bestowed on them.

Do you know anyone who has been lulled into a spiritual sleep? Someone who professes to be a believer and continues to use pornography (that is, to commit adultery—see Matthew 5:28), deceive, lie, fear, gossip, idolize, and complain? Some of these sins Paul listed in 2 Corinthians 10 as disqualifiers for eternal rewards. Do you know of some professing believers who are involved in carousing, drunkenness, sexual promiscuity, sensuality, strife, and jealousy? These are sins Paul warned his Roman readers about (13:11-13) when he told them to "awaken from sleep."

It is by the *goodness* of God that you are reading this book. If you haven't ever heard the truth about the Day of Judgment, you've been missing a wonderful encouragement for holy living. If this chapter has served as a wake-up call to you, then *praise the Lord*. Even though perhaps you have lived carelessly, you may still repent and reap a reward for overcoming and rousing yourself from your spiritual slumber!

What About Judgment Day and Unbelievers?

Whereas *believers* in Jesus Christ have the promise from God that they will *not* be disappointed in the Day of Judgment (Romans 10:11), those who have not trusted in Christ are going to be very disappointed, indeed, that they have ignored all of God's revelation of Himself. The passage of Romans 1:18-25 indicates that even those who have had no witness except through creation have no excuse for not believing. God has made His invisible attributes known through what has been made. However, those who have heard about Jesus and God's gracious offer of salvation through Him will be judged more severely for their unbelief and self-will (Romans 2:11-16).

God gives men many opportunities to prepare for the day when we will stand before Him. One day Jesus told a story that was intended, I think, to make us contemplate what we are doing with those opportunities. He was informed of two tragic events that had occurred in Jerusalem. His questions and comments were made for those in the crowd who were skeptics and unbelievers. Here's what Luke recorded:

> *Now on the same occasion there were some present who reported to Him about the Galileans whose blood Pilate had mixed with their sacrifices. And Jesus said to them, "Do you suppose that these Galileans were greater sinners than all other Galileans because they suffered this fate? **I tell you, no, but unless you repent, you will all likewise perish.***

Or do you suppose that those eighteen on whom the tower in Siloam fell and killed them were worse culprits than all the men who live in Jerusalem? **I tell you, no, but unless you repent, you will all likewise perish***" (Luke 13:1-5).*

Probably everyone in Jerusalem at that time was talking about these events. Most folks of Jesus' day were under the false impression that bad things happen to bad people, and if individuals are good and God is pleased with them, bad things *don't* happen to *them*. Sadly, many still think that today, even though it is obvious from tragedies like the destruction of the World Trade Center on September 11, 2001, and the great earthquake and tsunami in Asia in December, 2004, that the dead included both believers and unbelievers.

Jesus emphasized his point twice in the passage above. The bottom line of His message to His listeners was this: "God has been gracious to give you more time to repent and believe in Me. If you don't repent—think again about who I am and what I teach—you will perish." In those verses, eternal destruction is implied. His words were meant to be a wake-up call to unbelievers, skeptics, and procrastinators. Obviously, the eighteen people killed by the tower did not realize that they had failed to prepare for the Day of Judgment and that, for them, judgment was to happen on *that* day. We all know we're going to die; however, few of us know when or how.

How about you? If it is a "terrible thing to fall into the hands of the living God" for a believer who willfully sins against Jesus Christ and grace, what do you think "will be the outcome for those who *do not obey* the gospel of God?" (1 Peter 4:17). If you have not yet trusted in Jesus Christ and turned from your sins against God after having read this far, I believe I may safely assume that God has been speaking to you and *you know you are not ready* for the Day that is drawing near.

The biggest "storm of life" is the Day of Judgment, and there is only one place to anchor your soul and body when that storm blows. It is upon Jesus Christ, the Solid Rock. You either stand anchored into that Rock, or the Rock will fall on you and crush you (Matthew 21:44). God has provided Him for anyone who will come to Him in repentance and faith. Why delay seeking God? The rest of this book can wait!

Do You Feel Shaken and Without an Anchor?

It's time to anchor your faith into this part of the truth about Jesus Christ, the Solid Rock in the storms of life. Bow in His presence and confess your willfulness and your ignorance. If you've intentionally ignored God's Word about judgment, you might begin by thanking Him for forgiving that sin at the cross, when Jesus made purification for your sins. Continue with more confession about your willful sins against Him. Part of our confession, "[Jesus] runs all things by the Word of His power," implies that even your carelessness and slumber has a purpose in God's grand scheme of glorifying Jesus Christ. Our temptations and trials fit into God's plan. When we fail, it is no surprise to Him. He bore it on the cross! If Jesus runs everything by His power, then He could have prevented our recklessness. However, its occurrence means that God had a purpose for it. Give glory to God that you are now turning from your willful sinning and careless living to walk humbly in His sight, and all the more as you see the Day drawing near. Finally, ask the Holy Spirit to fill you and enable you to walk faithfully each day, applying your confession to all of life.

Although the *warning* was important, the author wanted to motivate his readers most by the hope of *reward*. As we proceed through the book of Hebrews, the theme of reward stands out as a great motivational word. In the next chapter, as we practice being anchored in Jesus, we will learn the greatest purpose behind God's training us to *draw near and hold fast* our confession through trials, suffering, and temptations.

Thirty-three

The Great Reward

I hope you have begun to realize the wonderful blessing God has provided to us in Jesus Christ! As we've studied the book of Hebrews, we've been reminded of vital truths that are foundational for living anchored on a solid rock in the storms of life. But these truths were not given solely for the purpose of equipping us in this life. God has much more in mind for us in eternity. *He plans to reward His people with a great reward in Jesus Christ.*

Having saved us by His grace through faith from the wrath of God that our sin deserves, God also is preparing us for the Day of Judgment. Usually the Day of Judgment plants fear and trembling in the heart, but God wants His people to come to that Great Day with a sense of anticipation and joy over His plans to reward us.

not ours

God Has Provided an Anchor in Jesus for the Purpose of Rewarding His People!

The "therefores" in the biblical epistles are important because they tell us what the previous truths are *there for*. Having given the warning in Chapter 10 of Hebrews, which we studied in the last chapter, the author motivated his readers with the hope of reward:

> *Therefore, do not throw away your confidence, which has a great reward. For you have need of endurance, so when you have done the will of God, you may receive what was promised. For yet in a very little while, He who*

is coming will come, and will not delay. But My righteous one shall live by faith; and if he shrinks back, My soul has no pleasure in him. But we are not of those who shrink back to destruction, but are of those who have faith to the preserving of the soul (Hebrews 10:35-39).

The author was not referring here to the *eternal* destruction or preserving of our souls. Remember that God determined our salvation in Christ before the foundation of the world. But in a previous verse (32) the writer had commended his readers for the way they had "endured a great conflict of sufferings." And in verse 38 he referred to the way we "live by faith" in this life, reminding us of God's displeasure if we shrink back in the midst of trials, for which he said we "have need of endurance." His encouragement to us is to exercise the faith God has provided us during those trials so that our souls will not "shrink back to destruction." What is the destruction? I think it is the fear or lack of peace that can shatter our sense of well-being and destroy our witness of Him. On the other hand, what is our confidence that our souls will be preserved? It is our confession. Please bear with me as I repeat it once more:

Jesus Christ is God's son, and He is our high priest.

After making purification for sins, He sat down at the right hand of the Majesty on high, where He intercedes for us and runs all things by the word of His power.

He will preserve us through suffering, trials, and temptation by giving us mercy and grace IF we will draw near to Him and hold fast our confession.

Drawing near and holding fast our confession has a great reward! In life, day by day, the preserving of our souls occurs when we stand on our confession. If we do not stand on our confession, our souls suffer—we do not enter into the rest of God. However, if when we find ourselves drifting and are warned or encouraged, and we then draw near to the throne of grace and anchor into our confession, we have reason to believe that God will immediately reward us by giving us grace for the people, situations, and events that try our faith every day. Be encouraged by this.

Draw Near! Hold Fast Your Confession! Be Rewarded!

Hebrews 11 is a great compilation of heroes of faith—men and women who believed God's word to them, who did not receive the reward in their lifetimes, and yet who did not drift, fall away, waver, or shrink back. Sometimes this chapter is called the great Hall of Faith. The author wanted to show by their testimonies how believers gain the approval of God.

Note, however, that approval is not the same as eternal salvation from sin. Believers gain God's approval by holding fast to the Word of God without wavering, regardless of the circumstances, and by looking to Christ for grace, mercy, and power in trials. Most of the people God used as examples of faith had times in their lives that we would not call stellar performances of trusting God. However, their faithfulness *was* demonstrated over the course of their lives. I want to encourage you to draw near and hold fast your confession over the course of your life also.

The first two verses of Chapter 12 explain why the author wrote what he did. I'm amazed at the skill and wisdom of this inspired man. In two verses he summed up eleven chapters!

> *Therefore, since we have so great a cloud of witnesses surrounding us, let us lay aside every encumbrance and the sin which so easily entangles us, and let us run with endurance the race that is set before us, fixing our eyes on Jesus, the author and perfecter of faith, who for the joy set before Him endured the cross, despising the shame, and has sat down at the right hand of the throne of God (Hebrews 12:1-2).*

We have all of these testimonies in the Scriptures of men and women whose faith did not waver because they could see the Day when Jesus Christ would sit at the right hand of God, as the high priest, over all things. They could see that Day, and their faith didn't shake. Though they did not see Him personally, just as we have not, they were anchored in the Christ, the Messiah of God, by faith (Hebrews 11:26)! Therefore, we also ought to 'run the "race" of our lives in the same way, by laying aside the sin that so easily entangles us. What sin is that? It is surely the sin of unbelief mentioned throughout the letter to the Hebrews.

How quickly are you entangled and encumbered by unbelief regarding Jesus' lordship over all things? How quickly do you forget that He is constantly interceding on your behalf when someone doesn't do what you want them to do? Or does what you *don't* want them to do? I've noticed that I can get entangled in a heartbeat. All it takes is a temptation or trial or some small inconvenience, and I've drifted away, not realizing or remembering that Jesus had a good purpose in it. Yet as I have practiced drawing near and holding fast my confession, I find that my recovery time is shorter and shorter. How encouraging it is to know when I am lacking peace and grace that I have a throne of mercy and grace I may go to—in a heartbeat!

What is to be our motivation for *drawing near* and *holding fast* during the race? The promise of reward! Of course, most of us know we should be motivated by a desire to glorify God, but have you ever thought that if you are rewarded, the glory ultimately does go to God? The author focuses our attention on how Jesus ran His race through great suffering, tribulation, and temptation: *He set before Himself the promise of God to reward His unwavering faithfulness in the midst of it*. That is why Jesus is called the Author and Perfecter of faith. He is both the heart of our confession and its author. Furthermore, He actually performed and perfected the practice of drawing near and holding fast until the end—without one drift, fall, or stumble. We may fix our eyes on Him as we draw near to Him and find mercy and grace in time of need.

Let's get practical as we consider *how* to draw near and hold fast. Let's simplify this a bit and bring the application home. Let's say you are a man who comes home from work hungry one evening. But your wife doesn't have dinner fixed on time. Here you can apply your confession and expect God to reward it. Instead of complaining, you remind and reassure yourself that you need this kind of trial in your life in order to practice drawing near and holding fast your confession. You give thanks to God, ask what you can do to help, and encourage her if she's had a lot of interruptions.

Because Jesus is in charge of *everything*, we can give thanks for *all things*, can't we? This comes down to the smallest details of our business and our work. The next time something small happens that you feel unhappy about, remember that you have not suffered to the point of shedding blood (Hebrews 12:4). Your suffering is small compared to Jesus'. Jesus suffered to the point of death, but He still endured. He who is seated at the right hand of the Majesty on high in reward for His faithfulness lives in you! Fix your eyes on Him and get anchored.

Our Father Disciplines His Children and Reproves Those Who Drift From Their Confession

The author knew that there are some who will make excuses for unbelief. I think that's one of the characteristics of unbelief that so easily entangles us. When we're suffering, it's natural to make excuses or place the blame on the human agent being used by God to give us practice. When we don't have grace or peace, it is easy to forget our confession and place the blame on someone else or on a particular situation. Of course, Jesus didn't do that.

The author had an interesting view of a lack of peace, mercy, or grace in any given situation. He considered coming short of grace as *discipline from our heavenly Father* for not practicing drawing near and holding fast:

> *You have forgotten the exhortation which is addressed to you as sons, "My son, do not regard lightly the discipline of the Lord, nor faint when you are reproved by Him; for **those whom the Lord loves He disciplines, and He scourges every son whom He receives."***

> *It is for discipline that you endure. God deals with you as with sons, for what son is there whom his father does not discipline? But if you are without discipline, of which all have become partakers, then you are illegitimate children and are not sons. Furthermore, we had earthly fathers to discipline us and we respected them; shall we not much rather be subject to the Father of spirits and live? For they disciplined us for a short time as seemed best to them, **but He disciplines us for our good, so that we may share His holiness.** All discipline for the moment may not seem joyful, but sorrowful; but to those who have been trained by it, afterwards it yields the peaceful fruit of righteousness (Hebrews 12:5-11).*

Using a classic parenting example, the author points out that the discipline of our heavenly Father is like that of a loving earthly father. The discipline he's referring to is *the training of our faith*. Our Father sends trials, suffering, and temptation through events and people in order to give us training in drawing near and holding fast our confession.

I've coached many beginning basketball players during my coaching career, but I was most diligent with my son. When Micah first started playing basketball, he was just a little-bitty guy. I first challenged him to see how many shots he could make out of ten. He could barely get that ball up to the ten-foot basket. Of course, he missed most of the time. He came in one day very frustrated because he didn't view his attempts to get the ball through the hoop as practice or training. He thought his self-esteem was on the line. I remember his saying, "Dad, I only hit one." I responded with, "Son, it's going to take practice. You need to keep shooting that ball over and over and over again, and the time will come when you will be able to hit five out of ten—maybe eight out of ten. But it is only going to come because you keep practicing."

That same principle is true in life. How are you going to have an unshakable faith in the midst of the storms of life? How will God reward you as He desires to reward you in the Day of Judgment if He doesn't give you opportunities to obtain it? We're not talking about earning eternal salvation; we're talking about gaining His approval and rewards in the judgment—*for His glory.* You must have repeated situations where you aim at the target. You need to be challenged by the storms. Situations beyond your control and difficult relationships are called for in a training program that has been designed for your growth and reward. The person who is trained in this way eventually learns to live in peace through any situation and within any relationship. It was through this kind of practice that the Apostle Paul "learned to be content in whatever circumstances" he was (Philippians 4:11). In fact, the peace and grace that God gives us to handle these situations are the down payment on the great reward to come!

If we learn in the midst of trials to hold fast our confession—to believe that all things are run by Jesus, who is seated at God's right hand and is able to preserve us to the end through the mercy and grace He gives us—then we will receive a great reward. In every present distress, grace and mercy sustain us. This will ultimately be *another* reason for us to bow before our Father and give Him glory and praise! The important truth we should grasp in this chapter is the author's teaching about discipline from our heavenly Father. It must occur. It shouldn't be taken lightly. In fact, I encourage you to make it your goal to *embrace* the daily encounters and situations that train you, knowing that as you become more gracious and loving through your practice, you will have more peace and God will be more glorified. He will reprove those who don't draw near and hold fast their confession. There is a reward to those who are so trained.

We Have a Responsibility to Others When We See Them Coming Short of God's Grace in Their Trials

Pursue peace with all men, and the sanctification without which no one will see the Lord. ***See to it that no one comes short of the grace of God;*** *that no root of bitterness springing up causes trouble, and by it many be defiled; that there be no immoral or godless person like Esau, who sold his own birthright for a single meal. For you know that even afterwards, when he desired to inherit the blessing, he was rejected, for he found no place for repentance, though he sought for it with tears (Hebrews 12:14-17).*

Although one may take verse 14 from a personal perspective, it appears by the context that the author had in mind the whole body of Christ. Each of us who are believers are to "chase after" peace with others, as well as after purification or holiness of life in the midst of suffering, trials, and temptations. We are not only to be on guard against our own drifting away from our confession about Jesus, but we are also to be on the alert for others who are being reproved by the Lord, so that we may help them. Coming short of the grace of God is evidence of God's *loving* reproof toward them. If they were drawing near and holding fast, they would have grace for the trial. However, if they are falling short of grace, they are in need of encouragement and assistance.

This is not the first time the author has stated our responsibility toward our Christian brothers and sisters. In Chapter 3 believers were told to encourage each other day after day. Do you know someone who has forgotten or drifted away from his or her confession and is being reproved by the heavenly Father?

One way you know that someone is not drawing near and holding fast is the presence of bitterness. If one believes that Jesus Christ is running all things through the word of His power and that His intercession is being answered, then bitterness has no base of operations in the soul. However, if one looks at a tragic situation or difficult relationship through the vision of his or her own comfort and happiness, or of what he thinks is "fair" or "good," then a root of bitterness will sprout and bear its bad fruit. Usually the person then places blame on those who are God's agents in the training process.

Whenever we don't believe that Jesus is in control of all things for our good, we nurture seeds of bitterness in our souls, and we will reap what we sow. Have you ever thought of bitterness as a loving reproof from the Lord for not drawing near and holding fast your confession? It is not a joyful thing, is it? Instead of complaining, we need to learn to confess the sin of unbelief and quit pointing the finger at anyone else. The Father will then send grace for the trial.

When Coming Short of Grace, Find a Place to Repent of Unbelief

There is another powerful insight from these verses that helps us know what to do ourselves or how to encourage someone else who is coming short of grace. Esau comes to mind as someone who failed to see the hand of God in his circumstances because he was blinded by his lust for temporal comfort and by bitterness. He didn't trust that God was in charge of all things when he sold his birthright to Jacob. Because he didn't trust God, he could only see *Jacob's* faults. From his point of view, Jacob was the one with the problems! Esau could clearly see where Jacob needed to repent, but according to the Holy Spirit, Esau could not find his own place of repentance. Consequently, he couldn't pursue peace with Jacob and couldn't receive the blessing.

Why didn't Esau have grace from God to deal with the situation rightly? The Holy Spirit through the author identified the problem as an inability to find a place of repentance. The context implies that Esau didn't believe God. The lesson is this: *God trains us to believe in Him and keep our minds fixed on Him. Furthermore, He rewards us with grace when we draw near and hold fast, and He reproves us by withholding grace when we are unbelieving and fail to find the place to repent of unbelief.*

How should we respond when we detect frustration, anger, and bitterness within others or ourselves? We should respond as a loved child who is being reproved—with repentance and faith toward Christ. When we have not believed that Jesus is running all things by the word of His power and that He is building our faith to make us like Christ, then it is wise to ask: Where is the place of repentance? Until we find the place to repent for not believing Jesus' word and trusting in His rule over all things, we should expect to come short of the grace of God. Blaming others out of bitterness only prolongs the trial and the frustration.

Believers in Christ Have Received an Unshakable Kingdom

As we read through the rest of Hebrews 12, we see that the author emphasized the glorious kingdom to which his readers had come. They had come to an unshakable kingdom. They were to live their lives in light of such stability and security.

> *But you have come to Mount Zion and to the city of the living God, the heavenly Jerusalem, and to myriads of angels, to the general assembly and church of the firstborn who are enrolled in heaven, and to God, the Judge of all, and to the spirits of the righteous made perfect, and to Jesus, the mediator of a new covenant, and to the sprinkled blood, which speaks better than the blood of Abel (Hebrews 12:22-24).*

The following warning may seem needless to you if you are hearing this for the first time and are excited about practicing *drawing near* and *holding fast*. However, apparently the first readers of the letter to the Hebrews had demonstrated some reluctance to respond to the truth and were in need of a final encouragement not to ignore what they believed about Jesus Christ:

> **See to it that you do not refuse** [reject] **Him who is speaking.** *For if those did not escape when they refused him who warned them on earth, much less will we escape who turn away from Him who warns from heaven. And His voice shook the earth then, but now He has promised, saying, "Yet once more I will shake not only the earth, but also the heaven." This expression, "Yet once more," denotes the removing of those things which can be shaken, as of created things, so that those things which cannot be shaken may remain (Hebrews 12:25-27).*

What does this mean to us? It means that God is going to shake our lives through situations and relationships until unbelief is shaken out and nothing remains but an unshakable faith in Jesus Christ. If it can be shaken, He is going to shake it. He can use any number of people to shake it. Limitless situations are at His disposal to train us to *draw near* and *hold fast* our confession.

Gratitude Flows From a Soul That Is Anchored in Jesus Christ

> ***Therefore,*** *since we receive a kingdom which cannot be shaken,* ***let us show gratitude,*** *by which we may offer to God an acceptable service with reverence and awe; for our God is a consuming fire (Hebrews 12:28-29).*

You'll find that the more you practice drawing near and holding fast, the more you will receive an abundance of grace to live for the glory of God. As we receive and experience the blessing of being in an unshakable kingdom, we want to express our gratitude to God. This is how we serve God, according to the author of Hebrews. We do so with reverence and awe because our relationship with God consumes our lives. I think of it this way: God has determined that His children will be anchored in Jesus Christ in this life. Unbelief is sin, and God is patiently working to remove this sin from our lives. He trains us every day, all of our lives, to practice drawing near and holding fast our confession in Jesus.

Do You Need to Find a Place of Repentance for Unbelief?

What is your response to God who has spoken through His Son? Have you fallen away from the living God? Do you need to find a place to repent of unbelief? If you can't love, if you are bitter, or if you are ensnared by lustful desires, I encourage you to repent of your unbelief—you have not believed that Jesus has been in control of all things that have occurred in your life. Repent and begin applying your confession. Fix your eyes on Jesus, and determine to pursue peace and holiness. Thank God as an offering of worship.

Do you need to encourage someone who has fallen away? God desires us to be a means of blessing to our brothers and sisters in Christ. If you know of someone who is struggling with depression or thoughts of suicide, or who is bitter at God or others, then you have what is needed to be a channel of blessing to them. Encourage them to *draw near, hold fast, and receive the reward* in Jesus Christ.

Thirty-four

Build on the Rock

We have made quite an excursion through this book, haven't we? Let's remind ourselves of where we've been.

We began by studying fourteen commonly misused scriptures and learning to apply some sound principles to studying God's Word. This helped us clarify the true nature of God and salvation through His Son Jesus Christ by eliminating commonly held misconceptions.

Next we looked at the nature and person of God and addressed His purposes for sin and the Fall. After seeing man's ruined condition before God and our reconciliation to Him through Jesus Christ, we concentrated on rethinking the way we live our lives as disciples of Jesus in the present kingdom of the heavens.

That led us to consider God's way of sharing the gospel with others and how we can be most effective in leading our children to Christ. As we approached the final segment of the book, we learned the importance of holding fast our confession of Christ and not drifting from it so that we might enter the rest God has for us. We worked to develop a healthy attitude of expectation toward the coming Day of Judgment, finally rejoicing in the promise of the great reward God has in store for His people.

Isn't God's Word amazing? Have you realized the consistency of thought and spirit which runs through all that we've studied? As you have read through *Anchored in Christ*, have you found the Holy Spirit strengthening each truth with other scriptures and truths you've read or heard before? Has your heart been awestruck with God's greatness, with Jesus' glory, and with assurance which comes from trusting in God's work rather than your own? I hope so.

My purpose in taking you through all these things has been to anchor your soul in Jesus Christ, so that you may stand firm and not falter through all the storms of life. The great nineteenth-century preacher Charles Haddon Spurgeon illustrated these inevitable storms, and the blessing God designs them to be, in one of his sermons:

> The bow of trouble shot David like an arrow toward God! It is a blessed thing when the waves of affliction wash us upon the rock of confidence in God alone, when darkness below gives us an eye to the light above.[43]

God designs the storms of life for our good. They separate our hearts' affections from things below and direct us to Him who is our greatest hope.

A Rock in the Storm

As we now reach the end of this book and what I hope has been a life-changing and exciting journey for you, I am reminded of a fitting story Jesus used as He concluded His greatest sermon, *The Sermon on the Mount*:

> *"Therefore everyone who **hears these words of Mine and acts on them**, may be compared to a wise man who built his house on the rock. And the rain fell, and the floods came, and the winds blew and slammed against that house; **and yet it did not fall, for it had been founded on the rock**. Everyone who hears these words of Mine and does not act on them, will be like a foolish man who built his house on the sand. The rain fell, and the floods came, and the winds blew and slammed against that house; and it fell—and great was its fall."*
>
> *When Jesus had finished these words, the crowds were amazed at His teaching; for He was teaching them as one having authority, and not as their scribes (Matthew 7:24-29).*

Jesus' words are the rock into which we may anchor our souls. We notice in this passage that it isn't enough to *hear* the words of truth; to build our house on the Rock requires that we *act* on the truth. We might think of it this way: Jesus is the rock upon which we build our house, and our acting on His words is how we anchor *into* the rock. Of course, the rain, flood, and winds Jesus had in mind figuratively speak of the Day of Judgment and the return of Christ; however, if the house can withstand *that* storm, it can also withstand *any* storm in this life!

Rest in Jesus Christ

I like the way the Apostle Paul, in writing to the Corinthians, explained his methods of evangelism and his message:

> *For I determined to know nothing among you except Jesus Christ, and Him crucified. I was with you in weakness and in fear and in much trembling, and **my message and my preaching were not in persuasive words of wisdom, but in demonstration of the Spirit and of power,** so that your faith **would not rest** on the **wisdom of men,** but on **the power of God** (1 Corinthians 2:2-5).*

As I have written this book and considered you, my readers, I like Paul have had many times of weakness, fear, and trembling. I've not wanted you to put your confidence in knowledge of the truth or to become proud that you know something others do not know—responses that would promote a kind of faith that rests in the wisdom of men. I've wanted you to learn to rest in Jesus Christ and His power to save and keep you.

Boast in the Lord

Instead of providing you some way to boast in a decision you have made or in your knowledge in any way, my goal has been to show you the absolute and sole worthiness of boasting in the Lord alone. How can God get all the glory if we are able to boast of even one thing we have done to gain our salvation or to persuade others to make a decision for Christ? I have prayed that as you have read through these pages, God would give you His Holy Spirit to work powerfully in your heart and life. My desire is that you would be amazed at the power of God revealed in and through Jesus Christ, His Son.

I hope you will review more thoroughly all the ground we have covered and meditate on what the Scriptures have revealed about our great God. He has been at work to fulfill His purposes for you and for the whole world since before He laid the foundations of the earth. In Christ, God has given us everything we need to live godly in this generation, anchored in Jesus Christ. The Apostle Peter wrote about this confidence that I have hoped would be revealed to and in you:

> *Grace and peace be multiplied to you in the knowledge of God and of Jesus our Lord; seeing that **His divine power has granted to us everything pertaining to life and godliness, through the true knowledge of Him who called us by His own glory and excellence.** For by these He has granted to us His precious and magnificent promises, so that by them you may become partakers of the divine nature, having escaped the corruption that is in the world by lust (2 Peter 1:2-4).*

The only explanation for the way we live, love, and hope is God's divine power. Where does that divine power come from? From the knowledge of God and of Jesus our Lord. To be anchored in Jesus is to apply the truth we have learned about God and His Son to our lives, moment by moment—who They are, what They have done, why They have done it, and what They have promised.

Thinking on these things means we take our eyes off of ourselves and fix our eyes on Jesus, the author and finisher of our faith. When sharing with others about our faith and the gospel, we don't boast about ourselves and what *we* have done, but about God and what *He* has done. As storm winds blow, we don't *try harder* to handle the situation or to hold on to Jesus; instead we draw near and hold fast to *what we know is true about Jesus.* As we do this, we discover that *He* has a hold on us. He is both the Solid Rock *and* the Anchor!

Practice

Drawing near and holding fast our confession takes practice. Here's a good place to begin: Perhaps as you've read this book, you've been grieved over the times you've failed in the past. Don't be discouraged. Keep going to your Savior. If you'll turn to Him now, He will comfort you in your griefs. His mercies are new every morning! He has promised to stand with you every moment, "even to the end of the age," as well as while you go through judgment on that final Day. Our confidence is in His mercy, His love, and His promises. For...

> *... **if God is for us, who is against us?** He who did not spare His own Son, but delivered Him over for us all, how will He not also with Him freely give us all things? Who will bring*

a charge against God's elect? **God is the one who justifies;** *who is the one who condemns?* **Christ Jesus** *is He who died, yes, rather who was raised, who is at the right hand of God, who* **also intercedes for us** *(Romans 8:31-34).*

I'm sure we all have things of which we are ashamed, and more will come our way; however, if we deal with those things in His presence *now* or *as soon as they happen*—relying on His mercy and grace—we can know we will find mercy even in the Day of Judgment. Where do we find such assurance and comfort? From two promises of scripture. First, the writer of Proverbs declared this confidence when he penned these words:

> *He who conceals his transgressions will not prosper, but* **he who confesses and forsakes them will find compassion** *(Proverbs 28:13).*

Aren't those encouraging words? And look at what the Apostle John wrote in his first letter:

> *If we confess our sins, He is faithful and righteous to forgive us our sins and* **to cleanse us from all unrighteousness.** *If we say that we have not sinned, we make Him a liar and His word is not in us. My little children, I am writing these things to you so that you may not sin. And if anyone sins, we have an Advocate with the Father, Jesus Christ the righteous (1 John 1:9-2:1).*

Think of it this way: God knows we are sinners and has provided what we need to be secure in His Son. When you stand in the Judgment, having confessed your sins, God will cleanse you of all unrighteousness. Think of the Judgment as the final, great cleansing. Yes, we will be *grieved* over our sins *temporarily*, but we will also be *washed* of our sins *eternally*! The tears will be dried by His gentle touch, and with His own hand He will lift us up into His glory. Why not begin right now to practice drawing near to God and holding fast your confession of Christ by applying this truth to your life?

For Your Future Happiness

I believe the reason I've written this book, and you are reading it, is for your edification, cleansing, and sanctification, as well as for your future happiness. If some wrong thinking has been confronted and exposed, and your mind renewed in the truth, let's shout, "To the praise of the glory of His grace!" (Go ahead and let 'er rip.) If you've been awakened from a spiritual slumber and you need to put off those "clothes of the night" and get dressed for "the Day," then to God be the glory! Put truth into action.

Spurgeon has another word of encouragement for us. "Do not treat God's promises as if they were curiosities for a museum, but use them as every-day sources of comfort."[44] My purpose for writing has been that as you have read this book, you would learn to live for the glory of God alone. May God fill you with His Spirit and a hope of glory as you begin practicing what you have been given by His mercy and grace. One day we will rejoice together in our glorified bodies at His throne in the new heaven and earth when these words in 2 Corinthians 6:16 through 7:1 will have been fulfilled:

> *"I will dwell in them and walk among them; and I will be their God, and they shall be My people. And I will welcome you. And I will be a father to you, and you shall be sons and daughters to Me," says the Lord Almighty.*
>
> *Therefore, having these promises, beloved, let us cleanse ourselves from all defilement of flesh and spirit, perfecting holiness in the fear of God.*

Anchored in Jesus, You Glorify God

I hope our time spent together in God's Word and your reading the thoughts God has given me to share with you have served to anchor your soul in Jesus Christ more deeply and consistently. I realize that if you have endured to this point, God has been with you. My goal has not been to answer all of your questions about doctrine and theology, but to be practical and lead you to think about the glorious confidence which comes when we view everything in life from a God-centered perspective and live life out of the fullness of relationship with the only true Source of Life—Jesus Christ, the Son of the living God.

In Charles Spurgeon's classic book of meditations, *Morning and Evening,* the following excerpt captures what my heart prays for you:

> We must not rest without a desperate struggle to clasp the Saviour in the arms of faith, and say, "I know whom I have believed, and I am persuaded that he is able to keep that which I have committed unto him." Do not rest, O believer, till thou hast

a full assurance of thine interest in Jesus. Let nothing satisfy thee till, by the infallible witness of the Holy Spirit bearing witness with thy spirit, thou art certified that thou art a child of God. Oh, trifle not here; let no "perhaps" and "peradventure" and "if" and "maybe" satisfy thy soul. Build on eternal verities, and verily build upon them. Get the sure mercies of David, and surely get them. **Let thine anchor be cast into that which is within the veil, and see to it that thy soul be linked to the anchor by a cable that will not break.**[45]

If God has been gracious to give you revelation through these pages and has equipped you to be more pleasing in His sight when you stand in the Day of Judgment, I rejoice with you, and we'll give Him the glory. I hope you have been encouraged in your faith and anchored in Jesus to a greater degree. If so, think about passing this book on to your friends and family who may also receive the same benefit.

Now the God of peace, who brought up from the dead the great Shepherd of the sheep through the blood of the eternal covenant, even Jesus our Lord, equip you in every good thing to do His will, working in us that which is pleasing in His sight, through Jesus Christ, to whom be the glory forever and ever. Amen (Hebrews 13:20-21).

Appendix

Study Guide for Small Groups or Sunday School Classes

Week 1

Assignment: Read Chapters 1-2

1. Read Joshua 24:14-27
   a. What is the danger of only using verse 14 in a gospel presentation without the context? P. 4
   b. What does a command reveal about the recipient of the command? P. 4
   c. What choices did Joshua hold before the men of Israel? P. 5
   d. Why did Joshua think the men of Israel could not serve the Lord? P. 5
   e. What verse reveals the heart attitudes of the people prior to Joshua's challenge? How so? P. 6
   f. What does verse 15 indicate about Joshua's heart? Where was his heart turned?
2. Read John 1:12-13
   a. How do these verses relate to the passage in Joshua 24? P. 10
   b. Why is verse 13 so important for understanding verse 12? P. 10
   c. Why is understanding that new birth is determined by God's will and not our wills important? Pp. 10-11
   d. What is the evidence that someone has "received" the Son as a gift from God? P.11

e.   Why can we say that man's will is never free, but is always in bondage? P. 12

Week 2

Assignment: Read Chapter 3

1.   Read John 2:23-John 3:21
2.   Discuss some illustrations of natural faith like those who believed because of the signs. Pp. 13-14
3.   List the characteristics of natural faith. P. 16
4.   What are the dangers of trying to "convince" someone to be saved? Pp. 16-17
5.   What are the dangers of affirming everyone who makes an outward profession of faith? Pp. 16-17
6.   List the characteristics of Spirit-born faith. Pp. 18-23, 29
7.   Discuss the implications to Nicodemus of Jesus saying that anyone may be saved from sins and be loved by God through faith. How would this conversation between Jesus and Nicodemus impact John's Jewish readers? Pp. 25-27
8.   Share your experiences with natural faith and supernatural faith.

Week 3

Assignment: Read Chapters 4-5

1.   Read Acts 2:4-38 and Acts 16:23-34.
2.   What did God do to arrest the attention of those He wished to convert in Acts 2 and Acts 16? Why is this important when applying the verses commonly used in gospel presentations? Pp. 34, 40-42
3.   What sign gave Peter understanding that the Holy Spirit was working in the hearts of the men at Pentecost? P. 36
4.   What sign gave Paul understanding that the Holy Spirit was working in the heart of the jailer in Philippi? P. 43
5.   What does *repentance* mean? P. 36
     Share about when God gave you repentance and you were "pierced to the heart" by the Holy Spirit.
6.   What are the dangers of a formulaic gospel presentation? P. 44
7.   What have you learned about "keeping in step with the Spirit" in the evangelism process? P. 45
8.   Pray together about people with whom you associate and for the

Holy Spirit's working in their lives. Also, pray for sensitivity and discernment on your part to keep in step with the Spirit.

Week 4

Assignment: Read Chapter 6

1. Read Romans 10:1-17.
2. What is "decisional regeneration"? Was it a surprise to you to discover that it has no biblical foundation? P. 48
3. How does the typical altar call lead one to believe his salvation depends on the choice of his will?
4. What was the Apostle Paul's concern for his Jewish brothers? P. 52
5. What does Romans 10:10 reveal about the relationship of faith to the heart? P. 53
6. What is the difference in interpretation between the King James Version, Today's English Version, and the New American Standard Version of verse 14? P. 54
7. What is the importance of the *however* in verse 16? P. 55
8. Where does faith come from? Why is this important? Pp. 56-59
9. If someone thinks his salvation depends on the faith they can muster in Christ, how will he live life? Pp. 56-57

Week 5

Assignment: Read Chapters 7-8

1. Read 1 Tim. 2:1-7.
2. Why would God's desire to save every single man be a motivation to pray for kings and those in authority? Why would God's desire to save all kinds of men be a motivation to pray for kings and those in authority? Which explanation is most consistent with the context of verses 1-4? Pp. 62-63
3. What do you think was most in the mind of the apostle: why we should pray for kings and those in authority or God wants to save everybody in the world? Discuss. P. 63
4. What is the theological significance of understanding the scope of the word "all"? If one didn't know the Greek construction rules, how could one tell from the context whether it means "every kind or variety" or "every single one without exception"? P. 63
5. What theological problem arises if the apostle had "every single one without exception" in mind? Pp. 63-65

6. Which of the three options of interpretation listed on p. 67 is consistent with the rest of the Scripture revelation? Why?
7. Read 1 Tim. 4:6-10.
8. What are some of the outward actions and bodily disciplines in which people trust today for preservation and sanctification? P. 70
9. What reasons can you give for interpreting the word that is commonly rendered *savior* in verse 10 to mean *preserver*? Why is exercising ourselves to godliness of more benefit than bodily discipline for keeping the saints from falling into heresy or apostasy? Pp. 70-71

Week 6

Assignment: Read Chapters 9 and 10

1. Read Titus 1:10-2:14
2. What problem in the church did Paul address when he wrote Titus? What was Paul's solution and safeguard to overcome the problem? Pp. 73-74
3. What kinds of people did Paul encourage Titus to exhort in sound doctrine? Pp. 75
4. What is the *grace of God* which has appeared? P. 76 Has this specific grace of God appeared to every single man in the world? Pp. 76-77
5. Read 2 Peter 2:1-3
6. How are these verses relevant to the church in general today? P. 82
7. Discuss the two terms for *master* used in Chapter 2. What is the significance of the distinction in words? Pp. 83-84
8. How do John 6:37-39 and 10:27-30 eliminate the notion that Peter was referring to false teachers who lose their salvation? Pp. 84-85
9. What is the primary warning of Peter in Chapter 2 of his epistle? Is it to teachers or to the body of Christ? P. 85

Week 7

Assignment: Read Chapters 11-12

1. Read 2 Peter 3:1-9
2. What was Peter's purpose in writing this section of his letter? Pp. 87-88
3. What is wrong with appealing to the emotions of lost people

that God really wants to save them, but it's up to each of them to choose Him? P. 87

4. Which of the following answers the question of the Lord's slowness (from our perspective) in keeping His promise to return? Discuss your answers. Pp. 88-90

a. He doesn't realize how difficult life is for those He loves.

b. He doesn't want anyone in the world to perish.

c. His perspective of time is different than our perspective of time.

d. He won't return until the last one of those He has loved has come to repentance and faith.

5. Since the Lord is being patient about His coming, how are we to live? P. 91

6. What do these verses tell us about God's love for those who are His? Pp. 91-92

7. Read 1 John 1:1-10

8. Of whom was John thinking when he wrote verse 9? What is the problem with telling *anyone* their sins are all forgiven if they will only confess them? Pp. 93-95

9. What vital truth are believers to draw from 1 John 1:9? Pp. 99-100

Week 8

Assignment: Read Chapters 13-14

1. Read 1 John 2:1-2 and the definitions of advocate and propitiation on P. 101.

2. Take a moment to meditate on the glorious truth of Jesus being your advocate and having made propitiation for your sins. Afterward, share what the Holy Spirit brings to mind with one another and then give thanks to our Lord.

3. Discuss the reasons we should *not* think verse 2 teaches that Jesus died for everyone in the world who has ever lived. Pp. 98-100

4. What was John teaching and why is it meaningful to John's first readers? Meaningful to us? Pp. 100-101

5. Read Revelation 3:14-22.

6. How has Rev. 3:20 been used in evangelistic presentations? Was that what the Holy Spirit originally intended for this verse? Pp. 103-104

7. To whom were these verses addressed and what is Jesus offering? Pp. 105-106

8. What would be the accurate use of these verses today? P. 107

Week 9

Assignment: Read Chapters 15-16 and the chart on p. 116-117.

1. What danger is there to listeners if they don't think about and examine what they hear? What does it mean to be a Berean? Read Acts 17:11. Pp. 111-113
2. Discuss the chart on Pp. 116-117. What has changed in your thinking about these verses?
3. Discuss the differences between a man-centered interpretation of Scripture and a God-centered interpretation. Pp. 121-123
4. What do the following verses teach us about God and His participation in the affairs of men? Rom. 11:36, 1 Cor. 8:6; Col. 1:16-17, Is. 46:5, 9-10, Is. 45:5-7
5. What are the implications of the truth that God is Spirit? P. 124
6. What does it mean to your faith that God is *infinite* in his Being, wisdom, power, justice, goodness, and truth? Pp. 124-125
7. What is the significance of God's eternality when you consider Jesus' death on the cross? Pp. 125-126
8. Why is your faith anchored by the fact of God's unchangeable Being and character? P. 127
9. Why is the fact that God's truth is infinite, eternal, and unchangeable important in today's culture? P. 133

Week 10

Assignment: Read Chapters 17-18

1. What do all philosophies and false religions have in common? P. 136
2. What truth lies at the heart of the evolution vs. intelligent designer debate? Pp. 136-137
3. How can we know who is the God of creation? Pp. 138-139
4. Why do people *want* to believe the miracles of the Bible are mythical? P. 139
5. How has God revealed Himself throughout history? P. 139
6. What is true about the Bible that is not true about any other piece of literature? Pp. 141-143
7. Why is the Bible the basis for determining truth? P. 142
8. What does it mean to be *God?* P. 143

9. What is the mystery of God's purposes? Read Eph. 1:7-10, Rom. 11:33-36, Col. 1:16-20, Rev. 5:12-13. Why is this important to your faith? Pp. 146-147

Week 11

Assignment: Read Chapters 19-21

1. Read Ephesians 1:11 and Is. 46:10. What are the implications of this truth to the affairs and events of history? P. 150
2. What examples other than those mentioned on page 150 illustrate how God's creatures act according to *their* mind and purposes?
3. What is the first foundational fact about the fall of man? P. 151
4. What is meant when we say, "God decrees something to occur"? Pp. 151-152
5. What is the second foundational fact about the fall of man? Read Rom. 5:12 and 1 Cor. 15:21-22. P. 154
6. What was the first element necessary for the Fall to occur? Pp. 160-161
7. What was the prevailing heart motivation in Adam? P. 160
8. What was the second element necessary for the Fall to occur? P. 163
9. What are four purposes of law? P. 165
10. Explain how God's grace cannot be defined without the presence of the law and sinners. Pp. 166-167
11. Why was it necessary for God's people to be "lost" in Adam? P. 167
12. What was the purpose for the tree of the knowledge of good and evil? How does this fit into God's purposes? Pp. 170-171

Week 12

Assignment: Read Chapter 22-23

1. What is the third element necessary for the Fall to occur? P. 173
2. What do Col. 1:15-16, Mark 1:25 and 5:13 teach us about Satan and his minions in relationship with Jesus Christ? Pp. 173-174
3. After reading 1 Sam. 16:14 and 1 Kings 22:20-23, discuss God's purposes for Satan in the lives of the wicked. Can you think of modern-day examples? Pp. 174-175
4. After reading Deut. 8:2-5, James 1:13-14, 1 Cor. 5:5, and 1 Tim. 1:20, discuss God's purposes for Satan in the lives of His people. Can you think of modern-day examples? Pp. 176-177
5. How has Jesus destroyed the works of the devil? Pp. 178-179
6. Review the 11 factors of God's purposes on Pp. 180-181

7. What is the third foundational fact about the fall of man? P. 183
8. Discuss various views of "sin" in contrast to a biblical definition of "sin." Pp. 184-186
9. Make a list of the effects of the Fall on the hearts of men as you read the following scriptures. Pp. 187- 198
Rom. 8:7, Jer. 17:9, Gen. 6:5, Eph. 2:1-3, Rom. 5:6, Rom. 6:17, 7:14, Gen. 8:21, Rom. 3:10-18, Ps. 36:1-4, Mark 7:14-23, Eph. 4:17-19, Rom. 1:18, 21-25

Week 12

Assignment: Read Chapters 24-25

1. What is the fourth foundational fact about the fall of man? P. 201
2. How is man on probation before God? When does a man become a reprobate? P. 202
3. Why does all of history exist? Why has God put up with millennia of evil and wickedness? P. 203
4. Read 1 Tim. 1:15-17 and Titus 3:3-6 and use them as inspiration for a time of personal and group worship and praise to God for what He has done through Jesus Christ. P. 204
5. Review the four foundational facts about the fall of man.
6. What dilemma does God face in justifying sinners? Pp. 207-208
7. Read Rom. 3:22-27 and 8:3-4. How has God justified Himself in forgiving sinners? P. 209
8. Read 1 Cor. 1:30-31 and Col. 1:20-22. What has God done for you by putting you into Jesus Christ? Pp. 210-211
9. What does a Christian do to be justified in Christ? P. 212
10. What are the evidences that a person has been justified and called by God? Read Acts 5:31, 11:13-18, 2 Tim. 2:24-25, 2 Cor. 7:9-11, Acts 15:7-9, 16:14, Rom. 6:17-18, 10:17, and Eph. 2:8-10. Pp. 213-219
11. What is the difference between the general call of the gospel and the call of God to salvation? Pp. 219-222
12. Share about experiencing God's call in your own life.

Week 13

Assignment: Read Chapter 26 and make a list of people who have taught you about life.

1. Share with the group some of those who have discipled you in your life. Pp. 227-228

2. What and where is the kingdom of heaven? Pp. 230-231
3. Read Matt. 5:3, 10, 19, 13:11, 52, and Phil. 3:20. What do these verses teach us about when we enter the kingdom of heaven? Pp. 232-233
4. Read Matt. 6:6, 9, 33, Acts 1:9-11, 7:49-56, 17:24-28 and 2 Kings 6:15-17. Where is Jesus now and how far away is He? If you understood Jesus' presence in the space around you, how would it affect the way you live each day? Pp. 231-232, 234-236
5. Read John 14:18-21. Where is the kingdom of God revealed today? Pp. 237-238
6. Read John 17:3, John 14:1-21, and Matt. 7:13-24. What is eternal life and when does it begin? How does one enter? Pp. 239-241
7. Read Matt. 28:19-20. How do we know this passage is not about salvation? What is Jesus commanding the disciples to do? Pp. 241-243
8. Read John 6:44-45 and John 14:16-24. Who is the primary *teacher* of new converts?
9. What have you learned about the Holy Spirit's purpose in your life?

Week 14

Assignment: Read Chapter 27 and ask God to make you aware of an opportunity to use the questions to build relationships from p. 267-268.

1. What false notions are most evangelistic tracts based on? P. 246
2. Why should Christians witness if salvation is all of grace? Pp. 247-248
3. What are the two kinds of witnessing that believers do? Pp. 250-252
4. What are the three ingredients necessary for effective evangelism to take place? Pp. 252-256
5. What is the motive in evangelism, and why is it important to our witness? Pp. 256-257
6. What is the order of understanding necessary for salvation to occur? Pp. 258-264
7. Share about an opportunity God gave you to ask a relationship-building question.

Week 15

Assignment: Read Chapter 28

1. Review what you've learned thus far about evangelism and salvation. P. 271

2. Read Proverbs 16:2 and Jeremiah 17:10. How does God teach your children about the power of sin? Pp. 272-273
3. Read 1 Timothy 1:8-11 and discuss how the Law of God may be used lawfully with children. Pp. 274-275
4. Read Proverbs 13:24, 22:15, 23:14, and 29:15. Share what you learned about using the rod and reproof from Pp. 275-278.
5. Why is it important that children's hearts be turned toward their parents? Pp. 278-279
6. Besides the promises mentioned on P. 281, what other promises of God can we give to our children?
7. Can someone explain the wisdom of God in having us wait for Him to fulfill His promises? P. 282
8. What are some of the dangers parents face in leading their children to Christ? Pp. 283-286

Week 16

Assignment: Read Chapters 29-30 and memorize the confession on pp. 290-291.

1. Quote the confession and give the verses from Hebrews that support each point.
2. How should we apply who Jesus is to each event in life? Give examples. Pp. 290-291
3. Why is it important for us to know that purification has been made for all our sins at one time? P. 292
4. Where is Jesus now and what is He doing on our behalf? Pp. 292-293
5. How should we apply the truth of what Jesus is doing now to each event in life? Give examples. Pp. 293-294
6. What is the value of trials, suffering, and temptation? Pp. 295-296
7. How does God preserve His people and under what conditions? Pp. 296-298
8. Read Hebrews 2:2-5 and 3:7-11. Why is it important that we not drift away from applying our confession when facing trials, suffering, and temptations? Pp. 300-302
9. What does it mean to fall away from the living God? Pp. 303-304
10. When you see someone going through a trial and they have no grace, what should you do? Pp. 304-306

Week 17

Assignment: Read Chapters 31-32 and continue memorizing the confession on pp. 290-291.

1. Quote the confession.
2. Read Hebrews 4. What has God promised to His people who draw near and hold fast their confession? Pp. 308-309
3. Review Hebrews 4:12-13. What "word" is the author speaking of? To what part of our confession do these verses refer? P. 310
4. Discuss Jesus' ministry to His people as their high priest. What means the most to you? Pp. 310-313
5. What is the importance of keeping the Day of Judgment "on the radar screen" for believers? How does this affect your daily walk? Pp. 315-318
6. Read the following verses and make a list of what you learn about what will occur on the Day of Judgment for believers. Matthew 12:36-37, Romans 2:2-3, 5-6, 11, 16, 14:10-12, 1 Corinthians 2:12-15, 2 Corinthians 5:10, and 1 Peter 4:17
7. Read Revelation 10:11-15. When will God wipe away our tears and remember our sins no more? Pp. 320-321
8. What is "spiritual napping" and what are its dangers? Pp. 323-324
9. Read Luke 13:1-5. What will occur to unbelievers on the Day of Judgment? Pp. 325-326

Week 18

Assignment: Read Chapters 33-34

1. Quote the confession.
2. Share how applying the confession in your life each day has affected you. Give examples.
3. What has God promised to reward in the Day of Judgment? Pp. 329-330
4. What sin so easily entangles us and how does the Heavenly Father discipline His children when they do not draw near and hold fast their confession? Pp. 333-334
5. What responsibility do we have to our brothers and sisters in Christ? P. 335
6. When you don't have grace in a trial, what should you do? Pp. 336-337
7. What is the "solid rock" to which we are anchored in the storms of

life? Pp. 340-341
8. How can you apply what you've learned about your confession to
    past failures? Pp. 342-344
9. What has been the value of studying *Anchored in Christ* for you?

Endnotes

Chapter 3

1. John Piper, *Future Grace*, Multnomah Books, Sisters, OR, 1995, pp. 210-211.

2. Leon Morris, *The Gospel According to John*, Wm. B. Eerdmans Publishing Company, Grand Rapids, MI, 1971, p. 206.

3. Dallas Willard, *Divine Conspiracy*, Harper Collins Publishers, New York, NY, 1998, p. 25.

4. W.E. Vine, *Expository Dictionary of Old and New Testament Words*, Vol. IV, Fleming H. Revell Company, Old Tappan, NJ, 1981, p. 230.

Chapter 4

5. Ibid., Vol. III, p. 279.

Chapter 5

6. D. Martyn Lloyd-Jones, *Romans: An Exposition of Chapter 10, Saving Faith*, Banner of Truth Trust, 1997, p. 135.

Chapter 6

7. Vine, Vol. IV, p. 230.

8. D. Martyn Lloyd-Jones, *Romans: An Exposition of Chapter 10, Saving Faith*, Banner of Truth Trust, 1997, p. 131.

9. Ibid., pp. 132-133.

Chapter 7

10. Vine, Vol. I, p. 46.

Chapter 8

11. James Strong, *Strong's Exhaustive Concordance of the Bible*, Abingdon Press, Nashville, TN, 1974, #4990 of the Greek Dictionary of the New Testament, p. 70.

Chapter 10

12. Richard Belcher, *A Journey in Grace*, Richbarry Press, Columbia, S.C., Second Edition, 2002, p. 178.

13. Ibid., p. 115.

Chapter 13

14. Merriam-Webster Online Dictionary, http://www.m-w.com.

15. Noah Webster, *First Edition of An American Dictionary of the English Language, Reprint of 1828 Edition*, Foundation for American Christian Education, San Francisco, CA, 1989, entry at *advocate*.

Chapter 16

16. *The London Baptist Confession of Faith 1689, Updated with Notes by Peter Masters*, The Wakeman Trust, London, 1981, p. 24.

17. William Hendriksen, *New Testament Commentary, The Gospel of John*, Vol. 1, Baker Book House, Grand Rapids, MI, p. 168.

Chapter 17

18. Prof. L. Berkoff, *Systematic Theology*, Wm. B. Eerdman's Publishing Co., 1939, 1941, p. 25.

19. Adapted from the article *"Who Made It?"*, Minnesota Techology, October 1957, p. 11.

Chapter 19

20. Lawrence O. Richards, *Expository Dictionary of Bible Words*, Zondervan Publishing House, Grand Rapids, MI, 1985, p. 214.

21. Wayne Grudem, *Systematic Theology*, Zondervan, Grand Rapids MI, 1994, pp. 47-48.

Chapter 21

22. *The Works of Jonathan Edwards*, Vol. One, "On the Freedom of the Will," Section IV, Banner of Truth Trust, Carlisle, PA, reprinted 1979, p. 39.

Chapter 23

23. Prof. L. Berkhof, *Systematic Theology*, Fourth Revised Edition, Wm. B. Eerdmans Publishing Co., Grand Rapids, MI, 1939, 1941, p. 227.

24. Berkhof, pp. 233-234.

25. Berkhof, pp. 231-233.

26. John F. MacArthur, Jr., *Ashamed of the Gospel*, Crossway Books, Wheaton, IL, 1993, flyleaf.

Chapter 23

27. Noah Webster, *First Edition of An American Dictionary of the English Language, Reprint of 1828 Edition*, Foundation for American Christian Education, San Francisco, CA, 1989, entry at *probation*.

28. Ibid., entry at *reprobate*.

Chapter 25

29. Lawrence O. Richards, *Expository Dictionary of Bible Words*, Zondervan Publishing House, Grand Rapids, MI, 1985, p. 372.

Chapter 26

30. Dallas Willard, *Divine Conspiracy*, Harper Collins Publishers, New York, NY, 1998, p. 271.

31. W.E. Vine, *Expository Dictionary of Old and New Testament Words*, Vol. III, p. 279.

32. C. S. Lewis, "What Are We to Make of Jesus Christ?" an essay in *God in the Dock: Essays on Theology and Ethics*, Eerdmans, 1970, pp. 157-158.

33. Dallas Willard, *Divine Conspiracy*, Harper Collins Publishers, New York, NY, 1998, p. 73.

34. Ibid., p. 27.

35. Ibid., p. 71.

36. Ibid., p. 41.

Chapter 27

37. John MacArthur, *Ashamed of the Gospel*, Crossway Books, Wheaton, IL, 1993, pp. 49, 65, 70.

Chapter 28

38. Norm Wakefield, *Equipping Men: Practical Tools for Life's Issues*, Message 12, "Heart Maintenance," The Spirit of Elijah Ministries, Bulverde, TX, 1998.

39. Brother Lawrence, *The Practice of the Presence of God*, Fleming H. Revell Company, Old Tappan, New Jersey, 1985.

40. Norm Wakefield, *Rising to the Call*, Message 1, "Having Ears to Hear," The Spirit of Elijah Ministries, Bulverde, TX, 1998.

Chapter 29

41. Lew Sterrett, *Sermon on the Mount: Self-Control*, (video) Miracle Mountain Ranch, Spring Creek, PA, 1997.

Chapter 31

42. *New American Standard Exhaustive Concordance of the Bible*, Holman, Nashville, TN, 1981, #3838 of the Greek Dictionary of the New Testament, p. 1672.

Chapter 34

43. *Spurgeon's Sermon Illustrations*, Charles H. Spurgeon, edited by David O. Fuller, Kregel Publications, Grand Rapids, MI, 1990, p. 11.

44. Ibid., p. 136.

45. Charles Spurgeon, *Morning and Evening*, Fleming H. Revell Company, Old Tappan, New Jersey 1984, p. 45.

OTHER RESOURCES AVAILABLE FROM
THE SPIRIT OF ELIJAH MINISTRIES

Equipping Men ....available on CD/DVD/MP3

Rising to the Call ....available on CD/DVD/MP3

Teenagers 101...available on CD/MP3

On Fire for the Gospel ....available on CD/MP3

Unshakable Faith ....available on CD/DVD/MP3

Marriage for God's Glory ....available on CD/DVD/MP3

Raised Up with Christ ....available on CD/DVD/MP3

Reality Check: It's Not About You ....available on CD/MP3

The Book of Revelation Bible Study (39 MP3's) ......available on MP3 DVD

Equipped to Love ....book by Norm Wakefield

Anchored in Christ ....book by Norm Wakefield

Walking Worthy Series for Men (Volumes 1-5) ....book series by Norm Wakefield

Glorious Grace...............................music CD or audio tape by Norm Wakefield

To order any of these resources or to find out more about them, please visit our website:

http://www.spiritofelijah.com

8/9/15

The first AIC book I had was out of order and I didn't notice until I got to pege 142 of it... So all of my notes from the first half of the book are in the other book I have. I pray I will learn much from this book and grow in spiritual wisdom and understand of God and His will for me.